PENGUIN BOOKS

THE HIGHLAND CLEARANCES

John Prebble was born in Middlesex in 1915 but spent his boyhood in Saskatchewan, Canada. A journalist since 1934, he is also a novelist, a film-writer, and the author of several highly praised dramatized documentaries for B.B.C. television and radio. During the war he served for six years in the ranks with the Royal Artillery, from which experience he wrote his successful war novel, *The Edge of Darkness*. His other books include *Age Without Pity*, *The Mather Story*, *The High Girders*, an account of the Tay Bridge Disaster, *The Buffalo Soldiers*, which won an award in the United States for the best historical novel of the American West, and *Culloden*, a subject he became interested in when he was a boy in a predominantly Scottish township in Canada. *Culloden* was subsequently made into a successful television film. Its natural successor, *The Highland Clearances*, was published in 1963 and *Glencoe* in the spring of 1966. *The Darien Disaster* was published in 1968, *The Lion in the North* in 1971 and *Mutiny: Highland Regiments in Revolt* in 1975. Many of his books are published in Penguins.

JOHN PREBBLE

THE HIGHLAND CLEARANCES

*'Since you have preferred sheep to men,
let sheep defend you!'*

PENGUIN BOOKS
in association with Martin Secker & Warburg

Penguin Books Ltd, Harmondsworth, Middlesex, England
Viking Penguin Inc., 40 West 23rd Street, New York, New York 10010, U.S.A.
Penguin Books Australia Ltd, Ringwood, Victoria, Australia
Penguin Books Canada Ltd, 2801 John Street, Markham, Ontario, Canada L3R 1B4
Penguin Books (N.Z.) Ltd, 182–190 Wairau Road, Auckland 10, New Zealand

—

First published by Martin Secker & Warburg 1963
Published in Penguin Books 1969
Reprinted 1969, 1970, 1971, 1972, 1973, 1974, 1975, 1976, 1977,
1978, 1980, 1982, 1983, 1984, 1985

—

—

Made and printed in Great Britain by
Hazell Watson & Viney Limited,
Member of the BPCC Group,
Aylesbury, Bucks
Set in Linotype Juliana

FOR SARAH

CONTENTS

MAPS

THE decision to write this book was made for me when I wrote the last sentences of my account of the battle of Culloden and its aftermath in the Scottish Highlands. I quote them here as an introduction and an explanation:

'Once the chiefs lost their powers many of them lost also any parental interest in their clansmen. During the next hundred years they continued the work of Cumberland's battalions. So that they might lease their glens and braes to sheep-farmers from the Lowlands and England, they cleared the crofts of men, women and children, using police and soldiers where necessary.'

This book, then, is the story of how the Highlanders were deserted and then betrayed. It concerns itself with people, how sheep were preferred to them, and how bayonet, truncheon and fire were used to drive them from their homes. It has been said that the Clearances are now far enough away from us to be decently forgotten. But the hills are still empty. In all of Britain only among them can one find real solitude, and if their history is known there is no satisfaction to be got from the experience. It is worth remembering, too, that while the rest of Scotland was permitting the expulsion of its Highland people it was also forming that romantic attachment to kilt and tartan that scarcely compensates for the disappearance of a race to whom such things were once a commonplace reality. The chiefs remain, in Edinburgh and London, but the people are gone.

Finally, we have not become so civilized in our behaviour, or more concerned with men than profit, that this story holds no lesson for us.

February, 1963   JOHN PREBBLE

I

THE YEAR OF THE SHEEP

'2,000 Men would not suppress the Insurrection'

MR MACLEOD of Geanies was 'much fatigued' this Sunday morning. He asked the Lord Advocate to excuse any omissions or inaccuracies in his dispatch, he was already half asleep. The paper on which he was writing was coarse and unsuitable, but he hoped that his lordship would excuse this also, it being the best that the butler could find while the family was at church. Mr Macleod could have waited until his host returned to Novar House, but that would have meant a delay in the Post, and great events demanded that Edinburgh should have early news from the North. And the news which Donald Macleod had to send was such that could give the Lord Advocate nothing but satisfaction, and do Mr Macleod nothing but good. So he was writing immediately, in his riding-boots and coat, his obstinate pen spitting blots over the paper in its haste. His body ached from two days in the saddle, during which he had led the Gentlemen of Ross (together with their 'servants and dependants armed') in an exciting man-hunt across the mountains beyond Cromarty Firth. 'It does much honour to the Gentlemen of the County,' wrote Mr Macleod, 'with what alacrity the greatest part of those within reach hurried out.'

Some of the Gentlemen, those who had not gone to church with Sir Hector Munro to give thanks for the preservation of their property, were resting now in Novar House, as pleased with their efforts as Sheriff Macleod. In the park outside, where the land fell in a green slope to the sea, were three companies of the 42nd Regiment, red coats and dark tartan lying in exhaustion on the grass. After a forced march from Fort George to Dingwall, and then on through the night to Strath Rusdale with cartridge and ball, they had been too tired to accompany the gentry on the last phase of the operation. Mr Macleod was naturally pleased that the civil power, by rallying the gentility, had been able to do something in this distressing affair without using the muskets of the military. Not that he wished the Black Watch to be anywhere but at his back today, and he asked his lordship to regularize this. 'Major Dalrymple has not at this moment received any official orders to put himself under my orders or to move from Fort George; and I can with truth assert that if this business was allowed to proceed one week more, 2,000 Men would not suppress the Insurrection which would ensue not only in this but in the Counties which surround us.'

Mr Macleod was in the forty-eighth year of his life, and his twentieth as Sheriff-Depute of the County of Ross. That he was to hold the office for another thirty-nine may be largely attributable to his behaviour this warm August weekend. Excitable and vain, proud of the Highland quality indicated by the words 'of Geanies' (though he had merely bought the acres that gave him the use of the designation), he was also hard-headed and shrewd. He had boyish dreams of generalship, and would later raise a regiment of militia as 'Colonel Macleod of Geanies'. But when reality, as now, demanded proof of his military ardour, he did very well indeed. Most men who are responsible for the preservation of Law and Good Order like to feel that they have at least once saved both from disaster. Mr Macleod had no doubt of it today. The times were persuasive. His thoughts, like those of the Gentlemen now snoring in Sir Hector's drawing-room, had been much concerned of late with affairs beyond the borders of the kingdom. In France the Commonality had risen against the lawful and divine authority of Government, inviting the rest of Europe to follow its example of insurrection and murder.

It seemed to Mr Macleod and others that faint tremors of Jacobinism were being felt beyond Dingwall, and that the Mob in the hills to the north might well be wearing red caps. So far Life had not been taken, but Property had most certainly been abused. The Lord Advocate was assured that Mr Macleod, however, did not value his possessions before his honour and duty.

'It may appear a little extraordinary, but I learned from some of the prisoners that they have not touched my farms, nor did intend to do it unless I opposed them by force, a threat which I very much despise.'

These prisoners were now guarded by a file of Highlanders outside Novar House. 'We discovered eight of the scoundrels either lying in the barley-corn or in the woods, and after a good deal of galloping over very bad ground we apprehended every one of them and delivered them over to the care of the Military.'

When the Gentlemen and their riding-servants then galloped on to Strath Rusdale they found it empty except for four frightened men, and these were also taken in arrest to answer for the seditious absence of their neighbours. In the dark glens below Ben Wyvis, the heather above Loch Morie, many more were undoubtedly hiding, but they would not be safe. 'We mean to refresh the men and officers till 6 at night when we return to Dingwall, and shall be ready tomorrow to proceed against the others if they are hardy enough to stick together, and have no doubt of bringing in all the ringleaders of this most unaccountable commotion.'

He had the names of eight ringleaders and he wrote them into his dispatch, adding the names of the twelve scoundrels who had been flushed from the barley or taken at their doors. He asked for Justiciary Warrants to be sent quickly. His lordship would understand that while he was engaged in 'this species of actual and fatiguing service' the work of gathering precognitions from witnesses was scarcely possible.

Of the twenty men he named more than half were called Ross. Among them were 'William Ross a Piper in Achlaich, William Ross at Gladfield, Donald Ross in Dounie, Walter Ross in Croick, George Ross in Easter Greenyard, William Ross Bain in Wester Greenyard'. All these were thus from one narrow valley, from Strathcarron in the north, and this should be remembered later.

The hills over which Mr Macleod's irregular horse had coursed for human quarry were the home of *Clann Aindrea*, the race of Andrew, the Rosses. Their roots were deep in the pleated land.

They had all sprung from the fertile loins of *Gilleon na h-àirde*, father of the Celtic Earls of Ross. They spoke the Gaelic only for the most part, and except for those who went to soldier in the King's Highland regiments they knew little of the world beyond their hills (certainly nothing of the principles of Jacobinism). Their way of life had already undergone great changes, and against the latest threat to it they had gathered like their ancestors. But this time the invader was not Clan Mackay fording the Kyle of Sutherland on a foray. To drive it from Ross they needed nothing but sticks, the high crying of their voices on the hills.

But at a place called Boath, Mr Macleod had found them. 'What effect this check may have,' he told the Lord Advocate, 'I cannot determine, it may make them more desperate, but a day or two will determine, and I shall not fail to acquaint your Lordship.'

The year was 1792. The prisoners whom the Sheriff took to Dingwall that Sunday evening, other men he was to pursue on Monday and Tuesday, and many more who had taken no part in this 'most unaccountable commotion' would remember the year and be inspired by it thirty, fifty, even sixty years later. They called it *Bliadhna nan Caorach*.

The Year of the Sheep.

'Servant of the servant, worse than the devil'

ALEXANDER MACDONELL of Keppoch, *Mac-'ic-Raonuill*, the matriculated student of Glasgow University, was killed by the musketry of Pulteney's Regiment on Culloden Moor. He and old Lachlan MacLachlan were the only chiefs to die that day, but in their deaths the finger of the future touched their class. Keppoch was in most respects typical, and he had once described Highland society by a single phrase. His rent-roll, he said, consisted of five hundred fighting-men. When dying he added some depth to the description, calling upon his clansmen as his children. The men who carried him from the field in his red plaid wept for more than they knew.

Although a fraction only of the clans had taken part in the last Jacobite Rebellion of 1745, all felt the results of its defeat. Bayonet and noose, the proscription of arms, of tartan and kilt, the abolition of the hereditary jurisdictions of the chiefs, the sequestration of their estates, began the destruction of the clan system. A memory survived, cocooned in the silk of songs, awaiting mutation in romance.

'Oh, how bitter the changes,' sang John Roy Stewart who had led a regiment in the charge at Culloden, 'that have left us to range in the storm!' But greater changes were to come, and what was yet to be lost was not always as regrettable as the singers were to claim. What was to replace it was not always as worthy as men like Sheriff Macleod of Geanies sincerely believed.

Until the middle of the eighteenth century a Highland chief with little silver in his purse could count himself rich if, like Keppoch, he had five hundred fighting-men to answer his call. The land was his, its ownership long since settled by the swing of a broadsword, and although most chiefs had realized that paper now carried more weight in Law than steel, their tribal or feudal levies still protected their title deeds. The land produced little, but it was enough for a people inured to famine, and money was needed only to buy the chief the luxuries that were his right. He lived in the twilight of his glens with his children, and sowed his earth with dragon's-teeth as much as with corn.

Since the basis of land-tenure in the Highlands before the Rebellion was this value of the tenant as a warrior, military requirements determined the manner in which a chief granted tacks, or leases, on his property. Save that which he held directly himself, all land was leased to his principal supporters, frequently blood-kin who officered the clan regiment and recruited companies among their sub-tenants. These tacksmen took titles from the land they leased, were Mac-This of That or The Other, and were as sensitive as sea-anemones in matters that touched their honour. Their rents were paid in kind or services, or were quit-rents that scarcely equalled the value of what they possessed. In many cases they may have held written leases, although after Culloden, when a black-cattle economy replaced a military order and the clan needed no majors and captains, the chief began to show an understandable reluctance to put his name to anything that gave something for nothing. Having ceased to be a king in his own glens, having lost by Act of Parliament the power of 'pit and gallows' over the clan, he slowly realized that he was now a landlord not a warlord, and that he needed paying tenants not officers.

For some years after Colonel Belford's cannon blew away the clans at Culloden chiefs and gentry continued to respect the beliefs of the clan, and encouraged the view that they were its custodian. This was not only because it enabled them to parade tartan and title in Edinburgh drawing-rooms. Their rights and powers under Scots law were becoming increasingly important to them, and the docile obedience of their people would make the hard necessities of the future easier to impose.

They began, willingly or unwillingly, the great betrayal of their children.

Highland society had been a pyramid. Below the chief, at its apex, the tacksmen leased their land to sub-tenants who paid for it in kind and service. They had no written leases and held their meagre patches of soil from year to year on the sufferance and goodwill of the tacksmen. Their insecurity of tenure was the greatest guarantee that they or their sons could be brought into the clan regiment when needed. Below them was a bottom stratum of landless men, the cotters, who screamed into battle in the wake of the charge.

The sub-tenants formed small communities or townships. Six or eight men might hold a farm in common, and whereas in the beginning, beyond their memory, each man might have had an equal share, now one had a third and another a sixth with the obligation to divide even that fraction among their sons at their death. The township held a portion of the glen and a tract of mountain pasture for thirty or forty black cattle, a small herd of thin and fleshless sheep. The best of the arable land was farmed in runrig, strips for which the sub-tenants periodically drew lots.

Payment in kind or service for this land could and frequently did turn a sub-tenant into the servant of his tacksmen and hold him in perpetual debt.

The cotter was from birth a servant. Tradition and customary right gave him a little grazing for a cow on the township pasture, a kail-yard and potato-patch by his round-stone hut, and for these he paid a lifetime of service to the sub-tenant. He was what other men were not, herdsman, blacksmith, weaver, tailor, shoe-maker, armourer, axeman and bowman in the last rank of clan. 'Gille ghille is measa na'n diobhal!' he cried bitterly after Cullo-den. The servant of the servant is worse than the devil. Bad is the tenancy, but the evil of the Evil One is in the sub-tenancy. His escape could come in his dreams, or in the sharing of glory with the chief when the Bard sang or the Piper played. He could escape further into the King's red coat, and die at Ticonderoga or Havana with the slogan of his clan on his lips.

Yet the life was something which he and the sub-tenants were themselves unwilling to change. Their attachment to the land was deep and strong. They had peopled it with talking stones, snow-giants, and mythical warriors of mountain granite. Their culture was virile and immediate, their verse flowered on the rich mulching of their history. They held to the spirit of the clan when the chief was bartering it for a house in Belgravia. They retained their respect for him long after he had lost his for them. They acknowledged his right to dispose of them as he thought fit, and their inability to throw up leaders from their own ranks made their destruction inevitable. De their na daoine? What will the people say? they asked, and did nothing. The land they jealously regarded as their own, though they had no title to it, wasted beneath them for lack of knowledge and lack of opportunity. The shared sub-tenancies fed upon themselves and grew smaller each year, it being the custom, for example, to dig great pits in arable land to make compost heaps. On one township in Easter Ross, five of its eighty good acres were scooped out and lost in this manner.

The insecurity of the people, their dependence on the good-will of factor, tacksman and laird, made them frequently subservient, scheming or dissimulating. The laird could punish them by driving them landless from the glen, the laird could reward them with a corner of his land. Such a people to whom the past was a present reality, a monoglot minority accustomed to making no decisions for itself, not only feared change but was a prepared victim of it. Beyond the mountains the Highlander was despised and hated. *Mi-run mor nan Gall*, he called it, the Lowlander's great hatred. And this hatred was to persist until Walter Scott and his imitators took the Highlander out of his environment, disinfected him, dressed him in romance, and made him respectable enough to be a gun-bearer for an English sportsman, a servant to a Queen, or a bayonet-carrier for imperialism.

The old structure began to crumble rapidly after 1770. The chiefs, said Thomas Douglas, 5th Earl of Selkirk, 'were reduced to the situation of any other proprietors, but they were not long in discovering that to subsist a numerous train of dependants was not the only way in which their estates could be rendered of value'.

The economy and the manners, the demands and vanities of the south, the need for money and more money, swept away the lairds' picture of themselves as fathers of their people, custodians of the clan. The old chiefs who had gone out in the Rebellion, or had stayed at home testing the political wind with their fingers, died one by one. Their sons developed into a class that forgot the Gaelic and agreed with the English that it was a barbarous tongue. They took wives from England and the Lowlands, and these women asked for more than homespun on their backs and stones for walls. They coveted town-houses in Edinburgh, carriages, horses, southern educations for their children. A chief's daughters, too, were no longer content with husbands picked from the cadets of neighbouring glens, but desired softer men from the south who expected more substantial dowries than an infusion of warrior blood.

There was no satisfaction to be got from living on the land of their forefathers, and towards the end of the eighteenth century three-fifths of the Hebridean lairds, for example, were already absentee landlords. With the blunt edge of the fancy dirks they wore at balls the chiefs cut the ties that had held them to the people. They were rich in land yet their wives were ashamed of their poverty when they went to an Edinburgh rout among merchants, lawyers, and Lowland lairds. Their sons were competing for majorities in English regiments, and needed money to buy their commissions or pay their gambling debts. They sank into debt with a self-indulgence that characterized the age. Dice-cup and wine-cup began their long drain on the Highland purse.

Money would be had from the land. Not from turning its stony soil, but from the cattle that could graze upon it. As Britain's wars and population increased, so did the need for meat. In thirty years the demand for black Highland cattle grew so great that prices doubled. Southern cattlemen began to lease grazing land in the hills, using the old drove-roads or cutting new ones from the far north and west to the great trysting-place at Falkirk. The administrators of estates forfeited to the Crown after the '45 had shown what could be done by larger farms, higher rents and the abolition of run-rig. Speculators who had taken leases on these estates (Donald Macleod of Geanies was one) had grown rich from their ruthless and energetic improvements. While the growing destruction of ridge-farming was undoubtedly economic and profitable, the merging of small holdings into large single units under one tenant increased the numbers of landless men. For them Improvement had little sympathy. Compassion makes expensive calls on the conscience, and it is a comfort to find it undeserved.

'They live in the midst of smoke and filth,' said Sir George Mackenzie of Coul, himself a great Improver. 'That is their choice.' And for all his Highland name he might have been a Sussex landowner when he added: 'They will yet find themselves happier and more comfortable in the capacity of servants to substantial tenants than in their present situation.'

To exploit the land that must pay his debts, carry his mortgages and support his family's ambitions, the chief had first to remove his tacksmen or bring them to heel as reasonable tenants, for they, not he, held most of his property. He removed them by refusing to grant them written leases when the old ones expired, preferring southern graziers who would pay to kinsmen who might not. Where tacksmen remained they competed among themselves for the land that fell vacant, passing on the rent increases (often as high as 300 per cent) to their sub-tenants. To tacksmen who were reluctant to put pressure on people who were, after all, their clansmen, the chief might send a peremptory order in which the past sounded like a clash of cymbals.

'You are to intimate to the whole tenants in your district,' wrote The Seaforth's factor to a tacksman in the Isle of Lewis, 'that they must sell no cattle this year until the rents are paid, to anyone who has not the factor's orders to buy; and if anyone attempt to buy with ready money, you are to arrest their cattle and not allow them to be carried out of the country until the whole rents are paid up. This on your peril.'

The tacksmen lagged behind the chief in the race to the future. Few of them had the means, opportunity or desire for southern education and southern dalliance, and thus were closer to the old ways, the old traditions and the old idea of their importance. They resented the rack-renting of their cousin or uncle the chief, though this resentment did not prevent them from transferring the burden to their sub-tenants. An English traveller, returning from an exhausting visit to the Highlands in 1785, wrote with smug indignation of what he had seen : 'The chieftain lets out his land in large lots to the inferior branches of his family, all of whom must support the dignity of lairds. The renters let the land out in small parcels from year to year to the lower class of people, and to support their dignity squeeze everything out of them they can possibly get, leaving them only a bare subsistence. Until this evil is obviated Scotland can never improve.'

Those who could not endure the increasing oppression of the chiefs, left Scotland altogether for North America, and thus began what Samuel Johnson saw and called a 'fever of emigration'. Often the tacksman's people, sub-tenants and cotters, would go with him, and he welcomed them not as fellow-seekers for liberty, but as future tenants on the land he hoped to acquire in Nova Scotia or the Carolinas. Among the people the poets lamented the passing of the tacksman. In Kintail lived John Macrae, whose father had been hanged on an apple-tree by the Duke of Cumberland, and before he left for America he sang a bitter approval of what the tacksmen were doing:

> Better not to dwell under lairds
> who will not suffer their tenantry,
> who will take gold from a crab's claw
> rather than from a good man.

These early emigrations were not the wretched, helpless exodus that was to come in the next century. The tacksmen took their little wealth and greater arrogance with them. In 1791 the Society for the Propagation of Christian Knowledge (seeking godlessness in the Highlands, but finding something more alarming) reported that 'The secretary was assured upon authority which appeared to him conclusive that since the year 1772 no less than sixteen vessels full of emigrants have sailed from the western parts of the counties of Inverness and Ross alone, containing, it is supposed, 6,400 souls, and carrying with them in specie at least £38,000 sterling.'

There were tacksmen who took their people away from rack-renting and greedy chiefs because they saw it as an obligation on their honour. They were few, of course, but among them was John Macdonald of Glenalladale, *Mac Iain Oig*, the son of Young John. His family was a cadet branch of the great Macdonalds of Clanranald, stubbornly Catholic and Jacobite in convictions. He resented the Presbyterianism and the land-grabbing of the Clanranald family. He grieved for the passing of the tacksman's old position and honour. He looked at the situation: 'I saw many of my friends whom I loved, like to fall into, and which the children could not avoid unless some other path was struck out for them.'

He struck out the path. He bought land on the island of St John in the Gulf of St Lawrence, and to it, in 1772, he took an expedition of 'opprest people', tacksmen and sub-tenants from South Uist, Moidart and Arisaig. 'Emigrations,' he wrote from Greenock before he left, 'are like to demolish the Highland Lairds, and very deservedly.'

In the Isles there were harsh memories of 1739 when Macdonald of Sleat and Macleod of Dunvegan had sold some of their
people as indentured servants for the Carolinas. And now Sir
Alexander Macdonald was squeezing his tacksmen from Uist
and provoking from his bard Ian MacCodrum an angry protest.
Seallaibh m 'an cuairt duibh is faicibh na h-uaislean . . .

> Look around you and see the gentry
> with no pity for the poor creatures,
> with no kindness to their kin.
> They do not think that you belong to the land,
> and although they leave you empty
> they do not see it as a loss.
> They have lost their respect
> for every law and promise
> that was among the men
> who took this land from the foe.

But there was something more in MacCodrum's words than
a lament for the passing of the tacksmen. He would not have
called them *truaghain*, 'poor creatures'. He was thinking of the
people, for if the chief had no pity for his kinsmen, none could
be expected by the commons. Already the people were becoming
vagrants, wandering southward from the hills to the Lowland
coast. John Knox, bookseller, book-writer and philanthropist,
wrote of those whom he saw when touring the Highlands in
the seventeen-eighties. 'I often met families or bodies of people
travelling to the ports. They generally edged off the road or hurried along as if shy of an interview.' Those whom he persuaded
to give such an interview told him that they had been driven
from their land by their chiefs, their cattle seized and their furniture taken in lieu of unpaid rents. 'Our fathers,' said a Lochin-
ver man, 'were called out to fight our master's battles, and this is
our reward.'

But the money to pay their masters' debts, dowries and dun-
ning tradesmen had to come from somewhere. In time black
cattle alone would not be enough, though they darkened the
braes of many glens. As Britain entered the long Revolutionary
and Napoleonic wars, the demand for meat became stronger.

And in the Highlands there was a new sound, a placid bleating that was to blot out for ever Keppoch's dying call to his children.

'Woe to thee, oh land, the Great Sheep is coming!'

IN TIME, WHEN mountain pastures were white with woollen snow, when there were only black droppings in valleys that had once sent a hundred broadswords to a gathering, Highlanders would call the sheep the laird's 'four-footed clansmen'. Lost in a Glasgow slum, fumbling with scaling-knives in a Sutherland fishery, or swinging an axe in a Canadian clearing, they would forget, if indeed they ever understood, that sheep were one symptom only of the pressures that had driven them from their homes, not the compulsion itself. Yet the choice made by their lairds was real, sheep instead of men, and this was the cause of their exile and of their sorrow.

Exile to the Highlanders was not a matter of miles. Once expelled from the glen they had occupied for generations it was of small consequence to them whether they travelled ten miles or four thousand. The loss was the same, the pain as great. Unprepared for change, they held to the old ways, of which an acceptance of the chief's authority was among the strongest. He might dispose of them as he thought fit, but he was also their only protector, and when he began to use the power and ignore the obligation they were helpless. Aware of betrayal, they sometimes walked into exile with the meekness of the animals that replaced them.

They still saw themselves as the chief's rent-roll, supporters of his military and political prestige. Though they could lament the prodigal expenditure of their lives in quarrels that did not touch them directly, their pride had roots in a warrior history. It was almost their only compensation in famine and poverty. And it was exploited. During the fifty years that followed Culloden the chiefs raised twenty-two splendid regiments for the

Crown. These were mustered as the clans had been gathered in the past, as much by threat of eviction as by appeal. The promises made to them were often broken, and it is not surprising that in eight of the regiments there were mutinies serious enough to be punished by drum-head courts-martial and the firing-squad. But no one could complain of the Highlander's courage. The wearing of the Government's black tartan kept old ardours warm. It also bred a new pride that was heard in the voice of the bard when the laird began to replace his clansmen with Lowland shepherds and Lowland sheep.

> When sheep are gathered at the fold
> and the people are gone,
> each landlord, with his crook
> in his cloak, will not sing
> as he once did, counting
> the rents at the table.
> If war comes to the Kingdom
> and the French sail across in their
> thousands, King George's throat
> will not be safe from their blades.
> When the Gael left,
> wanting clothes, money and food,
> the English were poorly protected
> though their bellies were full of meat.

There had always been sheep in the Highlands. Each township had a few score that grazed with the cattle on the pastures, or wandered wild and unwatched in the bogs. They were thin and white-faced, straight-horned and as small as dogs sometimes. Their fleece looked like hair, though selected parts of it produced a gentle wool when spun. They had no cash value outside the hills, and they were kept for their wool and their milk. Mutton from their starved flanks was the only meat eaten by the poorer families. The people gave each animal a name at lambing, and every night after milking it was brought to shelter. For they were blessed. Christ had spoken of Himself as a Shepherd, and of His people as sheep.

In the primitive husbandry of the old tenancies, the limited pastures, there was no room for a sheep economy, for a Lowland animal that would require six acres of mountain grazing in the summer, and sheltered valley floors for wintering. In the beginning southern sheepmen did not believe that their flocks could survive a Highland winter, yet by 1760 they were already leasing the grass hills of Perthshire and Argyll. North of the Great Glen, northward to the Atlantic, there was wide land awaiting sheep that could live upon it, and men who would develop it. The first of these men was a sailor, a vice-admiral home from the sea, Sir John Lockhart-Ross of Balnagowan who had started life and walked a quarter-deck for twenty-five years as plain John Lockhart. The name was changed when he inherited the disputed title of chief of *Clann Aindrea* and the more tangible property of Balnagowan, a broad swathe of mountain, loch and glen from the Dornoch Firth to the western coast.

In 1762, his forty-second year, he settled down at Balnagowan Castle, and took a long hard look at what he owned. It was not encouraging. Land and people were much as they had been for centuries, except that many of his tenants were absentee Lowlanders, sub-letting to the Highlanders. A methodical, patient man, a man used to waiting for wind and tide, he slowly began to change both earth and tenants. He enclosed barren hillsides, and paid southern labourers a shilling a day to plant them. He drained and reclaimed marshy valleys. He refused to renew the leases of the absent Lowlanders, and he raised the rents of the sub-tenants. He also brought sheep to the county of Ross.

On his journey northward he had passed through Perthshire, and he had seen the flocks of black-faced Lintons which graziers were now pasturing there. He was told that they not only survived the white winters and black frosts, but also produced three times as much meat as cattle on the same area. When he had gathered to himself all the troublesome leases on his property, Lockhart-Ross took one large farm under his immediate control and put a flock of Lintons upon it. The experiment was successful and having proved a point and being anxious to turn his attention now to other Improvements, he granted the lease of the farm to a southern grazier, Thomas Geddes, on condition that he continued with Lintons. Thus Mr Geddes acquired the distinction of being the first Lowland sheep-farmer to come north of the Great Glen. The prosperity that followed for him, and for the son who took the lease after him, showed that his journey had not been as suicidal as his Lowland friends had forecast. They were sending two hundred thousand sheep across the Border to England every year, and were anxious to send more. Armstrongs, Elliots, and Scotts, a 'fine stalwart race of men', they turned their eyes northward with quickening interest.

The county of Ross was admirably suited to a great sheep economy. It endured less snow and enjoyed warmer summers than some more southern counties. Through its immobile ocean of mountain waves ran valley troughs that followed the course of the sun. There were good pastures for summer and safe shelter for winter. The rock walls ran with sweet water. There were, of course, people as well, but men were already saying that since there were too many of them, anyway, they would be far better off elsewhere.

Mr Geddes received no welcome from the men of Ross whom Sir John had removed from the upland pastures. They shot his sheep at night, drove them into the lochs, and terrorized his shepherds. They faced him on the brae and spoke words that were gibberish to him. 'The strongest deer,' they said, 'will not live here in the winter.' But the black-faced Lintons did. Even so, a stronger, hardier breed was desirable, one that was less subject to disease and would give a greater yield of mutton and wool in proportion to the high acreage of pasture needed.

Such a breed already existed, and word of it reached the Highlands in the old way, on the lips of a seer who travelled from township to township, calling a warning. No kind thoughts now for Christ's blessed animal. '*Mo thruaighe ort a thir, tha'n caoraich mhor a' teachd*!' Woe to thee, oh land, the Great Sheep is coming!

The Great Sheep was the Cheviot. This animal was almost man-made, so well-bred that, according to Mr John Naismyth of Hamilton (who prepared a report on it for the Society for the

Improvement of British Wool), 'a flock of some hundred ewes may be found, almost any two of which might pass for twin-sisters'.

They came, of course, from the Cheviot Hills, the rolling downs that strike the natural border between England and Scotland. Once known as the Long Hill sheep, a distinct and hardy race of animals had grazed there for six centuries, strengthened now and then by thousands of Merinos brought from the Continent. But by the middle of the eighteenth century they were still lank and gibbety, long-necked and thin at the shoulders. It was a Cheviot farmer called Robson who began to turn them into the great beast that would become the four-footed clansman of the Highlands. He brought three rams from the Wolds of Lincoln and put them to his ewes, by which, said Mr Naismyth 'the carcase and figure was much reformed'. A Spanish ram bought later, Ryeland rams and ewes, added the strength of their loins to the line, and in twenty years Mr Robson's shepherds had produced a sturdy animal that yielded a third more wool and meat, and showed remarkable stamina in the harsh winters that blow on the Cheviots. It had also, Mr Naismyth thought it delicate to add, a 'countenance mild and pleasant ... the head and ears long, neat and slender; the neck high and full; the back broad, straight and strong-coupled; the shoulders and buttocks broad, and in due proportion to each other; the legs small, clean-boned, and of a very moderate length; a long leg like an inverted lever being thought to render the animal less vigorous in travelling through deep ground, or working for its food among snow'.

In producing this promising animal Mr Robson's shepherds had also created a mythology which, if it did not equal in subtlety that of the human race it was shortly to supplant, had much in common with its superstitions.

'Careful shepherds,' Mr Naismyth informed the gentlemen of the Wool Society, 'think it is a matter deserving attention at the time of copulation to keep the ewes as much as possible from beholding improper objects, that unfortunate resemblances may not be impressed on the young. Remarkable instances of this plastic sympathy felt by sheep at the time of conception, are mentioned, such as lambs brought forth with the manner and gesture of a hare or a cat, which probably had accidently crossed the field of love. But the following was a more unlucky instance: A number of black-faced hairy sheep, part of a drove which had been carried southward, straying back to their native home, passed, at the critical period, through the pastures of the fine-woolled sheep. The breeding ewes gazed with admiration at the savage-looking strangers, and, at yeaning time a good many lambs, exactly resembling them, were brought forth.'

Some years before Mr Naismyth entertained the Society with this fact and fiction, the Cheviots had gone north. Encouraged by the success of two Northumbrians who had brought the animal as far as East Lothian, other men had taken them on over the Highland line. In 1790 they were across the Cromarty Firth into Ross, and two years later they reached Caithness in the far north.

The man who took them there was Sir John Sinclair of Ulbster, a ruddy-faced, hawk-nosed Highland gentleman who had many remarkable ideas, not the least of which, according to some of his countrymen, was the claim that trews, not the kilt, were the ancient dress of the Highlands (as indeed they probably were, for gentlemen). The Sinclairs of Ulbster had bought much of their land from the Earldom of Caithness, after that house exhausted itself fighting Glenorchy Campbells for the possession of it, firstly in the field and secondly in the Courts. In the time of 'Agricultural Sir John', Caithness no longer had a noble chief, but a number of prosperous landowners of whom he was the most intelligent and progressive.

He was probably the only Scot of his age who used the word 'Improvement' objectively. Had he been listened to, had his example been copied, the half-century of evictions, burnings, riots and exile that followed might have been avoided. It was the kindly old man's tragedy that he brought the Great Sheep north for the benefit of his people, but was unable to prevent others from using it to oust theirs. He wrote copiously on the improve-ments that could and should be made on Highland estates to give work to the people and fulfilment to the land, illustrating his precepts with practical examples. He became, in time, Chairman of the British Wool Society, but before he advised Highland lairds to turn their attention to sheep be brought the animal to his own lands, 'thinking that any recommendation from a person who had tried no experiment himself, and who had scarcely what could be called a flock of his own, would not be much attended to'.

Five hundred breeding ewes and a proportionate number of rams were put upon one of his farms at Langwell (an estate which he had bought for £9,000). 'To the astonishment of the Shepherds, who were strangers to the country, and of the natives who thought that sheep were so debilitated an animal that they ought to be housed in the winter season, not one of the flock died from cold, disease, or hunger; and as they throve equally well in the year 1792, I resolved to carry on the plan with all the vigour and attention that was possible for a man immersed in so many other avocations.'

The Langwell experiment was so successful, in fact, drawing back a curtain suddenly on a dazzling future, that the British Wool Society offered flocks of fifty Cheviot rams and a hundred and fifty ewes at 36s. the ram and 20s. the ewe (with no other expense) to all Highland lairds who 'aspire to the character of being active and intelligent improvers'. There were many who were bankrupt enough to see in this the perfect description of themselves, and Sinclair's warm hopes for his country became bitter.

'Nothing can be more detrimental. . . . The first thing that is done is to drive away all the present inhabitants. The next is to introduce a shepherd and a few dogs; and then to cover the mountains with flocks of wild, coarse-woolled, and savage animals which seldom see their shepherd or are benefited by his care.'

He pleaded for slow and considerate change, for the encouragement of native shepherds among the Highlanders. He said that small tenants should be continued in possession, persuaded to join their holdings and capital, to hire a common herdsman and purchase a small flock of 300 sheep. Part of their rents should be taken in kind, in wool and mutton. It was an admirable proposal, but like most such proposals in economics and politics it argued that all men were as benevolent as the proposer. Lowland graziers were hungry for the land and its profits. Highland lairds had creditors at their doors and the rewards of sheep-farming were too tempting to share among their ignorant and inconvenient tenantry. Sinclair had himself given them cogent reasons to feel this way.

'The Highlands of Scotland may sell, at present, perhaps from £200,000 to £300,000 worth of lean cattle per annum. The same ground will produce twice as much mutton, and there is wool into the bargain. If covered with the coarse-woolled breed of sheep, the wool might be worth about £300,000, the value of which can only be doubled by the art of the manufacturer; whereas the same ground under the Cheviot or True Mountain breed will produce at least £900,000 of fine wool.'

So began the invasion of the Cheviot or True Mountain breed. They came up the old cattle roads into Argyll, Inverness, and Ross. They climbed where the deer died, they throve where black cattle starved. Land which had produced 2d. an acre under cattle now yielded 2s. under sheep. Four shepherds, their dogs and three thousand sheep now occupied land that had once supported five townships. Small gentry, lawyers, merchants, half-pay officers with a little prize-money took up leases on land they rarely, if ever, saw, and became Highland gentlemen with imaginary pipers and gillies at their tail. Thus did Donald Macleod of Geanies become a landowner in Ross, crossing Cheviot sheep with Merinos and writing to his friends about the rewarding results.

The presses were busy with pamphlets, books, advice and instruction on sheep-farming. Few of the men who read them, or wrote them, showed the public responsibility of Sinclair. Sir George Mackenzie of Coul (who advised Highlanders to be happy as servants of servants) burgeoned with advice on the future of the Highlands, which he saw as resting squarely on the broad shoulders of a Cheviot ewe. He had a great ambition to be accepted as a scientist and an economist. He was more frequently an ass. His passion for scientific research led him to sacrifice his mother's diamonds to prove 'by means of the concentrated solar rays that after all they were but a form of carbon'. This was undoubtedly of importance, though it may not have reconciled his mother to their loss.

On the subject of sheep he was listened to more thoroughly, perhaps, than John Sinclair, for he did not confuse his readers with philanthropy or concern for the Highlander. His book, A General View of the Agriculture of Ross and Cromarty, would have been more accurately described as A Landlord's View ('I am about to introduce a considerable flock of Cheviots, and I hope my example will soon be followed'). It was dedicated to his friend, Sheriff Macleod of Ross, 'whose life has been devoted to the service of the county, and whose exertions for its improvement have been unremitted'.

Among long descriptions of flora, fauna, geology, geography, domestic and agricultural economy, landlordism and peasantry, the book contained a stern dismissal of those who were protesting against wholesale evictions of tenants. 'We have heard but a few voices against the necessity of removing the former possessors to make way for shepherds.... The necessity for reducing the population in order to introduce valuable improvements, and the advantages of committing the cultivation of the soil to the hands of a few have been discussed by men much more capable of doing justice to these subjects than myself.'

This was an unusually modest acknowledgement from Sir George, but on the material advantages of replacing the many by the few he was quite positive. 'I have often set before my guests mutton of the Leicester, Cheviot and Forest and country breeds, taking care that none of it should be particularly remarkable for fatness, and they have mistaken one for the other.'

Sir George was a disciple of Improvement, and within the context of his age this made him progressive in thought and action. The responsibilities of land in a growing economy brought both profit and prestige to those who exploited it. A man who spent his time on his estates, increasing their yield, was giving greater service to his country than one who spent his at a gaming-table or, for that matter, at a writing-desk asking whether Men were not more important than Sheep.

From this noble premise it was logical to conclude that the Men of Ross were a seditious Mob.

'They have got a good many arms among them'

ROBERT DUNDAS, Lord Advocate of Scotland, was nephew to Henry Dundas, Home Secretary. The Dundases of Arniston had been providing great lawyers for more than a century and now, with Henry, they had moved into the jobbery of politics under the wing of William Pitt. Uncle and nephew were among the most hated men in Scotland. They ruled the country as Sultan and Grand Vizier, or as if, some men complained, it were 'a lodge at a great man's gate'. Although there was no family cordiality in the formal letters that passed between them in the summer of 1792 on the subject of Ross, Henry must have been concerned with the personal trials of Robert. There was rioting and mobbing in Aberdeen, Perth, Dundee and Edinburgh. The burning of the effigies of both Lord Advocate and Home Secretary was a popular entertainment. An Edinburgh crowd, interrupted in this by the reading of the Riot Act and by salutary volleys from redcoats, moved on to throw stones through Robert's windows. Driven from that, they went to St Andrew's Square, and threw more stones at the Lord Provost's house. Being a good Scot, he blamed the English for his townsfolk's lack of respect to his person.

'An evil spirit seems to have reached us,' he told Robert Dundas, 'which I was in hopes John Bull would have kept to himself.'

The evil spirit was Liberty. Notwithstanding the Lord Provost's complaint, Scotland was more active in its cause than England (where the people, in the name of 'Church and King', were more inclined to burn effigies of such liberty-lovers as Tom Paine and Joseph Priestley). There was, Henry Dundas was told by the Sheriff of Lanarkshire, 'an almost universal spirit of reform and opposition to the established government and legal administration, which has wonderfully diffused through the manufacturing towns of this country'. Earlier in the year a Society of Friends of the People had been formed in Edinburgh, taking oaths in the French style to 'live free or die'. Governments naturally qualify the word freedom, and when they suspect that it means that people wish to be free of them they exercise their lawful freedom to defend themselves. Thus young Thomas Muir, the articulate advocate who led the Society, was later arrested and transported.

But the evil spirit and the rioting continued, encouraged by the development of events in France. Though they were confined to the Lowlands, there was always the fear that in the mountains, the seat of Scotland's Mars, riot might too easily become rebellion. It was undoubtedly with this fear in mind that the Lord Advocate wrote to his uncle on 6 August. About the middle of July, he said, he had received reports of assault and riot in the County of Ross, whereby the property and person of a Mr Cameron had been much abused. He had not thought it necessary at the time to inform His Majesty's Ministers, believing that the trouble could be settled by the Civil Magistrates, with or without the help of three companies of the Black Watch which had been sent from Stirling to Fort George. 'But I am sorry to state that in this expectation I have been disappointed, and that the Inhabitants of that district are at present in a situation most disorderly.'

The trouble was in fact over, but with the delay in the Post from Dingwall he could not know this, and he told the Home Secretary that he had given orders for the remaining companies of the 42nd to march for Fort George immediately, 'which I trust will be sufficient for quelling these seditious disturbances'.

Of all the counties in the north, Ross had been most affected by the new sheep-walks. In Easter Ross the change had been sudden and sweeping. This peninsula of mountains between the Dornoch and Cromarty firths had become practical ground for the experiments pioneered by Sir John Lockhart-Ross, Thomas Geddes and Sir John Sinclair. An Ayrshire sheepman called

Mitchell had rented land from Davidson of Tulloch, Donald Macleod of Geanies had taken a long lease on land belonging to Balnagowan, and now two Cameron brothers from Lochaber, having put sheep on the lands of Munro of Culcairn, were moving further southward. They took a long lease on Kildermorie in the wild heart of Easter Ross.

The property belonged to Sir Hector Munro of Novar, a Colonel of the Black Watch, an indifferent major-general after some doubtful service in India, and the inactive Member of Parliament for Inverness Burghs for twenty-four years. His estates stretched northward from his yellow house on the Cromarty Firth to the green valley of the Oykel, where his cousin Culcairn's land began. He had been improving his property for some years. In Kildermorie he had reduced the number of tenants first to six, and then to none at all, renting it free of human occupants to the Camerons from Lochaber.

The men of Ross retreated sullenly before this bleating invasion. Part of their livelihood, and the increased rents they were paying, had come from the summer grazing of cattle belonging to farmers on the coastal lowlands of the country. For this they charged the owners 1s. a head, and to get the barest of livings they were forced to overstock the brown hills. When sheep ate into their pastures, and the roof-trees of their township were pulled down, they raised the grazing-price to half a crown a head, and then to a crown. Though they were in sympathy with the Highlanders, the farmers could not pay the money, and in 1792 they were already sending their cattle northward to Sutherland for the summer.

It was through Kildermorie and Strath Rusdale that the old seer had gone crying his warning against the coming of the Great Sheep. There were no Rosses now on Kildermorie, but they still held sub-tenancies in the strath, and when they drove their cattle up to the long moor at the head of the valley they could look to the west and see Glen Morie white with sheep belonging to Captain Alan Cameron and his brother Alexander. It was an old custom of the hills that men should not be too particular about the marches between grazings, and if the black cattle of

Strath Rusdale strayed on to the sheep-walk the Rosses let them go, thinking no more of it. But the Camerons sent a warning phrased in words suitable to a communication between Highland gentry and Highland commons. When next the cattle came upon Kildermorie they would be impounded against a fine.

They did stray, and the Cameron shepherds drove them into a fank at the western end of Loch Morie below the high heads of Meall nam Bo and Carn Beag. They were kept in the pen until the Rosses paid the fine. It happened again, and again, until the Rosses asked themselves who they were to take such treatment from Lowland shepherds. They decided to release their cattle by force, and a call was sent down the glen from Braentra to Ardross. All men were invited to the foray. The word was out against the foreigners from Lochaber. The word was out against sheep.

At Ardross the men of the township were cutting peat when the invitation came. They threw down their tools with enthusiasm. Led by a legendary giant called Alisdair Mor Wallace, they marched northwards up the banks of Alness Water, and from all sides of the strath men came bounding to join them. They climbed over the long moor, where the wind blows in a ceaseless tide over the grass, and they came down the shoulder of Carn Beag to the meadow at the head of Loch Morie. They came shouting and singing, crying taunts, and news of their approach reached Kildermorie long before they arrived. At the gate of the cattle-pen waited the Captain and his brother, their Lowland shepherds, and some of their people from Lochaber.

The Cameron brothers were big and powerful men, and the Captain, his blood stirring, had armed himself with a musket and with a dirk a foot long. There was little parleying before the Rosses flooded over the shepherds in an angry, scuffling mob. Big Wallace grappled with Captain Alan, and it is said that in the struggle the barrel of the musket was twisted like a reed. In a few minutes the Lochaber gentry were on their backs, and their people were flying in terror up the brae. The Rosses took their cattle home to Strath Rusdale, a piper playing a triumphant rant before them.

A brawl which would have made no stir at all fifty years earlier, now sent ripples of alarm southward to Edinburgh. The Camerons, their pride injured and their property rights abused, wrote in protest to the Sheriff. Mr Macleod wrote in his turn to the Lord Advocate who was not, at this stage, particularly worried, recognizing the incident as one tedious result of 'a measure very unpopular, the removing of the inhabitants from their small properties and dwelling-houses'. But when Sheriff Macleod wrote again to say that he alone would not be enough to bring the rioters to trial and punishment, and please could he have some assistance from the military, his lordship asked the Commander-in-Chief to put the Black Watch on the road northward. And he hoped, no doubt, that nothing more would be heard of the matter.

On Friday, 27 July, the Rosses of Strath Rusdale gathered for a wedding. Kinsmen came from all parts of Ross. They danced and they sang and they drank heavily. Fired by the crude whisky which they distilled themselves (in bland defiance of the King's rightful revenues), inflamed by the warrior challenge of the pipes and by the retold story of the rout at Loch Morie, they planned another foray that would rid them for ever of the Great Sheep and restore to them the home of their ancestors. They decided to call upon the men of Sutherland to join them in driving every ram, ewe and lamb, every Lowland shepherd and his dog from Glen Achany, Strath Oykel, Strathcarron and Strath Rusdale, from the east and the west southward to the Beauly Firth and over into Inverness. There, if they wished and had the spirit, the men of Inverness might drive them further, and others further still until the Great Sheep was returned to the land that had spawned it.

On Sunday, at the church doors in the parishes of Alness, Urquhart, Resolis and Kincardine, at the taverns in the parishes of Creich and Lairg (there being no preaching there that day), messengers called upon all men to gather that Tuesday along the banks of the River Oykel.

How many answered the call is not known, although Sheriff Macleod said there were four hundred. They went northward first, up Glen Achany to Lairg in Sutherland, and there they pressed the frightened Lowland shepherds into service before turning southward again. It was the largest drive the Highlands had known. Soon the hills on either side of the River Shin were covered with bleating, drifting animals. Men and women came to their doors to watch them pass, to offer water and encouragement to the drovers. The weather was warm and kindly, the earth soft beneath the feet of the exultant Highlanders.

'No act of violence or outrage occurred,' wrote David Stewart of Garth, who was at this moment coming north with his comrades in the 42nd Regiment, 'nor did the sheep suffer in the smallest degree beyond what resulted from the fatigues of the journey and the temporary loss of their pasture. Though pressed with hunger, these conscientious peasants did not take a single animal for their own use, contenting themselves with the occasional supplies of meal or victuals which they obtained in the course of their journey.'

Mr Macleod was less generous in his account of what the drovers were doing. He knew what was afoot as soon as the call went out on Sunday. 'Not one Constable has ventured or dared apprehend any of those who made the proclamation,' he complained bitterly to the Lord Advocate on Tuesday evening. 'They have kept their word and are this day gone from all quarters of the County on this extraordinary attempt.' The frightened constables had obviously larded their reports with their imaginations, for as a result of them Mr Macleod could see no hungry, conscientious peasantry coming south to Dingwall, only a dangerous and seditious mob.

'The most violent threats of denunciation were added against such as were luke-warm, or did not appear at the time or place appointed, such as killing their oxen in the hills, driving the sheep through the corn of many of them.... No Military Force is arrived, and by return of an Express I sent to Fort George, the 3 companies of the 42nd destined for that place are not expected before Friday or Saturday. I have no accounts whatever from the Commander-in-Chief or the rout or destination, which I think not a little extraordinary.'

His querulous dismay was perhaps understandable. The past was too close in the Highlands for a man holding his office not to fear trouble. Rusty weapons, hidden in defiance of the Disarming Acts, still lay beneath the divots of many cottages, and Mr Macleod may have had no doubt that these might soon appear in the hands of the men of Ross, if indeed they had not already. He told his lordship what he intended to do in the absence of the soldiers. The gentry of the country had been aroused, coming to Dingwall at the Sheriff's request. For all the priming of pistols, the arming of servants, there had been less ardour for the field than Mr Macleod had hoped.

'I proposed to attempt interrupting the Rioters with this Force if they thought it adequate, but they were decidedly of the opinion that it was perfectly inadequate, and that in the beginning of a commotion of this kind we were of no account to hazard a defeat which might be attended with the most dreadful and melancholy consquences to the Troops and to ourselves individually. They therefore advised me in the strongest manner not to move a man from Fort George until a sufficient force did arrive, and for the present to permit the deluded population to take their swing.'

It was obvious from the tone of his letter that the Sheriff did not share the gentry's view. And behind each word of it seems to stand the chimera of these days, a monster in a red cap waving hands of blood. He hoped his lordship would not treat the affair lightly, it was 'an actual, existing Rebellion against the Laws'. He did not know, could not say with certainty that the Rebellion had no 'Heads or Advisers', and he hoped that no Gentleman had been so ill-advised as to give it his encouragement and support.

As usual, he was writing his dispatch at the end of an exhausting day, and he wished his lordship to know this. After he had signed himself his lordship's most humble servant, he recalled something that he had forgotten, something that must surely make the Lord Advocate realize how serious the matter had become.

'PS. It was stated as an undoubted fact to the meeting that a person from Sutherland had come to Inverness a few days ago and had purchased gun-powder to the value of £26 Stg, and it is known that they have got a good many arms among them.'

'We are so completely under the heel of the Populace'

TWENTY-THREE alarmed gentlemen had met in Dingwall on Tuesday morning, summoned by Sheriff Macleod to hear from him the true and particular news from the glens, and to address His Majesty as 'Freeholders, Justices of Peace and Commissioners of Supply of the Shire of Ross'. For their President they naturally elected Sir Hugh Munro of Foulis, chief of his clan and the most notable man of the county, and between them they owned every acre and controlled every vote in Ross. The drovers in the hills were their clansmen and their tenants, but from the language they used the Men of Ross might well have been a revolutionary rabble from France.

From Mr Macleod they heard the worst confirmation of their fears. Constables in every part of the county were reporting 'disturbances and tumultuous associations', and every gentleman present saw his family in danger of bodily harm, his property in risk of pillage. They demanded exemplary punishment of the Strath Rusdale men who had outraged the rights and liberty of Captain Cameron, and so frightened themselves that when Sir Hugh wrote to the Lord Advocate that evening he said 'We are at present so completely under the heel of the Populace that should they come to burn our houses or destroy our Property in any way their caprice may lead them to, we are incapable of resistance.'

Desiring His Majesty to know the full extent of their alarm and loyalty, they drew up a series of resolutions, the preamble to which deplored both the assault on the brothers Cameron and the resistance of the Men of Ross to all legal enquiries into it. Such behaviour had been 'atrocity' enough, but the church-door proclamation of Sunday 'is considered by us as absolute sedition and setting the Laws and Government of this Kingdom at defiance'. In the gentleman's opinion, there was no just cause for the commotion. The Law was open to redress injuries suffered by all ranks. They declared, in their different characters of Magistrates and Landowners, that they had not until then heard of any grievance among their people. They were not ignorant, of course, of the fact that the introduction of sheep on to some farms was 'the pretext at present made use of to cover the crimes and outrages that are daily committed against all Law and Order', but no complaint had been laid before them by proper persons in the proper way.

Having thus polished their consciences, and declared their innocence before His Majesty, they presented to him the Resolutions agreed upon :

1st. THAT we shall exert ourselves in our private character as Landlords, to impress on the minds of our tenants and others on our properties the very dangerous tendency of the associations which subsist, and endeavour to prevail on them by every rational argument applicable to their interests and feelings to withdraw themselves from them, or warn them of their danger.

2nd. THAT we will afford our countenance, assistance and protection to the Sheriff in carrying through such proper and legal measures as may appear most likely to him to bring the ringleaders of the late and present tumults and disturbances to justice.

3rd. AND THAT we will never afford any protection or countenance to any who may presume to oppose the laws or regular administration of justice.

And so on, until they remained, jointly and individually the subscribed gentlemen of Ross. The list was impressive. There were the lairds of Foulis, Novar and Kindeace, Geanies, Culrain and Highfield, Tulloch, Scotsbean and Culcairn. And fourteen more. The meeting had been long and declamatory. The critical nature of the hour as much as the custom of the age demanded that each express himself with histrionic passion. The fear of one man took fire from another's alarm, and even Mr Macleod's assurance that three companies of the Black Watch were on the way was of no comfort. Although they had passed a resolution to prevail upon their tenants with rational arguments, they were of the private opinion that five hundred infantrymen and three troops of dragoons would be more effective.

No wonder the Sheriff told the Lord Advocate that he was 'perfectly exhausted with the business of this day'.

The week moved toward its end with no sign of redcoats and tartan on the Beauly road, but with daily news and rumours of the Rioters. They had crossed the Kyle of Sutherland southward into Ross, driving before them all the sheep of Colonel Baillie and Sir Charles Ross of Balnagowan. They were moving against Mr Mitchell's flocks in Strath Oykel. Men of the Sutherland glens by Lairg were with them, armed with muskets. Mr Macleod was now convinced that before the Black Watch reached Dingwall the Mob would already be howling through its streets, burning and killing. He decided that it was his duty to send word immediately to Simon Fraser, Sheriff-Depute of Inverness, not so much to advise that gentleman to bar his door as to ask him to summon up his gentry and send them north at once.

'You can be no stranger to the tumults, commotions and actual seditious acts that are going on in this County at this time,' he wrote, 'the flame is spreading; what is our case today, if matters are permitted to proceed, will be yours tomorrow. I understand a Mob of about four hundred strong are now actually employed in collecting the sheep, over all this and the neighbouring county of Sutherland. I intend to oppose them with what force I can collect – the Gentlemen of the County, armed with such of their servants and dependants as they can confide in, backed by three companies of the 42nd regiment. If you suppose you can raise any Volunteers hearty in the Cause of good Order and Subordination to join us, we shall feel much obliged to you; and request you may inform me here by Express tomorrow whether I may have any reliance on your assistance.'

Mr Fraser promptly appealed to his kinsman and chief, the Honourable Archibald Fraser of Lovat. As a boy, this old man had lain in the heather on Culloden Moor and watched his father's people go forward in a charge against the Royal line. He was a nervous, excitable man who seems to have needed little encouragement to see rebellion and riot behind every ben. He summoned forty gentlemen of the shire (thirteen of them of his own name) to meet under the presidency of the Sheriff. They drew up a series of resolutions which they ordered to be printed and circulated, and which declared their anxiety and their determination to give Mr Macleod all the assistance he needed. More confident of victory than the Gentlemen of Ross (being, perhaps, that much farther away) they resolved that if the jails of Inverness and Ross proved inadequate to hold all the prisoners that must be taken, then the Commander-in-Chief in Scotland should be asked to take the overflow into His Majesty's forts. They also told Mr Fraser that it was his duty to supply them with the necessary provisions and transport should they move northward into Ross.

Lovat sent these resolutions to the Home Secretary in London, with a covering letter so ill-spelt and ill-written that it is now almost unreadable. He asked for permission to draw arms and ammunition from the garrison at Fort George. If there were insufficient supplies there, he wanted some from Edinburgh, or even from Woolwich. Henry Dundas placed these martial demands before the King with the reassurance that the matter was in the capable hands of his nephew, and he wrote to the Commander-in-Chief in Scotland, warning him that if more soldiers must be sent to Ross then he was to take care that Edinburgh was not left unprotected before its own mob.

Unaware of the commotion and alarm they were causing among loyal gentlemen, the simple men of Ross and Sutherland came southward, driving six thousand sheep or more before them. On Friday, 5 August, they reached the scattered cottages of Boath seven miles from the Cromarty Firth and close by the elbow of Strath Rusdale. Here was a wide saucer of land, holding the warmth of the day's sun close to the sky. To the north was the green gash of the strath, to the west the brown flanks of Meall Beg and Meall Mor rose two thousand feet from the water of Loch Morie. The Great Sheep filled the gentle valley, moving restlessly in the evening light, boiling from corries of violet heather. Four hundred men, if Mr Macleod's figure is to be accepted, built their fires of peat and wrapped themselves in their plaids for the night. There was more yet to be done before they moved on to Beauly, and on Saturday morning all but fifty of them left the sheep at the trysting-place and departed for the west.

Sheriff Macleod was not without cunning. He had his intelligence service in the glens, the nature of which he did not think necessary to explain to the Lord Advocate. At two o'clock on Saturday afternoon he heard that the drovers had reached Boath, that the sheep were still there, and that most of the Rioters had left 'to collect Captain Cameron's and to go with them by a different rout and collect those belonging to Mr Mitchell, and proceed Monday and Tuesday with them by another Pass until they got the whole beyond the bounds of the County'.

To his relief, the three companies of the 42nd Regiment arrived almost at the same time as this information reached him. They were paraded in the streets of Dingwall, red coats dusty, bonnets nodding, the sun shining on oiled wood and polished steel. They were a reassuring sight to the frightened town, their scarlet-kilted pipers standing with one knee bent in the van of the platoons. Major Dalrymple, strapped about with broad-sword and pistols, placed his men at the disposal of Mr Macleod, remarking only that they were tired, and that while they would march upon the Sheriff's orders they were scarcely in a condition to go bounding over the heather after agile men who had slept well this week.

No one asked what the men of the 42nd thought of their present role. Some of them had been recruited in Ross, and all had more in common with the drovers than with Sir Hugh Munro and his lairds. Among the officers was one young lieutenant who found the duty distasteful. He had not been impressed by the talk of Riot, Sedition, Disorder and Insurgence. 'The manner in which the people gave vent to their grief and rage when driven from their ancient homes,' wrote David Stewart many years later, 'showed that they did not merit this treatment, and that an improper estimate had been formed of their character.' But he was a soldier, and his first loyalty and first love was his regiment. 'I was a very young soldier at the time, but on no subsequent occasion were my feelings so powerfully excited as on this. To a military man it could not be but gratifying to see the men, in so delicate and trying a situation, manifesting a full determination to do their duty against whomsoever their efforts should be directed; while to their feelings of humanity, the necessity of turning their arms against their friends and relations presented a severe alternative.'

There seems to have been no doubt in Mr Macleod's mind that the men of the Black Watch would, if ordered, advance with the bayonet against their kin, for in none of his letters is there any suspicion of their loyalty to the Crown. They were given no time, in any case, to reflect upon their duty. At eight o'clock they were on the road again, marching north-eastward up the firth toward Alness, trudging in the dust behind the hooves of the Ross-shire gentry. They were desperately tired, and even the fact that their Colonel, Sir Hector, was riding ahead could put no strength into their limbs.

To Mr Macleod their presence was enough, and knowing now that there were only half a hundred of the drovers at Boath, he was in high spirits. The gentry had gathered willingly upon the arrival of the Highlanders, and, said Mr Macleod, 'I added an order to the Magistrates of Dingwall to collect their inhabitants and to represent the urgency of the case and hoped that all who wished well to Good Order would attend upon me.' At five o'clock a score or more citizens were recruited in this way and put on the road with gentry and soldiers at eight. Ahead of them ran a screen of scouts, sending back messages to Mr Macleod. It took the column five hours to reach An Corran, a sickle-shaped braeside overlooking Boath from the south-east. Below, in the faint darkness of the northern night, could be seen the blue smoke of peat and the ghostly herd of sleeping sheep. Mr Macleod halted his troops and waited word from his scouts. The men of the 42nd, now beaten, fell out on the heather, exhausted.

The scouts brought back surprising news. The drovers had as good an intelligence service as the Sheriff, or his men had made too much noise, for before the forces of Law and Good Order had made their appearance on the brae the Men of Ross had fled. All of them, leaving the sheep where they slept and the embers of their fires still warm. Here was no armed band from Sutherland, no evidence of gunpowder bought boldly in Inverness for £26 sterling, but simple men running in fear.

'As the soldiers were a good deal fatigued,' said Mr Macleod, 'some of the Gentlemen agreed to accompany me on instantly to search the house and some wood that was in the neighbourhood, and with the assistance of our riding-servants, and about a dozen countrymen, we began our search.' They rode down at a gallop to the twisted stream that runs from Loch Morie to the Alness, and it was here that they drove eight men from hiding in the barley-corn. The Rosses ran, or stood in stupid fear until all were rounded up. Mr Macleod and other gentlemen splashed through the river and rode up Strath Rusdale for three miles. All but two of the houses were empty, and in these were taken John Ross *alias* Davidson, Donald Munro *alias* MacAddie and his sons, William and George. 'They had been out with the Sheep Drivers,' reported Mr Macleod, 'but returned home that night, all the rest of the inhabitants of that glen were still out with them.'

It may have occurred to some of the 42nd Highlanders, veterans of Brandywine, Germantown and White Marsh in the American Revolution, that here was a very sorry insurrection indeed, without a shot fired or a drum beating the advance. But as the Gentlemen rode to Novar House for breakfast their blood pulsed with pride. When Mr Macleod sat down to write his dispatch, without washing from himself the grime and sweat of the campaign, he wrote like a victorious general of an army in the field. The feeling that he had narrowly averted a calamity remained with him for the rest of his life, and the memory of it was to bring him out in arms again twenty-eight years from now.

The Men of Ross who had gone from Boath on Saturday to drive off the flocks of the Cameron brothers and Mitchell drifted back to their homes as soon as they heard the news. They closed their faces to the Sheriff officers who came seeking precognitions against the ringleaders, and they watched with bitter and heavy hearts as the Great Sheep came once more to the braes. The 42nd remained at Dingwall until the end of the month, and then it was recalled to the south, where, said David Stewart with thin sarcasm, it was 'actively employed against the Lowlanders who were rioting, and hanging, drowning and burning the effigies of those whom they called their political oppressors; a species of refinement in the expression of their sentiments towards their superiors to which the ignorant Highlanders have not yet attained'.

Mr Macleod found his ringleaders, or those whom he chose to call the ringleaders. They were: Hugh Breac Mackenzie, tenant of Acharn in the parish of Alness; Malcolm Ross *alias* Macrob, tenant in Alladale in the parish of Kincardine; Donald Munro *alias* Roy, tenant in Drumvaich in the parish of Kincardine; Alexander Mackay, tenant in Langwell in the parish of Kincardine; and William Cunningham tenant in Aulanguish in the parish of Kincardine.

At the bar of the Circuit Court in Inverness on 14 September they were charged jointly and severally with 'advising, exciting, and instigating persons riotously and feloniously to invade, seize upon, and drive away from the grounds of the proprietors flocks of sheep amounting to several thousands' whereby 'a daring insult was offered to the law, the public peace was disturbed, and the property of the lieges greatly damaged and at the mercy of a lawless and seditious mob'.

They could not have understood the charge, or, if they did, have recognized it as a fair and reasonable description of what they had done. Their actions had been passionate and impulsive, they had believed that by the arbitrary removal of the cause of their sorrow they would be able to recover their land and their old ways. They were defended by Charles Ross, a young advocate of their own country, but all his eloquence, putting their case in terms of common humanity as much as in Law, could not argue away the insolence of their assault on the sacred rights of property.

The accusations that had been made against the Men of Ross in the hysterical letters that had passed between Dingwall and Edinburgh – Sedition, Insurrection, Rebellion – demanded the extreme penalty if proved. The sentences passed were less harsh, although they were bitter and merciless. Hugh Breac Mackenzie was sentenced to transportation to Botany Bay for seven years. Malcolm Ross was sentenced to a fine of £50 and imprisonment until it was paid, which to a man with empty pockets could be for ever. Donald Munro and Alexander Mackay were banished from Scotland for life, and William Cunningham was sentenced to three months in gaol.

But one night as the five men lay in prison at Inverness, awaiting execution of their sentences, the door was miraculously opened, and in the morning they were gone. No one could or would say how it had happened. Although a reward of £5 was offered for the apprehension of each man, and an advertisement to this effect was published in the Edinburgh Courant of 3 November, they were never heard of again.

It was the end of the Ross-shire Sheep Riot. Never again would Highlanders gather to turn back the invasion of the Great Cheviot. Though they had a history of battles, one defeat could always persuade them to abandon a war, and their inability to create leaders from among themselves was to waste their anger in despair. For many years yet they would forcibly resist eviction from their homes, and in such resistance the women would be bolder than the men, but they now accepted the sheep as they accepted famine and pestilence. They were numbed by the betrayal of their lairds, and they could learn no lesson from the Year of the Sheep but that the great hatred of the Lowlander intended to destroy them.

For their part, the lairds, once they had recovered from the shock, realized that in future they could count upon the full power of the Law, backed by bayonets if necessary, to support them in removing their tenants and replacing them with sheep. They would not be slow in making use of it.

There was one more lesson to be learnt from the Year of the Sheep, although one man only seems to have recognized it and he, perhaps, the most unlikely. He was the Commander-in-Chief of the King's Armies in Scotland, Lord Adam Gordon.

On 15 July he had left Edinburgh and its mob in the care of his deputy, Lieutenant-General Leslie, and set out on his annual tour of the Royal forts in the Highlands, intending to relieve the tedium and discomfort of the duty (he was approaching seventy) with a long visit to the Duke of Gordon. But when he arrived at his grandnephew's home on Friday, 17 August, he found there a letter from the Home Secretary asking for his report on the affair in Ross, and making it plain that this was required immediately. Testily Gordon sent word to Sheriff Macleod and Sir Hector Munro to meet him the next day at Fort George, following the messenger himself at post-haste. He listened to Macleod and Munro throughout Saturday, and to all the gentry of Ross and Inverness who buzzed about him with talk of Sedition and Rebellion nipped in the bud.

On Sunday he wrote a private letter to Henry Dundas. Though he was an indifferent soldier, he was a wise old man, and in those few hours he had obtained a clearer picture of past, present and future than anybody in the country.

'If I was to hazard an opinion upon the matter it is a decided one,' he told the Home Secretary, 'that no *disloyalty* or spirit of *rebellion*, or dislike to His Majesty's *Person or Government* is in the least degree concerned in these tumults, and that they have solely originated in a (too well-founded) apprehension that the landed proprietors in Ross-shire and some of the adjacent Highland counties were about to let their estates to sheep-farmers, by which means all the former tenants would be ousted and turned adrift and of course obliged to emigrate, unless they could be elsewhere received.'

He agreed that the behaviour of the Men of Ross was a disgrace to any civilized country, and he did not argue against the lawful right of a proprietor to do as he pleased with his own property 'even if the Publick suffers thereby'. But there was something more to be considered.

'Everybody knows the wonderful attachment a Highlander has to his *native spot*, be it ever so *bare*, and ever so *mountainous*, and if these speculative gentlemen shall by any means, or from *avarice*, once dispeople their estates and stock them with sheep and that a bad season or two should follow, and the sheep be thereby destroyed, I am convinced no temptation under the sun will be able to bring inhabitants to such Highland property from any part of this world.'

2

THE YEAR OF THE BURNINGS

'That he was dull, there can be little doubt'

HE was coal and wool joined by a stately hyphen and ennobled by five coronets. He was a Knight of the Garter, a Privy Councillor, Recorder of Stafford, a Trustee of the British Museum, a Vice-President of the Society of Arts, and an Hereditary Governor of the British Institution. He was the Most Noble George Granville Leveson-Gower, second Marquess of Stafford, third Earl Gower and Viscount Trentham, fourth Lord Gower of Stittenham in Yorkshire, eighth baronet of the same place, and ultimately and pre-eminently for the last six months of his life he was the first Duke of Sutherland.

His red sandstone effigy, in a red sandstone toga, rears thirty feet from a pedestal seventy-six feet high at the top of Ben Bhraggie, which is itself thirteen hundred feet above the green water of the Dornoch Firth. Its back is to the glens he emptied, it faces the sea to which his policies committed five thousand people as emigrants or herring-fishers. For much of his adult life he had an annual income of £300,000, and he would have agreed with the *Gentleman's Magazine* that he 'expended this vast revenue nobly and munificently'. Other men helped him with the expenditure to the last. The owners of the steamer *Soho*, for example, charged him £700 for carrying his aged body from Wapping to Scotland.

He was the Great Improver. Where there had been nothing in his opinion but wilderness and savagery, he built, or had built for him by the Government, thirty-four bridges and four hundred and fifty miles of road. The glens emptied by his commissioners, factors, law-agents and ground-officers (with the prompt assistance of police and soldiers when necessary), were let or leased to Lowlanders who grazed 200,000 True Mountain Sheep upon them and sheared 415,000 pounds of wool every year. He pulled the shire of Sutherland out of the past for the trifling cost of two-thirds of one year's income. And because he was an Englishman, and spoke no Gaelic, he did not hear the bitter protests from the poets among his people.

Had he heard them and understood them he would have considered their complaint of small importance against the magnitude of the work he set himself. He had accepted the solemn duty to improve the property which inheritance and marriage brought him, and perhaps he may not be criticized for what he wanted to do, only for the manner in which it was done. He was the product of a class to whom Property was becoming a sacred trust and its improvement an obligation that must take precedence over all others. This class, owning the land, controlling the legislature, officering the Army, dividing mankind into Gentility and Commons, and transporting a child for the stealing of a handkerchief (because it was Property), sincerely believed that its own enrichment must bring a greater good to a greater number. And since the Marquess of Stafford on no occasion watched when his agents burned the timbers of his people's houses, and drove them to emigrant ships or to coastal villages that were like gulls' nests on the cliffs, it is understandable that he held to this view until his death.

His lineage was uniformly undramatic. The early Gowers were Yorkshiremen who moved to Stafford in the seventeenth century, marrying into the Levesons, coal-owning dsecendants of French wool-staplers. In three generations they had risen from a baronetcy to a marquessate, without doing anything significantly worthwhile to earn the elevation. 'I wish,' wrote Lord Ronald Gower, Stafford's grandson, 'I could think that their promotion was owing to deeds performed by land or sea; but if the truth must be told, the family have been more distinguished by their luck and their alliances than in the senate or in the field. For generations they appear to have wedded heiresses or co-heirs of peers; and in the marriage of my grandfather to the greatest landed heiress in three kingdoms their achievements in that respect may be said to have culminated.'

Stafford was born in Arlington Street in 1758, a delicate child who never successfully conquered his physical weakness. He went to Westminster and Christ Church, made the Grand Tour in the company of the usual divine, and reached manhood a bilious and rheumatic creature with a great hawk-nose drooping over a prim mouth. Artists did their best with this discouraging material. In his youth he was painted by Romney as a cavalier in silk and lace, but his face shows his disapproval of the deception. Later Opie saw him as a beaked and fussy old man in a snuff-coloured coat and an auburn wig. In 1808 James Gillray caught him shuffling through the snow to Christie's, and drew him with back bent, gaiters dragging, and pebbled glasses resting on the bridge of that sad nose. Only in Chantrey's sculpture has his face a nobility to equal his rank, and this may be due to the fact that it is still a hundred feet above eye-level even after one has climbed to the top of Ben Bhraggie.

'For that he was dull I think there can be little doubt,' wrote his grandson, 'I have searched in vain in his dispatches to find what manner of man (he) was. ... Neither have I heard that he ever did anything or said anything that was worth remembering; if he did it has been forgotten long ago.' Lord Ronald's judgement was something to be expected from a languid Victorian aesthete, but in the dispatches Stafford wrote while Ambassador in Paris during the Revolution there was nothing to dispute Gower's opinion. They were 'mere records of official dulness, hopelessly and lamentably dull, almost as dull as poor Louis XVI's entries in his diary'.

Lady Stafford, however, provided a colourful third dimension to the pasteboard character of her husband. A passport issued to her when they left Paris in 1793 described her as : 'Madame Elizabeth, Countess of Sutherland, wife of the Ambassador from England, aged 27 years, five feet high, hair and brows light chestnut, eyes chestnut brown, nose well-made, mouth small, chin round, forehead low, face rather small.'

She had been a Countess, and *Ban mhorair Chataibh*, the Great

Lady of Sutherland, since the age of six, the title secured for her by costly litigation following the death of her father, the last Earl. In her youth her beauty was remarkable. Plump and matronly in middle age, her appearance could still turn Byron's head for a second look when he saw her in a fashionable turban at Holland House. 'She is handsome,' he said, 'and must have been beautiful, and her manners are princessly.' She was Anglo-Norman by descent. She spoke no Gaelic and had inherited her family's contempt for the tongue, manners and customs of the Highland people. Although she became sentimental and over-romantic about them in the manner of Walter Scott (writing fancifully of witches and warlocks), she was as English in mood and taste as the furniture of a London drawing-room. English, too, was her passion for painting water-colours. She left hundreds of them when she died, tranquil monochromes of Sutherland scenes in blue, grey and sepia which, if they were the only record of the county during her lifetime, would give a very odd picture of it indeed.

Almost the whole of this great northern shire became her husband's when they married in 1785. In 1803 he inherited his father's marquessate and estates in Stafford and Shropshire, and also the vast fortune of his bachelor uncle, the canal-cutting Duke of Bridgewater. With more than a million acres and tens of thousands of tenants, he was now the richest and greatest landowner in Britain, drawing from them that monumental income of £300,000. Bridgewater also left him the finest private art collection then known, its nucleus the famous Orleans pictures brought from France during the Revolution. His wife encouraged him to add to the collection. He became the patron of Opie, Haydon and Lawrence, and he appeared at Christie's with the dogged regularity of a farmer going to market. He spent £30,000 in one year on paintings to be hung in Stafford House, and he bought a Rubens from the Doria Palace in Genoa for £3,000, a little less than half of what he was later to give toward the relief of destitution during a typhus epidemic in Sutherland. It was not necessary for him to give an opinion on the works he bought, to own them was enough. 'Lord Stafford deserves credit,' wrote his grandson, 'for having been one of the first owners of works of art in London to throw open his gallery to the public.' The gallery was Cleveland House.

More acres of paint and canvas covered his walls at Lilleshall in Shropshire, Trentham in Staffordshire, and Dunrobin ('Cock Robin Castle', sneered Henry Brougham) in Sutherland. Late in life, and almost as if he needed the wall-space, he acquired Stafford House. This splendid building, standing in the Mall, had been correctly described by its architect as 'a home fit for a Prince'. It had been built for the grand old Duke of York, who died before he could properly occupy it. The sons of George III were always prodigal with the purses of their friends. The Duke had borrowed £60,000 from Stafford toward the erection of the house, and his executors charged the Marquess another £72,000 for a ninety-nine years' lease upon it (annual ground rent, £758). Happily, the people, who were inclined to riot and mobbing where Royal Dukes were concerned, were not left out of the transaction. The purchase price was used to turn a section of Hackney Marshes into a recreation ground for them.

Wherever the Staffords lived in London their home became a centre for politics, society, and the Marchioness's marriage-broking. In his nightly *Memoranda* Richard Rush, Envoy Extraordinary from the United States, recorded a visit to them in language as plain as the good, plain republican clothes he wore to their assembly: 'The rooms were full. The Prince Regent, Royal Family, many of the nobility and others thronged them. It was past eleven when we arrived, yet fresh names were every moment announced.... The rooms abounded in ornamental articles which wealth had amassed and taste arranged. The paintings commanded admiration. Under light judiciously disposed, they made a magnificent appearance. There is said to be no such private collection in Europe. It comprehends the production of the finest masters of the different schools. These works of genius glowing from every part of the walls formed a high attraction.' Like everybody else, Mr Rush found it difficult to say more about the Marquess than could be put into a single sentence, one had to write about what the man owned rather than what he was, but it was easy to be fulsome about Lady Stafford. 'The Marquess is known to the country by the public character of his peerage and the posts he has filled. The Marchioness is not less known by her rank, for she is of the oldest of the realm. But this is not adventitious. She is also known by her cultivated mind, her taste in the arts, her benevolence to her tenantry; by virtues unostentatious and refined, that commend her to the love of domestic and social circles, and endear her name to strangers.'

When this was written, the Staffords were no longer the young and adventurous couple who had gone to Revolutionary Paris determined, as he wrote to his father, to '*brave la tempête*'. She had changed from a full-lipped, brown-eyed girl to a fat matron who amused Creevey by the way she moved 'her huge *derrière* by slow and dignified degrees about in her chair so as to come into action if necessary'. He was myopic, gouty, careless about his clothes, and desperately anxious for a dukedom (the only rank he could acquire, having inherited all others). He played politics with circumspection, approving of reform without haste, progress without a disturbance in the order of his society. He might have slipped into his grave and *The Dictionary of National Biography* without being remembered for anything more spectacular than his wealth and his art collection had it not been for his marriage and its consequences.

The dowry which the Countess Elizabeth brought to her English husband consisted of two-thirds of the shire of Sutherland, a corrugated land-mass of seventeen hundred and thirty-five square miles extending from Cape Wrath to the Dornoch Firth. For its size, the rental value of the property was paltry, little more than £15,000 a year, which Lord Stafford would have had no difficulty in spending in one morning at Christie's. The true worth of the estate lay in its potential.

In the eighteenth century the few visitors who came to Sutherland usually recoiled from it in horror, and decided that it was either the gates of Hell or the edge of the world. It was a wild country, a waste-heap of the glacial age, open to the wind and at war with a sea on three sides. Wherever one looked there were lonely, brooding mountains that seemed to be awaiting the resumption of Creation. In its occasional beauty there was an unutterable melancholy, a quiet sadness where tiny lochans held still fragments of the sky. To the north high cliffs scowled over the bend of the globe toward the Arctic. In the west long arms of land embraced the restless Atlantic. Arable land was limited to a coastal fringe varying in width from a hundred yards to a mile, the interior was a torment of rock and water, of narrow straths and lost streams. Few trees grew there, and those that did were crippled by winter frosts and by boisterous winds that blew with all seasons. It was a land that seemed to offer little to the Improvers, and for twenty years Stafford ignored it, and saw little of it except that which was visible from the ramparts of his lady's castle at Dunrobin on the southern coast of the county. Yet the mountain flanks were cloaked in abundant pasture for one of man's creatures. Cotton grass began its first rich growth with the spring thaws, followed by deer hair and by the alpine plants that had fattened Mr Robson's Great Sheep on the Cheviot Hills two hundred warmer miles to the south.

Though the lordship of Sutherland held most of the county, the remainder was divided among three or four great landowners only, Dempsters, Gordons, Macleods and Mackays, and of the last the greatest was the chief of the Mackays himself, Lord Reay. His estate was thirty-two miles wide and twenty deep, the far north-western corner of Scotland where the Atlantic rolls in impotent rage against a black cliff wall. Here the Mackays had lived for centuries, losing some of the land with each, and the six hundred square miles which Lord Reay now possessed were worth no more than £3,500 to him in rents. Two thousand red deer grazed upon them, walking among the sweet grass of the hills with the long-legged grace of ballet-dancers. The Northumbrian sheepmen who prospected in Lord Reay's country at the beginning of the nineteenth century argued that where one deer grazed ten sheep might profitably pasture, and that Lord Reay was robbing himself of another £3,000 by turning his back on wool, mutton and the future.

The people of Sutherland were a hardy and insular race, an amalgam of Norse and Gael, cut off from the outside world by its indifference to them and by the absence of a single road. They raised goats and black cattle, potatoes and inferior oats, brewed a rough beer and distilled a raw whisky for their dreams. They broke the earth with wooden ploughs, lived in crude huts of sod and stone and, in the opinion of one Lowlander called James Loch (whom they were shortly to hate as few men have been hated), they 'added little to the wealth of the empire'.

In 1801 there were about twenty-five thousand of them, and of these, by their proud and archaic reckoning, two thousand were fighting-men. They were scattered across the county in tiny clachans, in huddled townships, content with little, with their poor food, clothing and housing. Englishmen and Lowlanders who came to Sutherland on behalf of this scientific society or that, making uncomfortable journeys over moor and moss and bitterly lamenting the absence of a single decent inn, described the condition of the people with the same impatient contempt their grandsons were later to feel toward African and Indian. Even Sir John Sinclair of Ulbster, who could stretch tolerance and understanding further than most men of his class and time, accused them of congenital idleness. James Loch, soon to become Lord Stafford's Commissioner with as much power as that ever enjoyed by a Highland chief, wrote of how they had seemed to him before he set about turning them into industrious servants of the empire: 'Contented with the poorest and most simple fare and, like all mountaineers, accustomed to a roaming, unfettered life which attached them in the strongest manner to the habits and homes of their fathers, they deemed no new comfort worth the possessing which was to be acquired at the price of industry; no improvement worthy of adoption if it was to be obtained at the expense of sacrificing the customs or leaving the hovels of their ancestors.' In no country of Europe known to him, and at no period in its history, 'did there ever exist more formidable obstacles to the improvement of a people'. He blamed this distressing state of affairs on the potato which, he thought, 'enabled them with less labour than before to raise what was sufficient for the maintenance of their families, their pigs and their poultry'.

In an age when gentlemen beat children regularly to their lessons with a zealous belief in the righteousness of every blow, James Loch naturally thought it proper that the people of Sutherland should be pulled out of the past by the scruff of their necks. Those who resisted such treatment deserved just chastisement from a constable's truncheon or an infantryman's bayonet. By the logic of the Improvers' reasoning it *was* indeed criminal to oppose (for whatever cause) any reform of the tortuous system of land tenure in the Highlands. 'Few of the lower orders,' wrote Loch after he had swept away the anachronism, 'held immediately of their landlord. A numerous race of middlemen possessed the land, and along with the farms they occupied the inhabitants were abandoned to their control and management; services of the most oppressive nature were demanded. The whole economy of his house, his farm, securing his fuel, and gathering in his harvest, was exacted by the intermediate occupier from the dependants on his possession. It was a bad bargain indeed if the middleman could not contrive to hold that part of his farm which he had retained in his own hand, rent free.'

No one, of course, asked what the people wanted. Improvement was a moral obligation and scarcely a matter for debate. But suspicious of improvements that announced themselves in writs of eviction, the Highlanders of Sutherland may have desired to live as they had always lived, to do without roads, bridges, wheeled vehicles and the religions of their lairds; to wear the bonnet or cotton cap, neckcloth and coarse plaid, to operate illicit stills, to sing the Psalms in Gaelic and to believe in the Evil Eye. Their way of life, their apparent indifference to the stimulating rewards of industry, were the despair of the Improvers. 'It is a melancholy fact,' lamented Sinclair of Ulbster, 'that a poor tenant who rents land only to the value of 20s. or 30s., and whose labour could well be spared from his little farm many days in the year, will rather saunter or sit idle at home than work for 6d. a day, which would be a considerable addition to his own and his family's scanty meal.'

For all their exasperating sloth, their winter dreaming about their peat fires, their scandalous habit of living cheek by jowl

with their livestock, the Highlanders of Sutherland had one vir-
tue on which the nation greedily fastened. This was their courage
and their belief that nowhere in the world was there a fighting-
man to equal the Gael with a broadsword in his hand. The Countess Elizabeth was among the last of the Scottish chiefs who
raised their people for service in the Napoleonic Wars, but she
surpassed them all in her methods of recruitment. She made no
appeal for volunteers. She did not go among her clan with six
pipers, like the Duchess of Gordon, giving a kiss and a guinea to
every recruit. She imposed a form of conscription that would have
won Bonaparte's approval. She called for a census of her tenants
and sub-tenants, and when this was done five hundred able-
bodied young men among them were told that service in the
Sutherland Highlanders would be a test of their duty to the *Ban
mhorair Chataibh* and their loyalty to King George III. Though
parents may have grumbled bitterly about the choice they were
forced to make between the loss of a son and the loss of their
tenancy the young men went willingly enough.

They made an incredible regiment. 'They are all brave!' said
David Stewart of Garth. In nineteen years not one man of the
light company, for example, was punished for misconduct. And
many of those who survived the heat of South Africa, the fevers
of the West Indies, or American musketry at New Orleans came
home at last to find their glens empty, their homes pulled stone
from stone, and their families dispersed.

For Mr Sellar and Mr Young and Mr Loch had been busy, improving Lord Stafford's estates.

'If I had you in the field, and men binding you . . .'

IN May, 1809, Patrick Sellar and William Young boarded a
sailing-packet at Burghead on the Morayshire coast and took passage northward to Sutherland. They were distant kinsmen, still
young, and in high spirits. They felt, Sellar recalled later, as if
they were travelling to a land of unknown but exciting promise.

The little packet, now on its first regular voyage, and the harbour at Burghead were themselves an adventurous gamble. Sellar's father, William Young, and six other Morayshire men had bought the one and built the other with a view to opening up trade with the northern counties. Until then no one in Moray, Nairn and Inverness had given much thought to Sutherland or Caithness. 'The honest folk,' said Sellar, 'used to call the whole ridge of country which they saw on the opposite side of the firth "The Ross-shire Hills", and there was no communication betwixt the countries except when an occasional passenger would cross by boat, or a deer was brought to Burghead or Findhorn for General Grant of Ballindalloch.'

With the enthusiastic encouragement of Lord Stafford, the eight Morayshire speculators hoped that their little packet would soon carry more profitable cargo than a General's venison, but of all the voyages it was to make none would have more effect on the country of Sutherland than its first. And this because it carried William Young and Patrick Sellar.

Sellar was making the journey for pleasure and from curiosity. He was about thirty, a plausible and industrious advocate who had studied law in Edinburgh and whose 'conduct of business and character for humanity' was attested to by the Sheriff-Depute and by all whose briefs he had successfully handled. He was already the Procurator-Fiscal of Moray, and probably bored and ready for change and advancement. His intelligence was sharp and incisive, his ambitions in tune with his times. Yet in his convictions he was still one step behind his contemporaries. 'I came to Sutherland,' he was to remember, as a man tolerantly acknowledges a youthful folly, 'full of the belief that the growth of wool and sheep in the Highlands was one of the most abominable and detestable things possible to be imagined.'

William Young was burdened by no such prejudices. He had begun his business life as a corn-chandler, saving thereby a modest fortune of £700 with which he purchased a derelict property in Morayshire called Inverugie. It lay along the firth shore, a sanctuary for sea-fowl, covered for the most part with drifting sand and rotting sea-weed. Inventing a special plough, Mr Young (now 'of Inverugie') turned the white sand down and the black soil up, and by this and other improvements he soon made the property one of the most productive in the county. Those neighbours who had thought him mad to attempt the transformation were able to comfort their chagrin at his success with the knowledge that the effort had also left him penniless. There was only one man in Britain (so blessed with wealth that he was able to consider money of little importance) who could see that Mr Young's victory over the land was probably more significant than his defeat at the bank. Lord Stafford invited Mr Young to become Commissioner of his Sutherland estates, an invitation which the onetime corn-chandler accepted with understandable alacrity. And he was now travelling northward to take up his duties.

Stafford had begun the improvement of his wife's dowry two years before the first packet sailed from Burghead, planning the elimination of all middlemen, an end to run-rig, the establishment of large single-unit farms and the renting of them to southern sheep-farmers. An example had been set for him by some of the smaller landowners in the north – Mr Honeyman of Armadale, for example. They had already begun to clear away untidy and uneconomic townships, packing the confused and bewildered inhabitants off to the coast or to the emigrant ships at Greenock, and offering the emptied acres of cotton grass and deer hair to any Lowland grazier ready to meet the increased rental. In November 1807, the newly-formed Northern Association of Gentlemen Farmers and Breeders of Sheep (President: the Honourable Archibald Fraser of Lovat; Vice-Presidents: Sir Charles Ross of Balnagowan and Donald Macleod of Geanies) proposed, seconded and agreed to ask for a Royal Charter to extend their activities northwards to the counties of Ross, Sutherland and Caithness. At Beauly market Cheviot wool was selling at 36s. the stone, lambs at 11s. 6d. and 12s. The future was bright.

Parliament, its interest in Highland Improvements already committed by the beginning of the Caledonian Canal in 1800, offered to contribute half the cost of those roads and bridges sadly needed if trade and agriculture were to prosper. Landowners were expected to find the other half, and Lord Stafford, believing no doubt that all men should pay for the advantages they enjoy, instructed his agents to impose a poll-tax of 4s. on all his people, whether they possessed half an acre or ten thousand.

The Marquess and his lady were in Scotland that year to see the beginning of the great experiment. 'We travelled in wind and snow through the Highlands,' the Countess Elizabeth wrote to her son's tutor, 'and met Lord Stafford highly pleased with his journey and the improvements he saw in every part of Scotland; for he is seized as much as I am with the rage of improvements, and we both turn our attention with the greatest of energy to turnips, but cannot settle whether they ought to be broadcast or drilled.'

For ninety families, tenants-at-will in the parishes of Farr and Lairg, the problem at Whitsun, 1807, was not the proper cultivation of turnips, but where to sleep the night. What crops they had, potatoes or grain, were left on or in the ground when Lord Stafford's agents came to their doors with writs of eviction. They were offered smaller lots of land, ten, fifteen or twenty miles away on the coast, where, his lordship hoped, some of them might soon harvest the sea with more profit than the earth.

'The people had to remove their cattle and furniture thither,' remembered one who saw them go, 'leaving their crops on the ground behind. Watching this crop from the trespass of the cattle of the incoming tenants, and removing it in the autumn was attended with great difficulty and loss. Besides, there was also much personal suffering from their having to pull down their houses and carry away the timber of them to erect houses on their new possessions, which houses they had to inhabit immediately on being covered in, and in the meantime to live and sleep in the open air, except for a few who might be fortunate enough to get an unoccupied barn or a shed from some of their charitable newcome neighbours.'

These removals from Farr and Lairg were the first major clearances on the Stafford estates. They set a pattern for more and more that followed during the next two decades, except that with each new eviction the harshness and inhumanity of the officers ordered to execute it increased. It was as if the whole population of Sutherland was being shaken in a great cup, thrown out, and allowed to fall where it would on the coast or blow away to the other side of the world. 'Every means were resorted to to discourage the people, and to persuade them to give up their holdings quietly and quit the country,' wrote one man who was driven from Strathnaver. 'And to those who could not be induced to do so, scraps of moor and bogland were offered in Dornoch moor and Brora links, on which it was next to impossible to exist. . . .'

From the crenellated walls of Dunrobin Castle the Countess Elizabeth saw a different picture. Her interest in the Highlands had been rekindled after so many years of child-bearing, of Paris and London Society. 'We have been much occupied in plans for improvement,' she wrote. 'This country is an object of curiosity at present; from being quite a wild corner inhabited by an infinite multitude roaming at large in the old way, despising all barriers and all regulations, and firmly believing in witch-craft so much so that the porters durst not send away two old women who were plaguing us one day, believing them to be witches.'

Neither she nor her husband seem to have questioned the moral justice of what they were doing, nor can one expect them to have done so. Like all Highland lairds, they owned an uneconomic estate which in its present form (or even in the one they planned) could not support the steady and alarming increase in population. Since it was impossible for them to imagine peasant co-operatives (though Sinclair of Ulbster got close to it) and the equal sharing of the earth's wealth, the dispersal of surplus men, women and children to the colonies was both proper and necessary. Those who remained (in Stafford's opinion, the most industrious, diligent and praiseworthy) could find new employment in new ways. There was the coal-pit Stafford planned at Brora, the salt-pans, the brick and tile works, the herring-fisheries at Golspie and Helmsdale, into the creation of which he proposed to sink almost a quarter of a million pounds, which, even then, would still be less than one year of his income.

So the people of Sutherland began their great exodus from the interior, with no voice but the Gaelic of their poets to express their grief and bewilderment. The pamphleteers and journalists who were later to take up their cause were twenty years away. Ministers of the Church were silent or worse. According to Donald Macleod from Strathnaver, a literate son of the people, a stonemason who would soon prise at the rocks of Dunrobin with his pen, the churchmen of Sutherland were 'consenting parties to the expulsion of the inhabitants, and had substantial reasons for their readiness to accept woolly and hairy animals in place of human flocks'. With a few noble exceptions, the ministers chose the side of the landlords, who built them new manses, made carriage roads to their doors, and invited them to share in the new prosperity now and then with the grant of a few acres of sheep pasturage. In return the churchmen gave God's authority to Improvement, and threatened the more truculent of the evicted with damnation.

The Sutherland clearances really began with the arrival of William Young as Lord Stafford's first Commissioner. He soon had an active and enthusiastic recruit for his factor, Patrick Sellar. The young advocate quickly lost his early detestation of sheep-farming. Once ashore from the packet, and after a tour of the estates now leased by the Northumbrian stock-farmers, Atkinson and Marshall, he was, in his own words, 'at once a convert to the principle now almost universally acted upon in the Highlands of Scotland, viz., that the people should be employed in securing the natural riches of the sea-coast, that the mildew of the interior should be allowed to fall upon grass and not upon corn, and that the several hundred miles of alpine plants flourishing in these districts in curious succession at all seasons, should be converted into wool and mutton for the English manufacture'. He would not have accepted the term, but he was as much a colonist as those of his contemporaries who were preparing to dispossess the aboriginals of America, Africa and Australia to make room for meat, hide and wool on the hoof.

He had cogent arguments, too: 'Children of the white or Caucasian race of mankind come into the world without any covering or natural defence against the weather.... Let a man examine his wardrobe.... Is it too much to say that for every person born a certain number of sheep must be lambed? Thus does Providence in his wisdom and in his kindness to man give certain districts to provide cover and others to yield clothing to man.... In such matters I respectfully maintain that we cannot oppose nature without placing ourselves in a false position and being presently punished by diminished profit and increased suffering to mankind. On this principle, with a good conscience, I grow wool on mountains that are covered with peatbog, believing that I thereby benefit my fellow-men.'

And among his fellow-men he no doubt included those tenants-at-will in Dornoch, Rogart, Loth, Clyne, Golspie and Assynt to whom he and William Young gave their particular attention between 1810 and 1812. 'A large portion of the people of these parishes,' said Donald Macleod the mason, 'were in the course of two or three years, almost entirely rooted out, and those few who took the miserable allotments above mentioned and some of their descendants continue to exist on them in great poverty.'

Young and Sellar proceeded circumspectly, first securing the support of tacksmen and ministers who advised their people to go without protest, sternly warning them that it was the wish of their *Ban mhorair Chataibh* that they should obey her agents in all things. In this the tacksmen acted with more foolishness than sense, for after their tenants-at-will had gone, they too were evicted by Sellar and Young. There was no room in Improvement for obsolescent middlemen.

The first white wave of Cheviot sheep broke over the Assynt hills before the people there had time to obey the writs of eviction. To the sound of phrenetic bleating, they pulled down their house timbers and walked with them to the coast where the villages in which they were to live had not been built, the boats from which they were expected to fish had not been launched, the nets unspun. In the bitterness they felt, one of their poets cried out, apostrophizing Sellar and Young: *'Nam faighinn 's air an raon thu . . .'*

> If I had you on the field
> and men binding you,
> With my fists I would tear
> out three inches of your lungs!

From Assynt on the Atlantic coast, Commissioner and factor turned their attention to the parish of Kildonan, where this ran in a green and meandering strath from the inland plateau to the northern ocean, and it was here that resistance was first met. Sellar surveyed the land. Summons of removal were prepared against tenant and sub-tenant, and Sheriff's Officers were warned to make ready their delivery. The country was divided into lots and advertised, so that gentlemen from the south might inspect the property and make ready their bids. Never had the parish seen such a coming and going of foreigners, Lowland men and English, who rode along the banks of the Kildonan making notes in their record-books. This narrow valley, bordering on Caithness, was the country of Clan Gunn, a dour and hard people, more Norse than Gael, who had been made increasingly uneasy by the stories they had heard from Assynt, Farr and Rogart. Their reaction to the strangers in their glen was abrupt and angry, and news of it travelled far south to London, interrupting the Marchioness's season.

'I hope to be in Scotland this summer,' she wrote, 'but at present I am uneasy about a sort of mutiny that has broken out in one part of Sutherland, in consequences of our new plans having made it necessary to transplant some of the inhabitants to the sea-coast from other parts of the estate. The people who are refractory on this occasion are part of Clan Gun, so often mentioned by Sir Robert Gordon, who live by distilling whisky and are unwilling to quit that occupation for a life of industry of a different sort which was proposed to them. London is more full and gay, if possible, than usual. A great many foreigners from Russia, etc., *parlant bon anglais-russe.'*

The trouble occurred in March 1813, when a Mr Reid, the

Northumbrian manager of a southern sheep combine, visited Strath Kildonan with his notebook and inquiring tongue. He returned to Golspie, further down the coast, far earlier than was expected, declaring that he had been attacked by a mob of men and women, and put in great fear for his life. 'The factors,' said Donald Macleod the mason, remembering the affair thirty years later, 'eagerly jumped at this trumped-up story; they immediately swore in from sixty to one hundred retainers and new inhabitants as special constables, trimmed and charged the cannon at Dunrobin Castle which had reposed in silence since the last defeat of the unfortunate Stuarts.'

But the alarm was real enough. The people of Golspie, many of them newcomers from the south, had the townsman's old dread of the Highlander in arms, and the Year of the Sheep was close enough in memory for them to fear that Riot, Rebellion and Sedition was ever restless beneath Highland docility. At Dunrobin Castle, where his lordship's Commissioner and Factor had their headquarters, rumour quickly leap-frogged over rumour, beginning with Mr Reid's modest bound of truth. It was said that the men of Clan Gunn were marching down the coast toward Golspie, threatening to hang Sellar and Young, expel all sheepfarmers, and burn Dunrobin Castle. It is unlikely that the two Morayshire men believed these stories, but they knew that if the Gunns gathered to protest against the evictions there might well be serious trouble when the Sheriff Officers arrived in Kildonan with writs of removal. So Young sent messengers to the strath, inviting the people to Dunrobin, where their grievances would be heard and their happy future explained to them. According to Macleod, it was a trick. Young really intended to flush the malcontents into the open and frighten them with the power of Law and Good Order. In view of what followed, one may well believe this. The people of Kildonan, men, women and children, were six miles from Dunrobin when a sympathizer in Golspie sent them a warning that constables were waiting for them below the walls of the Castle, that soldiers had been sent for, and that some of them were to be arrested and charged with threats against Mr Reid's life.

Most of them wisely decided to remain where they were, but some who were more courageous (more desperate or more credulous) marched on, skirting the Castle and halting at last outside the Inn at Golspie. There they waited for someone to hear their grievances, and there at last came Commissioner, Factor and Sheriff at the gallop from Dunrobin, followed by a band of armed constables and several ministers of the county. Prompted by his lordship's agents, the Sheriff told the people that those who were guilty of mobbing Mr Reid would soon be discovered and punished, and that all of them would do well to disperse immediately. They were then scolded by the ministers, who used all the sonorous imagery of which the Gaelic is capable. Macleod said that the churchmen threatened 'the vengeance of heaven and eternal damnation on those who should presume to make the least resistance, no wonder the poor Highlander quailed under such influence'. Then, as if he believed that divine assistance might not be enough, the Sheriff began to read the Riot Act. Since this was in English, it was gibberish to most of the Gunns. They drifted away, more confused than afraid.

They went back to Kildonan, followed now by a powerful detachment of the 21st Foot, some artillery, and wagons loaded with cartridge and ball. The soldiers had come by forced march from Fort George, in response to the Sheriff's urgent plea for help, arriving too late to make a display of force outside the Inn at Golspie, but soon enough to pursue the people to their homes. The presence of the 21st in the Highlands at this time of uneasiness was probably no accident of posting. There is a cumulative security to be got from using one racial minority for the suppression of another, and although the 21st was nominally a Scots regiment* the men in its ranks were mostly Irish, pressed into service by force of famine. They had bitter memories of the Rebellion of '98 which a fencible regiment from Sutherland had helped to defeat. They marched northward after the retreating Highlanders telling all who would listen, or could understand, that they would have their revenge for Irish blood which Scots had spilt on Vinegar Hill.

*The Royal Scots Fusiliers.

But the sound of their drums alone was enough to end the little affair. The people of the strath went back to their homes to wait in listless resignation for the writs of removal. 'Dismayed and spirit-broken at the army of power brought against them,' said Donald Macleod, 'and seeing nothing but enemies on every side, even in those from whom they should have had comfort and succour, they quietly submitted to their fate.' The 21st took a few prisoners, men whom the Sheriff-Officers had smelt out, others who had looked too insolently, perhaps, at the King's Colours or the King's men, but since no reasonable charge could be brought against them, they were soon released.

At Whitsun large areas of Strath Kildonan were cleared and left to grass which, even after a century and a half, still grows greenest where the people had their tiny potato-patches. They were offered meagre lots of land on the cliffs at Helmsdale, the choice of becoming herring-fishers or leaving the country altogether. Ninety-six young men and women proudly chose exile – Gunns, Macbeths, Mathesons, Sutherlands and Bannermans from townships between Garlag and Borrobol. In early June they sailed from Stromness where they boarded the emigrant ship, *Prince of Wales*. Two months later they disembarked at Fort Churchill on Hudson Bay, and travelled southward by the waters of Lake Winnipeg to the prairie settlement which Lord Selkirk was building along the Red River. They endured a Canadian winter for which even Highland snows had not prepared them, and they wrote bitterly to their parents advising the old people to give up all thought of a second emigration.

Lord Stafford had no reason to doubt the efficiency with which his Commissioner and Factor were clearing human beings from those parts of his estate which, in Sellar's opinion, had been 'formed by nature to produce wool', but in 1813 he was beginning to see that his plans for Improvement (involving more than the collection of rents and the serving of writs) needed a creative mind greater than that possessed by either man. He found such a mind in James Loch, gentleman.

The *gentleman* is used with relevance. Social rank and the

abilities of those holding it were seriously debated by Stafford and Loch before they entered their contract, and probably neither of them, the one a descendant of wool-staplers and the other of Baltic traders, saw anything ironic in the discussion. Loch was at this time only thirty-three, a broad-shouldered, fair-haired young man with the type of resolute head that strikes well in profile on a coin. His home at Drylaw, a house and acreage near Edinburgh, had been bought by a seventeenth-century ancestor who had traded well with the Hanseatic ports, and the family had subsequently emblazoned it with modest arms and traced a real or imagined descent from a Norman de Loch or de Lacus. James Loch was called to the bar at Lincoln's Inn when he was twenty-six. He housed himself comfortably in Boswell Court, and built himself a profitable conveyancing practice of which he soon tired. He turned to estate management, showing immediate imagination and genius. He met Stafford at a dinner-party and it was there that they argued the question of whether or not it was possible for a gentleman to administer estates with success. Loch's advocacy of the positive answer, as much as of his own merits, was so persuasive that the Marquess made him Commissioner of all the Stafford estates, but most particularly of those in Sutherland. During the next forty years, for the rest of his life, he worked to complete the clearance of the interior, to carve the emptied lands into great sheep-farms, to build harbours, bridge rivers, turn cattle-tracks into macadam roads, and to so mould and control the lives of 'the ignorant and credulous people' that at one time the young among them had to go to his agents for permission to marry. 'In a few years,' he wrote, before a quarter of his long service was run, 'the character of the whole of this population will be completely changed.... The children of those who are removed from the hills will lose all recollection of the habits and customs of their fathers.'

This was 'the Loch Policy'. Behind it and the figure of its creator the Staffords became shadows, and Highlanders who had been reluctant to blame the *Ban mhorair Chataibh* for their suffering and exile could now hate the Lowlander Loch with all the passion their grief demanded. Men would debate the Loch Policy for a century, with admiration because it seemed to combine the best qualities of direction and *laissez-faire*, or with disapproval because it broke the spirit of a proud people and failed to bring the lasting prosperity it confidently proposed.

After an exploratory tour of Sutherland when he accepted the post, Loch confined his visits to a brief stay at Dunrobin with his family every autumn. He was content to work from Edinburgh or London, delegating the execution of his plans to Young and Sellar, and to the agents who followed them. He was a deskworker, at war with indolence, superstition, inefficiency, the obstinacy of a primitive people and the intransigence of the earth itself. Or so it seemed to him. A man must be inspired in a war, though he sits at a desk, and Loch's inspiration was his noble employer. He gave Stafford that adulation which was the fee paid by the lesser gentry of his time for the right to stand in the same drawing-room with their betters, but he also admired the Marquess and believed him to be an enlightened benefactor. The admiration, however, was laced with pedagogic instruction, betraying his inner belief that he was intellectually the better man. At this death a memorialist paid him a tribute that he would have appreciated : 'What a happiness it was for the Highlands that there was a man who had the courage to carry out his just conceptions of the duty of a great landowner !'

Loch's most relentless and implacable enemy was Donald Macleod the stonemason, a son of that 'ignorant and credulous people' for whom the Commissioner felt such impatient contempt and anger. He was born in Strathnaver, in the township of Rossal, some time toward the end of the eighteenth century, the son of a mason under whom he served his apprenticeship, and he came to manhood during the most terrible years of the Loch Policy. 'Every imaginable means short of the sword or the musket,' he wrote of those days, 'was put in requisition to drive the natives away, to force them to exchange their farms and comfortable habitations, erected by themselves or their forefathers, for inhospitable rocks on the sea-shore, and to depend for subsistence on the watery element in its wildest mood.... The country was darkened by the smoke of burnings, and the descendants were ruined, trampled upon, dispersed and compelled to seek asylum across the sea.'

If the portrait said to be his is a true one, the face fits the man he was, a broad forehead and shaggy brows, the uncompromising challenge of his eyes above the high cheek-bones, and a mouth of great compassion and understanding. Whatever he was like as a stonemason, he was a born journalist with an abundant share of the faults and virtues of the craft. He was courageous and incorruptible, his writing was wild, but never dull. In his old age he frequently repaired his memory with his imagination, as if he were afraid that the truth was not enough to arouse the nation's conscience. He was called, and is still called, a fanatic, by which men mean that there is something indecent in passion and something dangerous in anger. For such anger and passion he had good cause, and although they were rarely subjective his own suffering was great. He was hounded by the Stafford agents and brought before the justices. The persecution of his wife reduced her to incurable madness, and in the end he became an exile, like his kin and friends.

Until he and his family were driven like rats from Sutherland in 1831, he wrote nothing for publication, or at least nothing that any newspaper was willing to publish, but in his memory and his notes, his correspondence with Highlanders whom he dared not name, he stored a great arsenal of ammunition. His chance to use it came in 1840. Public opinion was changing; people were now uneasy about the value and justice of the great clearances. If newspaper editors were not ready to agree with what Macleod had to say, they were now willing to offer him a forum in which to say it. Between 1840 and 1841 the *Edinburgh Weekly Chronicle* published twenty-one of his letters which he later expanded into his *History of the Destitution in Sutherland-shire*.

From then on he wrote and wrote, not only the story of his own county, but of the removals and persecutions in other parts of the Highlands. But always he returned to the events of his youth, to *Bliadhna an Losgaidh*, the Year of the Burnings, when Patrick Sellar came to Strathnaver.

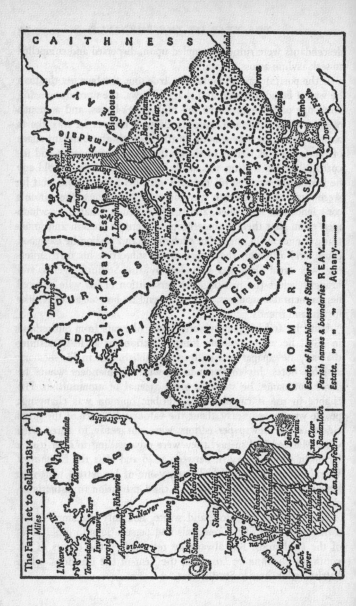

CAITHNESS

Bighouse
Armadale
Ben Griam
L. na Clar
DONAN
Ben Armine
CLYNE
Brora
Golspie
Embo
Dornoch Firth
GIOLSPIE
ROGART
Tongue
Ess⁵ Lhaghur
Str⁵ NAVER
R. Shin
Achany
Lairg
Skibo
Almahiarra
Ben Kilbreck
Achany
 C.

Durness
LORD REAY'S
DURNESS
Rosehall
Achany
Balnagown
CROMARTY

EDDRACHILLES
Ben More
ASSYNT

Estate of Marchioness of Stafford ∴∴∴
Parish names & boundaries REAY ——
Estate, ʺ ʺ ʺ Achany ———

The Farm let to Sellar 1814

0   Miles   5

R. Strathy
L. Naver
Strathy Pt
Armadale
Kirtomy
Farr
Torrisdale
Invernaver
Borgie
Rhinovie
Carrachan
R. Naver
Achnabourin
Dunveden
Rhifail
R. Borgie
Ben Stumino
Skail
Rossal
Rhiloisk
Rhiphail
Langdale
Syre
Dalchork
Ceann-na-Coille
Badinloskin
L. na Cullen
Grumby
Dalchaurd
Loch Naver
Esqual
Lon Khlnyschim
L. na Clar
Griam
Badanloch

'He would be a very cruel man who would not mourn'

ON Wednesday, 15 December 1813, twenty-seven tenants-at-will from Strathnaver, some of them with their families, gathered before the Inn at Golspie under the direction of their minister, Mr David Mackenzie. He was the missionary at Achness in their glen, and for such work as this day's the Staffords would shortly reward him with the great parish of Farr, a splendid manse for his home, a glebe consisting of the best land in the area, and a fine church from the pulpit of which he would translate and support each successive eviction order issued by his patrons.* He was here this day to translate Mr Young's Lowland English into the Gaelic of his parishioners, and to urge upon them that it was God's will that they should obey those whom He had placed above them.

In that bitter weather, the journey to Golspie from Strathnaver in the far north of the county must have been hard and cruel, but the people had come willingly and with anxiety, and perhaps in the hope that their presence alone would dissuade Lord Stafford's agents from proceeding with their eviction. Though they may not have known it, it was also their legal right to be there and to make their own bids when their land was put up for auction. This was the only occasion when Young invited those whom he proposed to remove to be present at a set, but since the affair with Clan Gunn some months before he may have been less concerned with the Law than with facing trouble before it grew too serious.

At last Mr Young came out of the Inn, well-wrapped against the cold, cleared his throat and read the formal notice:

---

*The Sutherland Estate appointed Church of Scotland ministers, as did many other Highland landowners, though the reintroduction of such patronage contravened the Treaty of Union. Under James Loch, the Sutherland Estate was to go further and forbid any other form of worship but that which it favoured.

Notice is hereby given to the tenants of Strathnaver and others on the old estate of Sutherland whose farms are to be set at Golspie this day – That Lord and Lady Stafford have directed that all the grounds from Curnachy on the north and Dunvieddan on the south side of the river down to its mouth, including Swordly and Kirktomy, with a sufficient quantity of pasture, is to be lotted out among them, and in which every person of good character will be accommodated. . . .

He waited until Mr Mackenzie had translated the notice and until it was clear that there was going to be no rioting or mobbing as a result. The tenants heard that by Whitsunday next they were to leave their homes and move to new plots on the harsh coast near Strathy Point which Lord and Lady Stafford, in their concern for their people's welfare, would graciously grant them. Mr Mackenzie then went inside the Inn to sign a declaration that he had translated the notice and that it had been understood.

There was no auction that day, or any day. One man only made a bid for the lease of the property, and he was Patrick Sellar. It was his second purchase of land on the Sutherland estates. In 1810, and shortly after becoming Factor, he had followed William Young's example and obtained the lease of the farm of Morvich on the east coast of Sutherland. Both men were to become great sheep-farmers, and it was in Strathnaver that Patrick Sellar made his fortune from wool.

The valley of Strathnaver is a green fold in the earth, the richest in that part of the country, a narrow, twisting glen down which the black water of the River Naver runs from south to north, from the loch of its name to the Atlantic Ocean. The people who lived there in 1814 were Mackays, by name or allegiance, though the Countess Elizabeth was their Lord. They lived in long stone houses roofed with sod. One end of the house was a byre, the other was living accommodation. There was no window-glass, the floors were uneven earth, and the smoke of the open hearths found its uncertain way through holes in the roof. The stone walls were sometimes plastered on the inside and plugged with clay to make them draughtproof. Scattered about such primitive buildings were dry-stone barns, outhouses and drying kilns. In such surroundings had Donald Macleod been born and bred.

The houses were grouped in a dozen small townships, north-ward down the strath to the sea and westward along the shore of Loch Naver. Because of the mission there, Achness was perhaps the most important to the people. It took its Gaelic name, *Achadh an Eas*, the cornfield by the cascade, from the brown stream that still falls in noisy delight from hills where once the Norsemen buried their dead. There was Rhifail, the enclosure in a hollow, the smooth dale of Dalvina, Skail the sheiling, and Syre where the young men had been asembled in the spring of 1800 for service with the Sutherland Highlanders. Along the loch, toward Altnaharra at its finger-tip, were Grummore and Grumbeg. On these fell the evening shadow of Ben Klibreck across the water, and if one stands among the few remaining stones of Grummore today the mountain takes the naked shape of a sleeping woman, the milky smoke of burning heather for her hair, and her head turned away from Strathnaver.

The tacksman of the property was Robert Gordon, whose an-cestors had come from Banffshire in the sixteenth century when a Countess of Sutherland married the son of a Gordon Earl. He was an old, simple man, who styled himself 'of Langdale' from the cottage and land he held on the west bank of the river. Most of the people in the strath were his sub-tenants, and while they did not speak ill of him, they expressed no surprise when he opened his door and offered the hospitality of his home to Patrick Sellar in the Year of the Burnings.

If Strathnaver were not the paradise some exiles believed it to have been when they remembered it in their old age, the words they used spoke their love and their longing for it. 'I remember,' said Angus Mackay, who was eleven when he was driven from the glen, 'I remember you would see a mile or half a mile between every town if you were going up the strath. There were four or five families in each of these towns, and bonnie haughs between the towns, and hill pastures for miles, as far as they could wish to go. The people had plenty of flocks of goats, sheep, horses and cattle, and they were living happy, with flesh and fish and butter, and cheese and fowl and potatoes and kail and milk too. There was no want of anything with them, and they had the Gospel preached to them at both ends of the strath.'

The property which Mr Sellar had acquired lay on the east bank of the river, a great loop of land twelve miles in length and seven at its widest. It was shaped like a tear. Its rich braesides mounted toward the waters of Loch nan Clar and the peaks of Ben Griam. Sellar anticipated no trouble from the people, believing, perhaps, that the stern handling of Clan Gunn in March, 1813, had shown them that bayonets and artillery would be brought against them if necessary. But he had been warned that the petty tacksmen of Sutherland might proceed against him, and that in particular he should beware of Mr Robert MacKid, the Sheriff-Substitute of Sutherland. Mr MacKid was a Gaelic-speaking Highlander who made great play of his attachment to the people, but who, since he was a middleman himself in a small way, was more probably a weapon which the tacksmen used in their doomed struggle against Improvement. One day toward the end of 1813, Hugh Ross, Procurator-Fiscal, took Sellar's arm in private and told him (as Sellar later claimed) that 'the Sheriff-Substitute was lying in wait to do me an injury, that he had learned this from the Sheriff himself so far back as the month of July, and he advised me to be extremely cautious in all my proceedings'. Sellar appears to have acknowledged the warning without acting upon it, but he was quick to remember it two years later, and to repeat it where it would do him most good.

On 15 January, the first rent-day of 1814, and in bitter snow-driven weather, Sellar arrived at Achness. With Mr MacKenzie the minister as his host, ally and interpreter, he gave notice to those tenants whom he wished to quit his property at Whitsun-tide. Others were told that their time for removal would come later, and still more of the people were warned that within four years Mr Young proposed to clear the whole of Strathnaver from Altnaharra to Dunvedin and place it under sheep. Meanwhile, a surveyor would come north as soon as the spring thaw permitted and would lay out those new lots on the coast where Lord Stafford had decided the people should now live. The surveyor did indeed come with the melting snow, but left immediately because of illness in his family, and although he returned in May his work was still unfinished when Whitsunday came.

Confused, uneasy, and stubbornly reluctant to leave the known for the unknown, the people remained where they were. In April beef prices had fallen with the end of the long European war, and the year ahead promised to be a hard one for all Highlanders who still lived on a black-cattle economy. In spring, too, fodder was always scarce, and now there was even less of it. As soon as the snows melted, Sellar's principal shepherd, John Dryden, had come to burn tens of square miles of dead heath so that cotton grass and deer hair might grow more richly for the coming sheep. Burning to prepare pastures was no new thing in the hills, but never had it been done here on so vast a scale. Much of the townships' muir-pasturage was burnt, and the Strathnaver cattle roamed raw-ribbed in search of food. There was more to make the people despair. In previous removals the evicted had been allowed to take their house-timbers with them for use in the building of new homes. Now it was learnt that the moss-fir was henceforth to be burned when it was torn from the cottages. The people were to be paid the value of the wood, or the value which Sellar set upon it, but this was no compensation at all in a land so sparsely timbered as Sutherland.

At the beginning of June, when most of the Strathnaver men were away in the hills looking for cattle that had strayed as far as Ben Griam for pasture, Patrick Sellar decided that it was time he acted. 'I waited patiently until the thirteenth of June, when it was then found necessary to cause the Sheriff-Officers to eject the tenants.'

He had arrived in Strathnaver a day or so previous to this date, accompanied by four officers and twenty men. He lodged in the 'rustic cottage on a knowe' belonging to Robert Gordon of Langdale. On Sunday, 12 June, he went to divine service in the mission-house at Achness with his host, and sat with him among the other petty gentry – Captain John Mackay of Syre, the Peninsular veteran who was Stafford's warm-hearted but ineffectual factor in Strathnaver, and William Gordon of Breacachadh, an ill-tempered, black-eyed man whose ancestors had also come up from Banffshire three centuries before.

While the Reverend David Mackenzie threatened the people with hell-fire for the slightest disobedience, Sellar seems to have been studying them with interest. After the service was over, he asked the two Gordons for information about them and was told that one man, a William Chisholm, at whom the Gordons pointed, was a very unsavoury character. He was no tenant, not cotter even, but, Sellar was later to write, 'a tinker who had taken possession of an extremely wild piece of ground in a morass among the mountains, and was accused by the tenantry of bigamy, theft and riotous conduct, and was put down in my instructions as a person to be expelled from the estate'.

The next morning the evictions began, and for a while Sellar stayed to watch. The burning of the house-timbers began as soon as a cottage was emptied, and even before if the occupants were laggardly. The smoke rolled oily and thick in the moist air. The bowl of the valley held the resonant noise of barking dogs, shouted orders, the crying of women and children. 'It would be a very hard heart but would mourn to see the circumstances of the people that day,' said Angus Mackay. 'He would be a very cruel man who did not mourn for the people. You would have pitied them, tumbling on the ground and greeting, tearing the ground with their hands. Any soft-minded person would have pitied them.'

He and his younger brothers were alone and asleep when the alarm came. Their parents had left the cottage early, driving their stock – sheep, cattle, a horse, two mares and a foal – northward to the coast, having been told that if any of their property was still on the ground at noon they would be fined. They told their young sons they would return for them soon, but before they came back the boys were aroused by a woman crying, '*Won't you wake up? Sellar is burning at Rhistog!*' Angus took his youngest brother, aged three, and ran naked toward the river. 'I took my brother on my back and through the river I went, and the water was that deep that when it came upon his back he commenced crying and shaking himself on my back, and I fell, and he gripped round about my neck, and I could not rise no more. We were both greeting, and took a fright that we would be drowned. There was a poor woman coming with her family up the strath, and she saw us and jumped into the river and swept us out of it.'

Betsy MacKay was sixteen and she lived at the river's edge by Skail. 'Our family was very reluctant to leave,' she remembered, 'and stayed for some time, but the burning party came round and set fire to our house at both ends, reducing to ashes whatever remained within the walls. The people had to escape for their lives, some of them losing all their clothes except what they had on their backs. The people were told they could go where they liked, provided they did not encumber the land that was by rights their own. The people were driven away like dogs who deserved no better, and that, too, without any reason in the world.'

Donald Macleod, by his account, was present in Strathnaver that day, though he wrote nothing of what happened to his home and family at Rossal. 'I was present,' he said, 'at the pulling down and burning of the house of William Chisholm, in which was lying his wife's mother, an old bed-ridden woman of nearly one hundred years of age, none of the family being present.' When Sellar came to Chisholm's little hut at Badinloskin to see the expulsion of this vagrant whom he had marked down after prayers the day before, Macleod told him that the old woman was too ill to be removed. 'He replied, "Damn her, the old witch; she has lived too long. Let her burn!" Fire was immediately set to the house and the blankets in which she was carried were in flames before she could be got out. She was placed in a little shed, and it was with great difficulty they were prevented from firing it also. The old woman's daughter arrived while the house was on fire, and assisted the neighbours in removing her mother out of the flames and smoke, presenting a picture of horror which I shall never forget, but cannot attempt to describe. She died within five days.'

That was Macleod's account, written thirty years after the event (later still, when he was in Canada, he was to add to it, saying that he had burnt his own hands while helping the old woman, Margaret Mackay, to safety). Chisholm and his wife, Henrietta, giving evidence in 1816, told a story no different in substance. The tinker said that one of Sellar's men had refused to carry the sick woman from the cottage, saying, 'He would not attempt it, even though they should take off his coat, as he would not be accessory to murder.' Sellar then ordered the cottage to be burned, laying faggots against it himself. Janet Mackay, Chisholm's sister-in-law, arrived then, and dragged her mother out in a blanket. The old woman cried, 'God receive my soul! What fire is this about me?' She never spoke a word more, said Chisholm.

All of Chisholm's little property was destroyed. His house, his furniture, and some growing corn amounting to twelve sheaves in harvest. He and his wife declared that three bank notes had also been burned with the cottage, for which he received no re-compense. Sellar gave him 3s., which the gypsy tinker took to be the value which the Factor placed upon his house-timber, but, he said, 'Twenty pounds would not have been enough.'

Thus William Chisholm's house burned. 'There was wind and it burned,' he said. 'The wood was thrown down before it was set fire to, and Sellar said "There's a bonfire for you!"'

Among the crowd which watched this burning was a boy of fifteen, George Macdonald,* who was then called away to drive his father's cattle northward. He lived at Rossal, where, he said, every house was burned after he had gone. He saw the black ruins some days later. 'I cannot remember the number, but I would say there were about twenty. There were four other town-ships near this, each with about the same number of houses, all of which were burnt on the same day. My father, when his own house was set on fire, tried to save a few pieces of wood out of the burning house, which he carried to the river about half a mile

---

*Macdonald's account, with some others quoted here, is taken from the evidence given before the Napier Commission of Inquiry in 1883 (see Acknowledgements). It is sometimes claimed that not too much weight should be given to this evidence, since the witnesses were not under oath – a contention that throws more light on the probity of those who make it than on the Highlanders themselves.

away, and there formed a raft of it. His intention was to float the wood down the stream and build a kind of hut somewhere to shelter his weak family, but the burning party came that way and, seeing the timber, set fire to it, and soon reduced the whole to ashes.'

Sellar left Strathnaver before the eviction of the twenty-seven sub-tenants, their families, dependants and cotters, was completed. He was satisfied, he said, that the people were suffering no hardship or injury. As late as Thursday that week the burning continued, the smoke moving with the wind and withering the spring-green growth of barley and oats. 'Many deaths ensued from alarm, fatigue and cold,' said Donald Macleod. 'Some old men took to the woods and precipices, wandering about in a state approaching to, or of, absolute insanity; and several of them, in this situation, lived on a few days. Pregnant women were taken with premature labour, and several children died. To these events I was an eye-witness....' There is no recorded evidence to support his passionate and grieving accusations (two deaths only can be charged against the evictors), but there was no conscious dishonesty in what he said. 'I was a neighbour of Donald Macleod,' declared George Macdonald, 'and can conscientiously say that he was a truthful and honest man. His book, I am sure, contains the truth, having read some of it myself, most of which I could substantiate.'

The recorded facts make harsh enough reading. John Mackay's pregnant wife, when the burners tore down her house at Ravigill, climbed to the roof and fell through it in an absurd attempt to protect her home, and so was brought to terrible labour. John Mackay's cry of protest, when he saw Patrick Sellar watching, was that the law of the country must surely have been changed for such things to be done with the approval of Sheriff-Officers and Factor.

Like the tinker Chisholm's mother-in-law, old Donald MacBeth was brought to death a month – six months, a year, it does not matter – earlier than he might have been as a result of that week. Mortally ill with cancer of the face, he lived at Rhimsdale with his son Hugh. On the Saturday Sellar came to Strathnaver, Hugh

MacBeth went to the Factor. He said that he had to leave the valley for his god-mother's funeral, and he asked that his house and his father be spared until his return. 'No,' said Sellar, 'De'il a ane of them shall remain!' Hugh MacBeth's father-in-law, who was present, declared that this was cruel, and Sellar cocked an eye at him, asking his name and writing it down in his pocket-book. Before MacBeth left for the funeral on Tuesday, he took the divots from the roof of his house leaving the couples and side-trees standing, hoping that this might mollify Sellar. When he returned, four days later, he found his father lying in the open among the stones, with only a low clay wall for protection against the weather. The old man died soon after, and whether it was from cancer or exposure seems a quibble.

The day after the burning of Skail, John Mackay, searching the hills for his cattle, found another old man of his own name lying helpless beneath some birch-trees. The only house left standing in the township was one which John Dryden, Sellar's shepherd, had marked for his future residence. Mackay knew that there would be no shelter there, so he left the old man where he was, beneath the birch-trees, speechless, lost in shock, and John Mackay could not say, when asked, whether he had found shelter across the river or whether he died where he lay.

Grace Macdonald, a girl of nineteen living by Langdale, took shelter up the brae with her family when the township was burnt, and waited there a day and a night, watching Sellar's men sporting about the flames. When a terrified cat sprang from a burning house it was seized and thrown back, and thrown back again until it died there. 'There was no mercy or pity shown to young or old,' said Grace Macdonald; 'all had to clear away, and those who could not get their effects removed in time to a safe distance had it burnt before their eyes. They were happy in Strathnaver, with plenty to take and give, but all are very poor now.'

William Morrison, who was fourteen, wandered through the glen and watched twenty houses burning at Rossal, he said, and two more at Dalvina, Dalmalaran and Achphris. 'But surely it was cruel!' he cried in his old age, 'For people to say that there was no cruelty or harshness shown people when they were burnt off Strathnaver is a glaring lie, which no amount of flowery language can hide!'

At Ceann-na-Coille, the first township north of the loch-end, there lived a schoolteacher, or a man who had enough book-learning to act as such when his work on the land gave him the time. His name was William Sutherland, and because of his small education, perhaps, the townships entrusted him with the collection of rents on term-day. He had a son and six daughters, one of whom remembered that when the burners came all the men of Ceann-na-Coille with the exception of her father were away after their cattle in the hills. 'When the company arrived to set fire to the house,' she said, 'he requested that in consideration of his service to the House of Sutherland, by going with the rents of the townships to Dunrobin, they would be good enough to spare the outhouse whither we might retire during the night; and that he himself would set fire to it the next morning. This was ruthlessly refused, and we had to remain all night on a green hillock outside, and view our dwelling smouldering into ashes.'

For days after the burning was over the homeless people remained in the glen. They sat on the hillsides among what they had been able to salvage from the ruins. They put canvas over their heads for protection against the night rain. Across the river from the township of Rhiloisk a little girl sat and watched and remembered: 'For some days after the people were turned out one could scarcely hear a word with the lowing of the cattle and the screaming of children marching off in all directions. Everything was burnt that they could lay their hands upon, in some cases the hens in the byres were burnt. I shall never forget that awful day.' She was eighty-two when she said that.

The men had returned with the cattle, which now wandered unhindered over the crops of young barley, the green potato patches by the roofless houses. Murdo Mackay's corn-kiln at Ravigill, which all the township used, had been pulled stone from stone, although it was a custom of the country that an out-going tenant was entitled to the use of his kiln until he had manufactured his waygoing crop. William Gordon's three barns at Skail, the finest in the valley, were also destroyed, and here too custom should have given the tenants the use of all barns until the harvest's end. But this year there would be no harvest; before barley or oats ripened Mr Sellar's Great Cheviots would be among the crops.

At last the people left for the coast. 'When they came down from the strath to the sea-shore,' remembered George Macdonald, 'they suffered very much from the want of houses. They hurriedly threw up earthen walls, stretching blankets over the top to shelter them, and cooped up in a small place like this, four or five families spent the following winter. No compensation was given for the houses burnt, neither any help to build new ones. Having brought with them large flocks of cattle and there being no food for them, they almost died the first winter.... Some people were removed three or four times, always forced farther down until at last the sea-shore prevented them from being sent any farther unless they took ship for the Colonies, which many of them did.'

Among the evicted were many old soldiers whose natural dignity of race was stiffened still further by a pride that took them beyond the edge of starvation before they would beg. One of these was Iain Ban Mackay from the township of Rhifail. He had served with the Reay Fencibles in the Irish Rebellion, marching up Tara Hill under heavy musket-fire, and for his courage and conduct that day he carried with him a letter of commendation from his colonel. After being driven from Rhifail in 1814 he and his family were removed five times more before they at last reached the coast, building themselves a hut of stones on the cliffs above Tongue. During the winter of 1816 the county suffered badly from a potato famine. Iain Mackay had given his last spoonful of meal to his sick daughter before he stomached his pride and asked Lord Stafford's factor for food. The factor closely examined him, demanding proof of his character, questioning his ability to pay for the charity he asked. When Mackay had agreed to give his one milk-cow in exchange, he was allowed a boll of meal. On this the family contrived to live until spring.

But perhaps, as Lady Stafford wrote to a friend that same winter, 'Scotch people are of happier constitutions, and do not fatten like the larger breed of animals.'

Nearly seventy years later Mackay's granddaughter, Annie, spoke of the effect which those times had on her family. 'I remember my grandmother, a sadly-depressed woman with a world of sorrow in her faded blue eyes, as if the shadow of the past were always upon her spirit. I never saw her smile, and when I asked my mother for the cause she told me that that look of pain came upon my grandmother's face with the fires of Strathnaver. Even when my mother was in her last illness, in May 1882, when the present was fading from her memory, she appeared again as a girl of twelve in Strathnaver, continually asking "Whose house is burning now?" and crying out now and again, "*Save the people!*"'

Improvements? asked Donald Macleod bitterly:

'Mr Dempster of Skibo has improved, and his factor from being a kitchen-boy has become a very thriving gentleman. These are the kind of Improvements that have taken place, and all would go merrily if they could get entirely rid of the small tenants. Mr Loch says that the Sutherlanders were in a "state of nature". Well, he and his coadjutors have done what they could to put them into an unnatural state!'

'The laws of the country imperiously call upon me!'

THE Procurator-Fiscal had been quite right. Robert MacKid, Sheriff-Substitute of Sutherland, had indeed been lying in wait for Patrick Sellar, and the Strathnaver evictions of June 1814 gave him his opportunity to spring. MacKid was a Highlandman, but his sympathies were less with sub-tenants and cotters than with that dying class of middlemen to which he belonged,* and whose creature he seemed to be. The middlemen were a great trial to Stafford, for much of his vast estate was still encumbered

---

* He rented the farm at Kirktown, parish of Golspie, from the Sutherland Estate.

with them, and the proposal to be rid of them along with the sub-tenants, said Sellar, 'made my duty no sinecure'. But there were a number of them who would not lie down or go away when bribed or threatened, and Mr MacKid was soon to be put into the lists as their champion against Sellar, and against Lord Stafford through the Factor.

MacKid was a lawyer by profession, practising first at Fortrose and later at Tain. In 1809, when the Sheriff-Substitute of the county was drowned with seventy other people aboard the Meikle Ferry, Mr MacKid became his successor. He liked to make speeches boasting that trial-by-jury was rare in Sutherland because crime was unknown except by name, but when the shire got the most famous trial-by-jury in its history Mr MacKid was responsible for it.

He was a fussy, money-ridden man with a large family of three sons and three daughters to whom he was sentimentally attached. In his nature there was a boyish and adventurous longing for the old days when any deer that started from the heather, any hare leaping, any bird rising was the rightful target for a Highland-man's gun. He was, in fact, grievously addicted to poaching on Lord Stafford's estates. 'I mean,' complained Sellar fretfully, 'to killing hares on the corn at breeding time, to shooting partridges by the covey when sitting close together in time of snow; and to otherwise destroying the game without either certificate or liberty from the proprietor. He had met with several checks from the keepers, from myself, and in one instance from the Marquess of Stafford; none of which checks were, I believe, calculated to compliment this man of authority, or to flatter his vanity.'

When MacKid was caught for a third time at his poaching, and was unable to talk his way out of the act, he wrote to the Staffords, begging them not to prosecute. 'Lord Stafford's answer passed through my hands,' wrote Sellar later. 'I cannot do it justice, but it was somewhat to this effect – that, including the Sheriff, there were seven poachers detected in different parts of the county and contained in the same report; that whatever differences might exist between the condition of the culprits, the quality of the offence was the same; and therefore, in granting the Sheriff's request his Lordship had directed me to discharge the whole.' But Robert MacKid did not forget that Patrick Sellar would rather have seen him in the Tolbooth.

All this took place before the burnings in Strathnaver. The evictions there were reported briefly by the Press, and without comment, except by the *Military Register*. The interest which this newspaper and its readers took in the affair was something more than a feeling that injustice had been done. It was edited and published from Pall Mall in London by a Scotsman, Robert Bisset Scott, an officer in the Tower Hamlet Militia, a military writer, and later a free-lance warrior in Portugal's wars. He had begun the paper in 1814, acquiring a healthy circulation for it among retired and half-pay officers, particularly in the Highlands. Therefore Scott had a strong and partisan concern for their affairs. In the past, when Highland regiments had been raised for the Crown, they had been clan levies, officered by junior kinsmen and tacksmen of the chiefs. Those who served well were rewarded, as was the custom, with grants of land. But now the raising of recruits and the commissioning of officers followed the normal procedure governing all regiments of the line. Officers returning impoverished and land-hungry from the Napoleonic Wars found no grants of land awaiting them, and in many cases no grateful chiefs to welcome them. The land they had hoped to receive (and often the land they believed they already possessed) was being sold for sheep-walks, and they were of no more importance than any English half-pay officer condemned to penury in Bath or Cheltenham.

The *Military Register* became their spokesman against Improvement and eviction long before Waterloo : 'The present war is a war of liberty ! O then let us not suffer petty local tyranny to destroy such hopes either in the army, or those sources from which are to be drawn our future armies.' It published full accounts of the events in Strathnaver, written by a correspondent who signed himself '*Miles – a Highlander of Sutherland*', and who, from the detailed nature of his information later, would appear to have been a close confidant of MacKid if not the Sheriff-Substitute himself. The *Military Register* was read aloud at cottage doors in the parish of Farr, fomenting a demand for the prosecution of Patrick Sellar. Encouraged, perhaps, by this sympathy from the south, the people drew up a petition to Lady Stafford, complaining of the injury, cruelty and oppression they had suffered. Having been assured by Sellar that there were no grounds for complaint, she replied to them : 'That if any person on the estate shall receive any illegal treatment, she will never consider it as hostile to her if they have recourse to legal redress as the most secure way to receive the justice which she always desires they should have on every occasion.'

It is surprising that the petition even reached her. 'In the rare case of any of the noble family coming to the Highlands during the period of the removals,' said Donald Macleod, 'they came only to the castle and stopped there, where the old tenants were strictly denied access while the new occupiers had free personal communication with the proprietors. When any memorial or petition from the former could be got introduced there was no attention paid to them if not signed by a minister, and this was next to impossible as the clergy, with one honourable exception, had to take the other side.'

When the people heard no more from the Marchioness (she believing Patrick Sellar) they wrote to her son, Earl Gower. He passed the petition to his parents, and this time Stafford replied that he was 'desirous that the tenants should know that it is always their [the Staffords] wish that justice should be impartially administered.' He told the people that he had ordered William Young to place both their petitions before Mr Cranstoun, the Sheriff of Sutherland, to take what steps he thought fit. Thus encouraged to believe that justice might be theirs, the men of Strathnaver began to collect funds for the prosecution under the guidance of the *Military Register*, which regularly published the anonymous donations received (in March, 1816, a total of £27 2s. sterling was reached).

In the spring of 1815, when Mr Cranstoun appeared to be laggard, the people wrote to him too, 'requesting that he would bring Mr Sellar to justice'. The Sheriff's reply showed that he had no intention of burning his fingers. He said 'that if the tenants mean to take a precognition *immediately* it will proceed before the Sheriff-Substitute, as my engagements will not permit me to be in Sutherland until the month of July'. He thus handed the matter to Mr MacKid, who had surely been active in the affair long before this.

The Sheriff-Substitute went to work with enthusiasm, setting out for Strathnaver at once and 'at considerable personal inconvenience and expense, and with much patient perseverance', he later told Lord Stafford. He said that he examined forty witnesses in Strathnaver, 'and it is with the deepest regret that I have to inform your Lordship that a more numerous catalogue of crimes, perpetrated by an individual, has seldom disgraced any country, or sullied the pages of a precognition in Scotland ! ! !'

It was not, however, his responsibility to collect such evidence. This should have been done by the Procurator-Fiscal, but Hugh Ross was away from the country for lengthy periods at this time, and MacKid was in no mood to await his return or the Sheriff's. So he travelled to Strathnaver on his own, without even the Sheriff-Clerk to be his penman. The people spoke freely and bitterly of the dark days of the burnings, and from their evidence came the picture of Margaret Mackay crying '*O teine!* Oh, fire !' as she was carried out in her blanket; of old Donald MacBeth lying for four days in the wind and rain by a clay wall, of their deaths, of the burning cottages, destroyed barns and broken kilns.

Back from the north toward the end of May 1815, MacKid wrote to Lord Stafford, informing him that his Factor Patrick Sellar was now a prisoner in the Tolbooth at Dornoch and that a statement would shortly be taken from him too. He was there, said MacKid, because 'the laws of the country imperiously call upon me'. Meanwhile he could tell his lordship something of the nature of the crimes with which the Factor was almost certain to be charged : 'Wilful fire-raising; by having set on fire and reduced to ashes a poor man's whole premises, including dwelling-house, barn, kiln, and sheep cot, attended with most aggravated circumstances of cruelty, *if not murder* ! ! !'

So far as MacKid was concerned, the Factor could stay in the

Tolbooth until his trial. He refused bail, and Sellar's friends had to apply to the Court of Judiciary in Edinburgh for an order that it should be accepted before they could get the Factor out of MacKid's hands. The *Military Register* expressed 'the utmost astonishment of the country' that bail should have been granted, and accused Sellar and his friends of threatening to commit Mac-Kid himself on charges of false imprisonment. This although Margaret Mackay's scorched blanket had been displayed in public!

The *Register* also published a long letter from *Miles* in which he gave a full account of the charges against Sellar. He could not understand why the authorities were so slow in proceeding against Sellar in the face of such terrible evidence.

All this, Sir, is charged to have been acted in a country where there is always a resident under-Sheriff; in a country where, in every district is at least one Magistrate, and yet, this *alien* for 12 months stalks abroad, without even the semblance of a judicial inquiry into his conduct. *Oh fie, fie upon it!* But such, Sir, are the effects of remote local tyranny.

Eleven months of argument and delay passed before Sellar was brought to trial (and then, it was said, at his own request in order to clear himself). The *Register* kept up its fire during these months, and Robert Scott wrote an editorial in which he demanded: 'The Sutherland people *must have justice*! We know nothing comparable to the cruelty of their case but the Massacre of Glencoe.' The circulation of the *Military Register* in Sutherland was stopped by the factors. *Miles* accused them of opening the mailbag before it reached the Post Office and taking from it whatever they wanted. 'The Factors of Sutherland,' he said, 'had much rather see both the *Register* and precognitions burnt by the common hangman, and you and me, Mr Editor, in the middle of the piles for having given an honest disclosure to their foul misdeeds and the wrongs of a brave people!'

At last, on Tuesday, 23 April 1816, and at ten o'clock in the morning, Patrick Sellar appeared before the Circuit Court at Inverness, and before the Lord Commissioner of Justiciary, Lord Pitmilly. There was a jury of fifteen men. Eight of them were local landed proprietors, two were merchants, two were tacksmen, one was a lawyer, and most were magistrates and Justices of the Peace. All were old enough to have vivid and unnerving memories of the Year of the Sheep.

The Court was crowded, and according to the marathon custom of the day the trial lasted without a break until one o'clock on Wednesday morning. Sellar was charged, primarily, with 'CULPABLE HOMICIDE, as also OPPRESSION and REAL INJURY', and with 'wickedly and maliciously setting on fire and burning'. The charge was long and the Advocate-Depute, Mr Home Drummond, was nearly two hours in reading it. The homicides involved were the sad and premature deaths of the aged Margaret Mackay and Donald MacBeth. Sellar heard that he was charged with saying, 'The devil a man of them, sick or well, shall remain!' He heard that 'all the persons whose houses, barns, kilns, mills and other buildings were burnt and destroyed, or caused and procured to be burnt and destroyed by you, the said Patrick Sellar, all as above described, did sustain great loss.' He heard that he was accused of burning 'heath and pasture on which a number of small tenants and other poor persons maintain their cattle'. He was told that he 'ought to be punished with the pains of law to deter others from committing the like crimes in all time coming'. And then Mr Drummond sat down and the trial began.

Of the forty witnesses whom MacKid had examined, fifteen only were called for the Crown. Nine were called for the defence, though more were waiting ready outside the Court. These nine were Sheriff-Officers and servants who had accompanied Sellar to Strathnaver, and they would have been very stupid men not to realize that, in one sense, they were on trial too. The Factor was also armed with letters from gentlemen of the county and others, in which he was described as 'a person of the strictest integrity ... incapable of any cruel or oppressive action ... a most respectable character ... of a humane disposition'. The only report of the trial that exists is that prepared by Patrick Robertson, who was junior Counsel for Sellar, and while it seems full enough within the space it allows itself, it fails to report the *arguments* of counsel. It does report, however, that Mr James

Gordon, counsel for Sellar, used these words when he addressed the jury of landlords:

'The question at issue involves the future fate and progress of agricultural and even moral improvements in the county of Sutherland; that (though certainly not so intended by the Public Prosecutor, whose conduct throughout has been candid, correct and liberal), it is nevertheless, in substance and in fact, a trial of strength between the abettors of anarchy and misrule, and the magistracy as well as the laws of this country.'

When Lord Pitmilly came to sum up ('in a very clear and able manner', thought Mr Robertson) he told the jury that it was unnecessary for them to consider any of the charges except that relating to the death of Margaret Mackay. He directed their attention to the evidence given by her son-in-law, the tinker, William Chisholm. He said that Chisholm's evidence, corroborated though it had been by others, should be matched against that given by witnesses for the defence, and if the jury had any difficulty in striking a balance then they must take into account the character of the accused. The implication was clearly that against the word of a man so nobly commended as Patrick Sellar, of what value was the evidence of a caird, a thief, and a bigamist?

With that the jury retired, and when they returned fifteen minutes later it was to declare the Factor innocent, an opinion which Lord Pitmilly happily shared. He looked across the court and said, 'Mr Sellar, it is now my duty to dismiss you from the bar; and you have the satisfaction of thinking that you are discharged by the unanimous opinion of the Jury and the Court. I am sure that although your feelings must have been agitated, you cannot regret that this trial took place; and I am hopeful it will have due effect on the minds of the country, which have been so much and so improperly agitated.'

And in Strathnaver there was an old woman, simple of mind, who would be thrown into a fit by the arrival of any stranger, of a man who appeared to carry authority in the set of his shoulders. She would roll her eyes, hug her body, and cry out, 'O shin Sellar! There's Sellar!'

With the Loch Policy vindicated, as much as his own character,

Sellar spent the summer of 1816 removing those tenants on his new estate on Strathnaver whom he had allowed to remain in 1814. He did this with caution, burning no roof-timbers and destroying no barns until the people were gone. He told them they might return to harvest their small crops, but before the grain ripened he had four thousand sheep on the land, from the River Naver to the twin peaks of Ben Griam. And winter came early that year, as hard and as cruel as any winter that the oldest tenant could remember. It began in October with heavy snow-falls and a great and bitter cold. Without barns or shelter, the people were unable to gather or store the harvest they cropped before the first snows.

'I have seen scores of these poor outcasts,' said Donald Macleod, 'employed for weeks together, with the snow from two to four feet deep, watching their corn from being devoured by the now hungry sheep of the incoming tenant; carrying on their backs, horses being unavailable, across a country without roads, on an average of twenty miles to their new allotments on the sea-coast, any portion of their grain and potatoes they could secure.'

Others came down from the north to dig what they could from beneath the snow and eat it there, cooking a few potatoes among the ruins of what were once their homes. 'Many severe diseases made their appearance, hitherto unknown in the Highlands, typhus, consumption and pulmonary complaints, bloody flux, bowel complaints, eruptions and rheumatism.'

Patrick Sellar did not forget Mr MacKid. His pride and dignity had been hurt by the days he had spent in the Tolbooth at Dornoch, while a clerk's pen scratched down his cold declaration of innocence. He remembered the gloating with which MacKid had written to Stafford. His acquittal was not enough, nor was he satisfied when the Sheriff-Substitute resigned his office in disgrace. In the summer of 1817 he began a suit for damages against the wretched man. MacKid was broken. From Drummuie, to which he had fled with his family, he wrote to Sellar in cringing humility, denying all that he had once charged against the Factor.

'I gave a degree of credit to those misstatements of which I am now thoroughly ashamed and which I most sincerely and deeply regret.' He allowed that Sellar would be entitled to exemplary damages, but pleaded with him not to prosecute. 'I shall not only acknowledge it as a most important obligation conferred on me and on my innocent family, if you will have the goodness to drop your law-suit against me, but I shall also pay the expense of that suit. . . .' He promised to pay any further sum which Sellar might choose to exact in compensation, believing this would be less than it would cost him to fight the suit which had already saddled him with heavy expense He said that Sellar was free to make whatever use he wished of this letter, hoping only that he would not publish it in the newspapers. The little man, mindful perhaps of the faith which the people of Strathnaver had placed in him, wished to retain some public respect.

More in disgust than compassion, Sellar withdrew the suit. 'I have no wish to distress Mrs MacKid and her family,' he said. He accepted MacKid's offer to pay what expenses he had incurred, and demanded £200 sterling beside. The money was paid. Robert MacKid left Sutherland, going north to practise law in Caithness, where, said Donald Macleod, 'every malignant influence followed him from the ruling powers of the former county'.

'Nothing but the sword was wanting . . .'

'IT IS SAID,' reported the *Scotsman* in June 1819, 'that a posse of men (with legal warrants be it observed) are parading the county of Sutherland and ejecting poor Highlanders from the homes of their fathers.' It was true. The burners had come again to Strathnaver. Lord Stafford's agents* were clearing all remaining tenants, tenants-at-will, cotters, tinkers and vagrants from both banks of the river and the loch, from Achness of the cascade

---

* Patrick Sellar had retired from Stafford's service in 1818. In less than ten years since he boarded the Burghead packet he had become one of the most prosperous sheep-farmers in the north.

to the water's end at Altnaharra. Included in the removals was Robert Gordon of Langdale, who had been Sellar's host in the Year of the Burnings. Mr Gordon seems to have forfeited any consideration this hospitality may have earned him by being grievously in arrears with his rent. Had he not been in debt to the proprietor, James Loch would certainly have found a way to be rid of him. The Englishmen who had taken a lease on the land, Atkinson and Marshall from Northumbria, were waiting to extend the great sheep-walk they had held in that part of the country since 1812 – the mountain pastures of Ben Klibreck between Loch Naver and Loch Choire.

First warning of the removals reached Strathnaver in October 1818, when a man came running to the manse at Achness, arousing the Reverend Donald Sage. This young man was new to the mission, having been appointed when David Mackenzie left to enjoy his reward of the Parish of Farr. 'I can yet recall,' Sage wrote in his *Memorabilia*, 'the deep and thrilling sensation which I experienced as I sat at the fireside in my rude little parlour when the tidings of the meditated removal of my poor flock reached me from headquarters. A tenant from the middle of the strath had been to Rhives, the residence of Mr Young, paying his rent. He was informed and authorized to tell his neighbours that the rent for the half-year, ending in May 1819, would not be demanded as it was determined to lay the districts of Strathnaver and Upper Kildonan under sheep.'

Many of the people in the strath, with the innocence that was at once their weakness and their strength, refused to believe the news, despite the fact that across the river they could still see the smoke-black stones of the townships Sellar had destroyed in 1814. They said that the *Ban mhorair Chataibh* would not permit her people to be persecuted further, but there were some who were less credulous. William Mackay, commonly known as Achoul ('and a distinguished member of my congregation', said Sage), was an old man of ninety-two who could remember the skirmish fire of musketry when the Jacobites came to Dunrobin in his youth. Until 1812 he had been a tenant-at-will on the south slope of Ben Klibreck, but had been removed to make room for the Northumbrians' sheep. He came to Grummore and buried his wife, Janet, in the churchyard at Achness, speaking his own valediction over her: 'Well, Janet, the Countess of Sutherland can never flit you any more.'

Whatever their hopes or fears, the people were not left long in doubt. 'Summons of ejectment were issued and despatched all over the district,' said Sage. 'These must have amounted to up-wards of a thousand, as the population of the Mission alone was 1,600 souls, and many more than those of the Mission were ejected. The summonses were distributed with the utmost pre-ciseness. They were handed in at every house and hovel alike, be the occupiers of them who or what they might, minister, cate-chist, or elder, tenant or sub-tenant, out-servant or cotter, all were made to feel the irresponsible power of the proprietor.'

He himself received notice of eviction. He was thirty years of age and had been born in the manse of Kildonan beyond Ben Griam, where his father was still Minister. He was a warm-hearted and generous man, weak in the ill-deserved admiration he felt for the gentry, but strong in his concern for the common people. His *Memorabilia*, edited and published by his son seventy years later, contain his bewildered indictment of the great landowners and the policy of removals, but there is no evidence that he spoke out against them *at the time*, and when his people expected him to follow where they went, he abandoned them. For this, perhaps, he should be understood rather than blamed. He had to cut his clerical cloth according to the tailoring demanded by his superiors. He had a conscience and a sense of injustice, and they were rare enough among his profession.

Physically frail, he found life in the bleak valley of the Naver very hard. From his youth he had prepared himself for such a ministry, rising early and going for long walks in the mountains before dawn. He despised comfort, sleeping without a feather-bed or English blankets, choosing a mattress of straw and one home-spun blanket only. His house at Achness stood at the foot of a weeping brae and in the middle of a fen. Its walls were of stone and lime, the roof thatched with divots, and within it were four rooms only – a kitchen, a parlour with a bed in the wall, a closet and a bedroom. They were sparsely furnished with carpets and chairs which Sage had bought from Robert MacKid when that beaten man sold his property and went to Caithness (Sage was much attached to MacKid, and had been tutor to his teeming family). In addition to the house he rented a small farm from Atkinson and Marshall for £5 sterling a year, and this gave him corn and fodder for a horse and two cows.

The meeting-house by the manse was now almost a ruin, stone and divot trembling above a floor of damp mud. Sage had preached his first sermon to Strathnaver in the open, with the wind rolling down Rowan Tree Hill behind him and catching up the Gaelic and English of his words. Throughout the winter of 1818 to 1819 he preached vehemently and passionately to the doomed people, seeking to reassure himself as much as them that their future was God's will. When the end came there was no resistance from the people. There was a typhus epidemic in the north of Scotland, and Strathnaver had been affected with the rest. 'The factors,' said Donald Macleod, 'taking advantage of the broken spirit and prostrate state of the people, people trembling at their words or even looks, betook themselves to a new scheme to facilitate their intended proceedings.' Young's men went from house to house some days before the date of eviction, demanding that the people put their names or marks to a bond promising passive obedience.

On the Sunday preceding the ejectment Donald Sage preached his last sermon, once more in the open, this time on a grass clearing before Robert Gordon's house. 'I selected a text which had a pointed reference to the peculiarity of our circumstances, but my difficulty was how to restrain my feelings. . . . I preached and the people listened, but every sentence uttered and heard was in opposition to the tide of our natural feelings.' Before he could finish his sermon, minister and congregation broke into weeping. When the officers arrived, two days later, Sage had already left Strathnaver. He gives no explanation in his *Memorabilia*.

Thirteen days before the May term the burners came like an army – Factor and Fiscal, Sheriff-Officers and constables, shepherds, fox-hunters and servants from Dunrobin. According to Donald Macleod, the warrants for eviction had been granted by

Captain Kenneth Mackay of Torboll, an officer of Volunteers and an extensive sheep-farmer, who was acting for the Sheriff's office in this part of the country. 'He was all the time residing in his house, situated so that he must have witnessed a great part of the scene from his own front windows. Therefore if he did not immediately authorise the atrocities to the extent committed (which I will not assert) he at least used no means to restrain them.'*

The destruction was begun in the west at Grummore as the party approached it from Altnaharra on the Lairg road, and messengers were sent ahead to all the other townships warning the people that they had an hour in which to evacuate their homes and take away what furniture they could. 'I saw the townships set on fire,' recalled Roderick Macleod, who was a boy at the time. 'Grummore with sixteen houses and Archmilidh with four. All the houses were burnt with the exception of one barn. Few if any of the families knew where to turn their heads or from whom to get their next meal. It was sad, the driving away of these people. The terrible remembrance of the burnings of Strathnaver will live as long as a root of the people remains in the country.'

The widower William Mackay was burnt out of Grummore, and walked far from his Janet's grave to die alone in Wick. Robert Mackay, whose whole family was sick with fever, carried his daughters on his back for twenty-five miles, 'first by carrying one and laying her down in the open air, and, returning did the same with the other till he reached the seashore'. At Grummore, too, when Donald Mackay, a boy, was driven from his home with his parents, he ran naked and terrified into some bushes and stayed there, watching the flames and refusing to come out. By the loch-side an old man, also of Clan Mackay, crawled into the ruins of a mill unseen. His dog kept the rats from him and he survived for

---

*The Captain may have felt he had no reason to love the people. Eight years before, he and his Volunteers had been called out to suppress a riot caused by the thoroughly unpopular appointment of a Murdoch Cameron to the ministry at Creich. His martial dignity had been offended when an old woman of seventy, resenting his naked broadsword, had shattered it with a stone.

a few days by licking the dust of meal from the floor. 'To the best of my recollection,' said Donald Macleod, 'he died there.'

The timber of three hundred buildings burned in the thin May sunshine. The valley was filled again with terrible noise, the crying of women and children, the hysterical barking of the dogs which the Northumbrian shepherds had brought with them. 'Nothing but the sword was wanting,' said Macleod, 'to make the scene one of as great barbarity as the earth ever witnessed.' At Ceann-na-Coille, George Munro the miller also had most of his family sick with fever. He carried them to a damp kiln not far from the Achness meeting-house, and there they watched their house burn. In the same township lived an old woman who had been evicted from Rhimsdale across the river five years before, and who was known as *Bean Raomasdail*, the Woman of Rhimsdale. 'In her house,' said Sage, 'I have held diets of catechising and meetings for prayer, and been signally refreshed by her Christian converse.' She was a paralytic, unable to walk or lie. Night and day she sat in a chair, and any movement caused her great pain. Lord Stafford's agents, said Sage, told her neighbours that 'she must immediately be removed by her friends, or the constables would be ordered to do it'. Her family lifted her from the chair, and four of the strongest boys in the township wept as they carried her out in a blanket. She was taken northward to the coast, 'and her cries never ceased till within a few miles of her destination, when she fell asleep.'

At Grumbeg the first house met with belonged to Widow Henney Munro, an old woman who had marched beside her husband in the Peninsular campaigns until he was killed or died of sickness. When she returned to Strathnaver the people had built her a cottage, given her a cow and pasture. She now pleaded for her home and was told that 'if she did not take her trumpery off within half an hour it would be burned'. And so it was burned, for she could drag her bed, presses and stool no further than the gable, and 'the wind blew in the direction of the furniture and the flame, lighting upon it, speedily reduced it to ashes'.

At eleven o'clock that night Donald Macleod climbed to high ground above the strath, probably to the top of the little hill at

Rossall behind the ruins of his home, and from there he counted two hundred and fifty buildings burning, 'many of the owners of which were my relations, and all of whom I personally knew'. The townships burned in a long line for more than ten miles, from Grummore on the loch northwards to Skail. He said the fires were still alight six days later, and that at one time the wind sucked great clouds of smoke down the funnel of the glen and out to sea, blinding a boat that was tacking up to an entrance of Torrisdale Bay.

One man refused to go north to Bettyhill and the unprepared allotments on the coast. He was John Mackay, the catechist at Achness, an old man of eighty who earned a living by making leather gaiters for the men of the townships. When he was burned out he walked to the south-east, inland over the hills toward Kildonan and away from the sea he feared. The rest of the people made their way down to Bettyhill and huddled on the quayside there. A small sloop was berthed against the stones, discharging a cargo of quicklime, and her master agreed to take some of the evicted to Caithness if they had a mind to go. Twenty families went aboard, said Macleod, 'filling deck, hold and every part of the vessel. Many of these persons had not been on sea before, and when they began to sicken a scene indescribable ensued. To add to their miseries, a storm and contrary winds prevailed, so that instead of a day or two, the usual time of passage, it was nine days before they reached Caithness. All this time the poor creatures, almost without necessaries, most of them dying with sickness, were either wallowing among the lime and various excrements in the hold, or lying on deck exposed to the raging elements.'

Donald Sage's *Memorabilia* confirm Macleod's claim that Strathnaver still burned six days after the torches were set to it. He came by the glen the following week, on his way to Tongue from his father's manse in Kildonan. 'Of all the houses the thatched roofs were gone, but the walls, built of alternate layers of turf and stone remained. The flames of the preceding week still slumbered in their ruins and sent up into the air spiral columns of smoke; whilst here a gable and there a long side-wall might be seen tumbling to the ground from which a cloud of smoke, and then a dusky flame, slowly sprang up.' The remains of his little manse at Achness became the home of a foxhunter employed by Atkinson and Marshall. Some of the timbers of his meeting-house were used in the improvement of the long road from Lairg to Tongue. Others were built into a new inn at Altnaharra. A year after Strathnaver was cleared, a woman who had once lived in it paid it a visit, and on her return she was asked what she had seen. 'O chan eil ach sgiala bronach!' she cried, 'I have seen the timbers of our church covering the inn. I have seen the kirk-yard filled with tarry sheep and Mr Sage's study turned into a kennel for Robert Gunn's dogs, and I have seen a crow's nest in James Gordon's chimney-head. Sgiala bronach!'

Donald Macleod did not complain of Mr Sage's unexplained absence when his parish would appear to have needed him most, but the stonemason bitterly attacked other ministers of Farr and Tongue who gave the people no comfort at this time. 'The clergy, indeed, maintained in their sermons that the whole was a merciful interposition of Providence to bring them to repentance....' Macleod said that shortly after the evictions the Staffords, or James Loch on their behalf, sent a message to the Reverend David Mackenzie at the manse of Farr, asking him if the people were comfortable and provided for. 'The answer returned was that the people were quite comfortable in their new allotments and that the change was greatly for their benefit.'

Also cleared at the same time as the townships along the Naver was the upper strath of Kildonan nearby, most of it lying within the limits of Achness mission. This long glen, from its narrow opening on the North Sea coast at Helmsdale, curved in a green bow north-westward to Loch nan Clar, Badenloch and the borders of Patrick Sellar's fine new sheep-walk. From the highest point of the valley the black ribbon of the Helmsdale River fell eight hundred feet to the sea. It was an enclave of Highland history. St Donan had a cell in its rock walls. Norsemen had stormed up it to the inland heart of the country. Gunns and Keiths had fought bloody brawls on the lowland meadows, and had left their memory in the names they gave to their land – Bealach nan *creach*, the Pass of the Forays, *Loch nan cuidhean*, the Lake of the Snow Wreaths. Viking tumuli were thick in the strath, from its mouth to its rise, and Clan Gunn's black cattle scratched their backs on stone slabs that marked a warrior's death. Within the glebe of the manse in which Donald Sage had been born an Abbot had once built his home. It was gone beneath a scrub of stunted whin even in Donald Sage's time, but his father's house and church still stand below the heather rise of Ben Dubhain, on a green grass field embraced by the river. The old minister's grave, and the graves of his two wives, are in a walled kirk-yard by the flat field in which the chiefs of Clan Gunn were once buried. But the valley is empty.*

Many of the people of the lower strath, close by the sea, had been burnt out in 1813 when the Irish of the 21st came up from Dornoch, demanding vengeance for Vinegar Hill. More had gone in 1815 and in the slow years following. Now it was the time for Loch to clear away the rest, to drive them down to Helmsdale, where his workmen were building herring-stores, curing-sheds and harbour offices, all bearing the Stafford arms and the date of the year in grey Highland stone. And if the people were too lazy (in Loch's opinion) to leave the plough for the trawl, then they might walk to the emigrants' ships at Wick and Thurso, and the country would be well rid of them.

'The whole inhabitants of Kildonan parish, with the exception of three families,' said Donald Sage, 'nearly 2,000 souls, were utterly rooted and burned out. Many, especially the young and robust, left the country, but the aged, the females and children, were obliged to stay and accept the wretched allotments allowed them on the seashore and endeavour to learn fishing.'

---

*An exile from Kildonan, whose ancestor armed himself with a flintlock to scare away the sheepmen, writes to me: 'What is the position in Kildonan today? Six alien proprietors owning land and water (where once hundreds of good, happy people lived), a red Post Office van, a score of gamekeepers and shepherds. In addition to deer, grouse and salmon, the proprietors do quite a side-line in sheep and cattle. They sometimes open baby shows and strut at Highland games, and the people think it fine.'

'The idle and lazy alone think of emigration'

WHILE his ground officers were clearing Strathnaver and Upper Kildonan, and as the Great Cheviot moved in thousands to the braesides of Badenloch and Borrobol, Mr Loch was finishing a book seven hundred miles to the south in Bloomsbury. It was published the following year: *An Account of the Improvements on the Estate of Sutherland belonging to the Marquess and Marchioness of Stafford, by James Loch, General Agent of the Sutherland Estates.* It was a long and confident justification of the Loch Policy over the preceding seven years, and of its proposals for the future. It became the great apologia of the Improvers, with an armoury of statistics for their use. It was to hold its own against a minority of doubt, scepticism and disproval for the rest of the century, and still has its supporters. Nowhere in its pages did Loch refer to himself as the creative and responsible mind, he wrote as if all had sprung god-like from the noble brow of his master. Yet his proud satisfaction can be read behind the figures of herrings barrelled and fleece sheared, of roads, bridges and harbours built, even of people removed. Improvement was the century's Crusade, and in this book James Loch defined its cause: 'To emancipate the lower orders from slavery has been the unceasing object of the Highland Proprietors for the last twenty years.'

All crusades have their troublesome Saracens, however, and before the book came off the press in Covent Garden 'Old Mother Stafford' (as Henry Brougham was now calling her) was sending her friends long and exculpatory letters. 'We have lately been much attacked in the newspapers by a few malicious writers who have long assailed us on every occasion. What is stated is most perfectly unjust and unfounded, as I am convinced from the facts I am acquainted with, and I venture to trouble you with the enclosed. .... If you meet with discussions on the subject in Society, I shall be glad if you will show this statement to anyone who may interest him or herself on the subject.' The enclosed statement was something Loch must have prepared at the request of the Staffords (who were being uncommonly sensitive to public opinion), a paraphrase of the important arguments and facts in his book.

In an age when every educated and landed gentleman was his own economist, sociologist, agriculturalist, scientist and Improver, Loch's arguments came like a soothing syrup. By the simple arithmetic with which men comfort their consciences it was obvious that against the removal of a few thousand people (to much better conditions) must be set the production of hundreds of thousands of pounds of wool and mutton. Loch allowed that there was opposition from tenants and sub-tenants, but saw it as 'formidable obstacles to the improvement of a people arising out of the prejudices and feelings of the people themselves'. Stafford's critics were claiming that 15,000 men, women and children had been torn from their homes, but this figure was almost the total population of his Sutherland estates. Loch said that the number of *families* removed between 1810 and 1820 did not exceed 600, by which he probably meant that this was the number of writs of eviction issued. In addition there were 408 families who, in his opinion, should not have been on his lordship's property at all, for they were squatters, refugees from other clearances with no right or title, and they were justly driven from the county. Assuming an average of five to a family this makes a conservative estimate of five thousand persons evicted. Loch's calculations do not include the removals carried out by Sellar and Young before 1810, and they do not include the cotters and out-servants who could not be counted among the squatters.

No one can ever know the correct figure. It was less than fifteen thousand, but probably considerably more than Loch claimed.

Justifying the remorseless removals, Loch set down the demands of Progress and Improvement: 'To render this mountainous district contributory as far as it was possible to the general wealth and industry of the country, and in the manner most suitable to its situation and peculiar circumstances. To convert the former population of these districts to industries and regular habits and to enable them to bring to market a very considerable surplus quantity of provisions for the supply of the large towns in the southern parts of the land, or for the purpose of exportation.' This, he thought, as if the idea were not his, was a 'wise and generous policy and well calculated to increase the happiness of the individuals who were the object of this change, and to benefit those to whom these extensive domains belonged'.

Loch's figures spilled tumultuously across the pages of his book in support of all this. Half a million pounds of wool were being exported annually, and more than two hundred thousand sheep grazed from Farr to Ross. Ninety miles of road were made or under contract. Bridges were being built at Dornoch and Helmsdale, and another planned for Bonar. Coal was now coming to the county from Newcastle, timber from Speyside, slates from Abderdeen, bricks from Peterhead and lime from Sunderland. A seam of coal had been struck at Brora. The estate was to have a brewery, a pier at Dunrobin where the Burghead packet might berth on its weekly call. Three excellent inns were now open on the coast. Lime was being quarried locally, and a tileworks and brickworks would also make imports from the south unnecessary. Carpenters, masons, smiths, mechanics and merchants were being attracted to the county from the Lowlands.

The herring-fishery at Helmsdale would be a model for all. Here one hundred and forty boats were already catching twenty thousand barrels of fish a year. Here were seventy coopers and five hundred and twenty women to stave and fill the barrels. Cargoes from Helmsdale were travelling to the Baltic, and even to the West Indies. In the beginning the people had at first hired themselves out to fishermen from the south, but when the curing and store-houses were built at Helmsdale in 1814 the mountain people began to captain and man their own vessels, and 'their success was much greater than could have been expected from the efforts of men unacquainted with the management of a boat'.

What man could not prefer such improvement to the state of affairs before, when the wretched people of Kildonan, for example, had to kill their cows to keep themselves alive in winter, slaughtering as many as two hundred in one season, and also as many horses because there was no fodder for them. Now seven hundred new tenants had been placed at Helmsdale. 'Their turf hovels after having, in the first instance, given place to cottages built of rough stones without mortar, are by degrees changed into neat houses constructed of stone and lime. A greater attention to cleanliness commences to be an object; and the cow and the pigs begin no longer to inhabit the same dwelling with the family.'

Another advantage of the Loch Policy had also been welcome. The removal of the people from the interior had struck a hard blow at an old Highland custom – the illicit distilling of whisky. To all respectable people this was uplifting news, for the practice had a terrible effect on the moral fibre of the mountaineers, 'nursing them in every species of deceit, vice, idleness and dissipation'. To regularize the consumption of whisky among his tenants, to secure for the farmers a regular market for the grain they had been selling to the illegal stills, Lord Stafford was proposing to build a distillery at Brora.

Loch closed his book with a justification of the Policy of Improvement in Sutherland and with a summary of its objects:

First: Nothing could be more at variance with the general interests of society and the individual happiness of the people themselves than the original state of Highland manners and customs.

Second: The adoption of the new system, by which the mountainous districts are converted into sheep pastures, even if it should unfortunately occasion the emigration of some individuals, is, upon the whole, advantageous to the nation at large.

Third: The introduction of sheep farms is perfectly compatible with retaining the ancient population in the country.

Fourth: The effect of this change is most advantageous to the people themselves; relieving them from personal services, improving their industrious habits, and tending directly to their rapid increase and improvement.

Lastly: The improvements ... have had constantly for their object the employment, the comfort, the happiness of every individual who has been the object of removal; and that there is no single instance of any man having left this country on account of his not having had a lot provided for him; and that those who have gone have been induced to do so by the persuasion of others, and not from themselves, and that in point of numbers they are most insignificant.

Such a bland assumption of rectitude was an invitation to Loch's critics to rush into print themselves, and the first away was a grumbling, sceptical English journalist named Thomas Bakewell of Spring Vale near Stone in Staffordshire. Loch's book had scarcely begun to circulate when Bakewell had his own in the bookshops: *Remarks on a Publication by James Loch, Esq., entitled, etc.* . . . It contained some plodding but telling sarcasm on the subject of Loch's modesty. 'How adroitly does he avoid that egotism which is so hateful to an enlightened mind. In almost every page we hear of the Marquess or the Marchioness – Lord and Lady Stafford, the proprietor or the landlord having done this or that to promote the comfort and happiness of their people, when it is well known to be Mr Loch himself that has done all these great things.'

He reminded Loch, 'you told me that the present Marquess of Stafford was fully aware of the value of popularity as a means of avoiding much evil, and of doing much good in society, and that, as his Lordship's Agent, you considered it your duty to observe that line of conduct which should effectually secure his popularity.' Observing Stafford's great English estates from the gate of his own tiny plot, Bakewell could not see that Loch had done anything there to win his master friends. 'I have seen periods of alarm and danger since you became agent; I have heard an old servant much attached to Lord Stafford lament that if a mob were to arise in these parts the first object of it would be to destroy Lord Stafford's property. I have, too, heard it declared that Lord Stafford could not be seen and known in one part of Shropshire without danger to his life.' The Marquess, however, rarely ran such risk of mobbing. In twenty years his English tenantry saw his face but once, at a ploughing match, when one of his farmers came to him and said that though he had lost the contest he had at least seen his landlord face to face, 'and that's what neither me nor any of my family ever did before'.

It was Bakewell's opinion that Loch's work in the Highlands

was probably no better than his activities in Staffordshire where he was well-hated for his evictions. 'He ejected a poor man, his wife and six small children from their humble cottage upon Tittensor hills, in a cold season of the year, the wife having been brought to bed one month and three days at the time of the eject-ment being executed. . . . I found them encamped in the open air like gipsies.'

It was Loch's apparent hypocrisy, encased in its burnished shell of righteousness, that angered Bakewell. He derided the Commissioner's claim to be improving the lot of the people. 'His eye, like the bright luminary of day, darts its rays upon the sides of the mountains, pierces the deep glens, and peeps through the rafters of these filthy hovels and sees men, their wives and dirty bairns, their cows, pigs, dogs, cats, and a great variety of vermin, all inhabiting the same apartment. His first object is to drive out that master-piece of sloth and uselessness – man and all his re-tinue. The huts are destroyed; the smoke of the burning moss timber quickly mingles with the clouds. The potato patches are soon converted into beautiful pasture grounds.'

David Stewart of Garth was another, if more cautious, critic of the Loch Improvements. Since the days when he had marched northward with the 42nd in the Year of the Sheep he had become a distinguished and veteran soldier. Now he was finishing his *Sketches of the Highlanders*, a loving tapestry of the manners and traditions of the clans, the valour of their regiments. The two honest volumes of this work were to become source-books for a romantic mythology that would anaesthetize the conscience of Scotland long after the people described in them had been driven from their hills. Publication of the *Sketches* followed close on Loch's book, and Stewart was unable to do more than put his comments into footnotes. Two are worth quoting. The first pricks the conceit of Loch's claim that the coastal fisheries of Sutherland had been created to give employment to the people removed from the interior.

'We may turn to an advertisement in the Inverness news-papers, describing sixty lots of land to be let in that country for fishing stations. To this notice is added a declaration that "*de-*

cided preference will be given to strangers". Thus, while on the one hand the unfortunate natives are driven from their farms in the interior, a decided preference is given to strangers to settle on the coast.'

The second examines Loch's frequent and flattering references to his master's philanthropy in the times of hunger and destitution that came with the Improvements. Stewart pointed out that the people of Sutherland had supported one family of earls through seven centuries and twenty generations, implying that it ill became the Countess Elizabeth (or her English husband) to think of them as a burden. The amount of poor relief paid by the parishes *before* Mr Loch began improving things had been less than £5 a year for every thousand of the people. And Lord Stafford's charity, when one looked into it, appeared to be a canny trick of giving with the one hand and taking back with the other. 'It has been stated that the starving population have been relieved by remittances to the amount of several thousand pounds in money, grain and meal; but it was not said that good security (or cattle) was taken for payment* of this relief, and that, except in cases of great destitution, where all property had been disposed of to resist a similar calamity, the whole remittances were paid up.'

Seventeen years after the publication of Loch's book, his Policy was again subjected to analysis and bitter criticism, this time by a Swiss, Simonde de Sismondi, one of the greatest social scientists of that age. 'There is something so absurd and revolting,' he said, 'in interpreting as a form of progress the destruction of the happiness, of the liberty, of the very existence of a race in the interests of wealth.' Being no Highlander like Stewart or Macleod, with their clansman's lingering wish to excuse the Chief everything and blame his agents for all, Sismondi aimed for the Countess Elizabeth herself :

'Mr Loch meanwhile insists that the Marchioness of Stafford had shown a great deal more humanity than any of her neighbours. She has concerned herself over the lot of those she has

*P. 84. Iain Ban Mackay of Rhifail in Strathnaver, who had to give his milk-cow to Stafford's factor in exchange for a boll of meal.

removed. She has offered them asylum in her own country, and while she has taken back from them 794,000 acres of land which they had possessed from time immemorial, she has generously left them about 6,000 of these, that is, two acres per family. These 6,000 acres available for use as a refuge for the small tenants were formerly waste, and yielded nothing to the proprietor. All the same, she has not made a gift of them. She has assessed them at an average of two shillings and sixpence an acre, and no leases have been granted for longer than seven years.'

Sismondi had no patience with the peculiarly British philosophy of *laissez-faire*, which argued that a man should be free to do what he wished with his own property within the law. 'If the Marchioness of Stafford was indeed entitled by law to replace the population of an entire province by twenty-nine families of foreigners and some hundreds of thousands of sheep, they should hurry up and abolish such an odious law, both in respect of her and of all the others in her position.' He recalled that in Switzerland the law gave the peasant a guarantee of ownership in perpetuity 'while in the British empire it has given this same guarantee to the Scottish lord and left the peasant in insecurity. Let anyone compare the two countries and judge the two systems.'

Later still in the replies to Loch's book came the stonemason's, and what Donald Macleod had to say, if less literary than the others, was more moving because he was speaking of and for his own people. He could speak a name and touch the shoulder of an old friend. Sismondi knew that the coastal allotments were worthless land, but Macleod had *seen* them – the bitter, rocky stretch between the mouth of the Naver and Strathy Point, for example, where there was no safe harbour, where the wind came without interruption from the Arctic Circle, and where men were now expected to live on what an inhuman sea chose to offer them. These men Donald Macleod knew. William Mackay who was sucked away by the waves while inspecting his little lot, and while his wife and children watched. John Campbell who was also drowned the same way. And Bell Mackay, a married woman who was taken by the sea while making salt. Robert Mackay, who fell and was killed when collecting plovers' eggs for his starving family. 'And John Macdonald, while fishing, was swept off the rocks and never seen more.'

There were improvements, Donald Macleod admitted. 'Roads, bridges, inns and manses to be sure, for the accommodation of the new gentlemen, tenantry and clergy, but those who spoke the Gaelic tongue were a proscribed race, and everything was done to get rid of them, by driving them into the forlorn hope of deriving subsistence from the sea while squatting on their miserable allotments where, in their wretched hovels, they lingered out an almost hopeless existence.' The harbours of which Loch was so proud, said Macleod, were often inadequate, and in one year along thirty miles of coast a hundred boats had been destroyed by the sea for want of a safe anchorage. 'It is lamentable to think that while £1,210,000* were expended on the so-called improvements, besides £500 subscribed by the proprietors for making a harbour, not one shilling of the vast sum was ever expended for behoof of the small tenantry, nor the least pains taken to mitigate their lot.'

The coastal strips were narrow patches on the cliff's edge, or bordered by bogs and morass. The arable soil was thin – so thin in fact, said Macleod contemptuously, that in any dispute over its ownership one man could have taken away his share in a creel. 'In many places the spots the poor people endeavoured to cultivate were so steep that while one was delving, another had to hold up the soil with his hands lest it roll into the sea, and from its constant tendency to slide downwards, they had frequently to carry it up again every spring and spread it on the higher parts.'

Seed was often blown into the sea before it could get a grip on such soil. Salt-blast and mildew destroyed the shafts of green before they grew a few inches. The cattle which the people had brought with them from the emptied glens strayed homeward, on to the new sheep pastures, and were impounded until fines for trespass were paid. Because they had little, if any, money, the people were asked to pay the fines in kind, in 'bed and body clothes, watches, rings, pins, brooches, etc., many of these relics

* In this arguable figure he presumably includes grants made by the Government as well as sums spent by the proprietors.

of dear and valued relatives'. When the fines could not be paid, the stock stayed in pound. 'It was nothing strange to see the pinfolds, of twenty or thirty yards square, filled up to the entrance with horses, cows, sheep and goats, promiscuously for nights and days together, in that starving state, trampling on and goring each other.' Other cattle strayed into the hills and were lost. 'I have myself seen many instances of the kind where the animals were lying partly consumed by dogs, though still alive, and their eyes picked out by birds of prey.'

The people occasionally struck back at the Great Cheviot flocks, now and then stealing a young ewe or killing a ram. The gentry formed themselves into an Association for the Suppression of Sheep-stealing in Sutherland, and transported any man found guilty of it. Stafford offered £30 for information that would lead to the conviction of an offender, and one of the Northumbrians, Atkinson or Marshall, was prepared to pay £1,000 for the capture of the ringleaders. The money was never claimed.

Sismondi said that while Loch had written a great deal about the prosperity and physical changes his employers were bringing to Sutherland, he was curious to know what had happened to those people whom the Commissioner had spoken of (almost in an aside) 'as having abandoned the mountains of Kildonan and the valleys of the Naver and Helmsdale rivers, and as having left the country altogether'. The observation was ironic. It was well known what had happened to them.

On 29 July 1819, the *Inverness Courier* published the following announcement:

At a numerous meeting of the late Tenants on the Estates of the Marquess and Marchioness of Stafford, in the County of Sutherland, and their Friends, held at the Meikle Ferry Inn, Sutherlandshire. 12th June, 1819

IT WAS UNANIMOUSLY RESOLVED

1. That from the peculiar and hard situation of the Tenants who have been removed from the Farms on the Estate of Sutherland, they have felt themselves under the grievous necessity of forming a Resolution to abandon their native country and to emigrate to America.

2. That being in general destitute of money to support them at home, even for a short period, they are compelled to hasten their departure, in order to save the small remnant of their effects, to enable them to encounter the many difficulties and hardships which they clearly forsee await them; and that numbers of them will not be able to muster as much money as will pay their passage to America. In these circumstances many of them will find it impracticable to get a variety of matters settled antecedent to their departure. For this purpose and also for the general benefit of their ill-fated brethren, themselves and their relations in Sutherlandshire, and in foreign countries, they shall and do now form themselves into a Society to be called the SUTHERLAND TRANSATLANTIC FRIENDLY ASSOCIATION.

This organization, which was to have a short and unhappy existence, was almost entirely the child of its self-appointed Secretary, Mr Thomas Dudgeon of Fearn in the county of Ross. It was broadly hinted by the Press that it had been formed to sustain the flagging fortune of Mr Dudgeon himself, and when, in six months' time, he tried to use it for the recruitment of an alarmingly unofficial militia, Sheriff Macleod of Ross warned all men high and low to have no truck with him. Of his true motives there is no longer record, and it would be uncharitable to judge him on the opinion only of those who wanted no troublesome demonstrations of sympathy for the evicted. His advertisement in the *Courier*, however, is of great importance. It shows how strong was the feeling for emigration among the people of Sutherland, how great the compulsion of their despair, and how wide the sympathy was for them among the ordinary population.

The tenants of Strathnaver and Kildonan were not the first to go to America from the Highlands. Emigration had begun three-quarters of a century before as a trickle, and would continue until it was a torrent forty years from now.* But these early Sutherlanders have a particular significance. They were the only Highlanders of the Clearances who were offered the choice between leaving the country or adapting themselves to the plans of the Improvers. They chose exile. They were young, and they

*See Part Four, The White-sailed Ships.

believed that by emigration they might preserve their identity as a community and their dignity as a race.

After the first eviction of the Gunns from Kildonan in 1813, the people sent a deputation to London, led by an unknown minister, perhaps, or a sympathetic advocate, to seek help from the Government and ask redress. The Home Office had no power, and probably no desire, to stand against Lord Stafford. But there was one man who seems to have listened to them – Thomas Douglas, Earl of Selkirk, who was settling the plains of Canada along the Red River Valley. He had some Highlandmen there already – Macleans and MacGillivrays, MacEacherns and Livingstones from Mull, Lewis and Argyll. He saw the Sutherlanders and was impressed. 'They are determined on emigrating in a body,' he wrote to the Governor of his settlement, 'They are a fine body of men. I feel quite as much interested in their success as if they were in my own employment.'

Seven hundred of them applied for grants of land in Selkirk's settlement, which suggests that all and more of the evicted were anxious to go, and which makes nonsense of Loch's claim that the worthless only preferred to emigrate. Selkirk could take a hundred, no more, and these made the party that sailed from Stromness on the *Prince of Wales*, in convoy with the *Eddystone* which carried servants and officials of Selkirk's settlement, and under the protection of a sloop-of-war. Selkirk was no philanthropist, he made it clear that the sea-passage would cost each emigrant £10. The money was paid, and many of the people were able to bank more with Selkirk, to be drawn upon when they reached Canada.

The first year was hard, a winter to be suffered, a country to be broken, bands of Indians and half-breeds to be fought, and some emigrants wrote to their parents at home, advising them against coming the following summer. More left the flat, hill-less grasslands, and went east to where Macdonnells from Glengarry had been settled for thirty years. But in 1815 there was another emigration from Sutherland to the Red River Valley, this time from Upper Kildonan and Farr. Donald Sage was to have gone with them, as their minister and at a salary of £50 a year, to be paid by Selkirk. His father pleaded that he be allowed to remain in Scotland for another year, when his Gaelic would have improved, and to this Selkirk and the emigrants agreed. He never went, and after the last evictions from Strathnaver he left Sutherland altogether. 'Without our minister,' declared one emigrant before the Justice at Red River, 'we would not have come!'

The spiritual leader of the 1815 emigrants, in place of Donald Sage, was James Sutherland, *Seumas Buidhe*, the Yellow-haired James, who lived at Ceann-na-Coille on the Helmsdale River. His family had gone with the first party in 1813. The Church gave him authority to marry and to baptize until the arrival of a minister. He did not stay long at the Red River Settlement, his family had left for the East before his arrival, and he soon followed them.* Those Sutherlanders who did remain in the Red River and Rainy Lake country were perhaps the best – Mathesons. MacBeths, Bannermans, Gunns and Mackays. They faced the harsh land with courage. They carried muskets in their hands as they walked behind their ploughs. They fought Métis and Cree to defend the Red River Colony, and they called their land Kildonan. It is still called Kildonan.

Their going had not disturbed Mr Loch. 'The idle and lazy alone think of emigration,' he said.

_____

*His great-grandson, Angus Sutherland of Helmsdale, a teacher at the Glasgow Academy and a leader of the Sutherland Association, was to become the people's first Member of Parliament when the radicals of the county elected him in 1885 to take the fight of the crofters to Westminster.

3

THE GENTRY WITH NO PITY

'There is no need for 500 men and 3 fieldpieces'

MR MACLEOD of Geanies, now known in Dingwall as 'that
fine old country gentleman of olden times', was still Sheriff-
Depute of the County of Ross and as ready as ever for the mili-
tant defence of Law, Good Order and Property. On the evening of
28 March 1820, in the library of his ugly house overlooking the
Moray Firth, he wrote a letter to declare that prompt action
(largely his) had once more saved this part of the Kingdom from
riot, anarchy and revolution.

> ... and I have further to state that an application was made by me
> to the Lord Advocate of Scotland for such military aid as might be
> deemed sufficient to enforce the execution of Laws against those who
> were actually in arms to oppose them.

He must have remembered similar letters written by him nearly
thirty years ago in the Year of the Sheep, and on the same unhappy subject : the Men of Ross and their Seditious Commotions.
That circumstances now forced him to defend himself before
the public and in the Press like this, was a sad indication of the
changes which time could bring. Some things, however, had
not changed. In 1792 there had been no doubt, in the minds of
Ross-shire gentlemen at least, that their tenantry had been inflamed by the treasonable activities of the Friends of the People
and by the poisonous philosophy of Jacobinism. And now for
some months it had been apparent that 'John Bull's evil spirit'
was coming north of the Border again. The death of George III,
in January 1820, was followed by demonstrations in England
against the person and Ministers of his unpopular successor, and
by dragoons swinging sabres against the mob. At the beginning
of March the Highlands heard the most unnerving news of all.
London peace-officers and Coldstream Guards had broken into a

barn in Cato Street, where Arthur Thistlewood and a physical-force remnant of Spencean Philanthropists* were plotting the murder and *beheading* of the entire Cabinet.

Highland landowners, heavily committed to eviction and clearance, may have felt that they had special reason to fear the land-nationalization schemes of these Spenceans whom the Government had accused of planning insurrection in 1817. Long before the discovery (if that is the word for it) of the Cato Street Conspiracy, murder and revolution had been darkly rumoured throughout the whole country, and southbound mails from the Highlands had carried frequent resolutions of loyalty to Throne and Parliament (which was the lairds' way of declaring that what they had they intended to hold). The temper of these resolutions, with their promise of armed support for the forces of Law if called upon, had been reassuring to Sheriff Macleod and other officers of the northern shires. Less comforting had been an advertisement published in the *Inverness Courier* just before Christmas:

LOYAL HIGHLANDERS!

The present crisis calls upon all LOYAL SUBJECTS to rally round the CONSTITUTION of our country. Highlanders from 18 to 40 years of age, are invited to attend a MEETING of the

SUTHERLAND AND TRANSATLANTIC
FRIENDLY ASSOCIATION

which is appointed to hold at GOLSPIE in Sutherlandshire, on Tuesday the 4th of January, at 10 o'clock a.m. for the purpose of evincing their firm attachment to His Majesty's present Government, by an officer of their services in a Military capacity.

Thomas Dudgeon, Secretary.
Fearn, December 20, 1819.

---

*Thomas Spence (1750–1814), an odd, bitter and unsociable bookseller with a passion for spelling-reform, had published his ideas of corporate land-tenure in 1775. His followers were politically simple and never strong. The Government made them scapegoats, crying wolf in their direction whenever its popularity needed stimulation. Finally, by the use of agents, it trapped them into the Cato Street Conspiracy.

The last thing the authorities wanted at this time was Mr Dudgeon's help. He was already in bad favour for his attempt to organize sympathy for the evicted tenants from Lord Stafford's estates, and now he wished to place arms in the hands of the Populace, of those very people against whom the Forces of Law might have to proceed at any moment. Sheriff Macleod and others in the counties of Ross and Inverness promptly dissociated themselves from any schemes this crazy man might have, and in Sutherlandshire prompt steps were taken to discredit his Friendly Association and to destroy it if possible. Robert Nimmo, who had succeeded MacKid as Sheriff-Substitute, issued a Public Notice on New Year's Day, signed by himself and twelve Justices of the Peace, one of whom was Patrick Sellar. The Notice warned the people that the meeting called by Dudgeon was illegal, and that his Society was suspected of dark aims beyond those it openly expressed.

We therefore consider it our duty as Magistrates of this county to warn the loyal and peaceable inhabitants of this jurisdiction of the impropriety of their being participants of such a meeting, or of the consequences thereof.

The Address of the county of Sutherland is already before His Royal Highness the Prince Regent, offering the most cordial support in defence of our King and Constitution; and the people know well that, as on every former occasion, they will be called upon whenever their services may be required, and that in a legal and proper manner, and without the interference of men of doubtful principles, totally unconnected with the county.

This seems to have scotched Mr Dudgeon's meeting and anything he may have hoped to come of it. Two weeks later the *Courier* reported that his Friendly Society was at an end, and later still that all its funds (£58 collected in pennies and sixpences from the people) had gone into Mr Dudgeon's pocket with the exception of £8. But more yet was to be heard of the gentleman from Fearn.

The year moved toward spring and the gentry's nervousness increased with each alarming report from the south. The cry for Parliamentary reform was audible even in the Ross-shire hills. The monster Liberty, now known as Democracy, was questioning the right of landowners to dispose of their acres and their people as they wished, and the Cato Street affair had shown that the land-reformers were ready for brutal murder. In Easter Ross, where new clearances were being planned for this year, the proprietors declared that in the event of resistance from the tenantry they would make one landlord's cause the cause of all, and they secured a promise from Sheriff Macleod that he would march to their assistance with musket and ball.

The landowners could see no reason for complaint. Wool was making them rich. Wool had forced up the value of land all over the Highlands. In five years the sale-price of the Castlehill estate had risen from £8,000 to £80,000. Redcastle, which had been sold for £25,000 in 1790, was shortly to be sold again for £135,000. Fairburn, which had yielded a rental of £700 in 1800, was now worth £80,000. In July, 1817, an Annual Sheep and Wool Market had been opened in Inverness, with the encouragement and support of staplers from Huddersfield and Leeds, woollen manufacturers from Aberdeen, and merchants in Liverpool. At its most prosperous, 100,000 stones of wool and 150,000 sheep would change hands at this market. Joseph Mitchell, the road-builder, said that a thousand farmers and buyers attended it every year, transacting business worth £400,000 : 'The burly south-country feeder stands at the street corner in deep conversation and about to strike a bargain with that sharp, lynx-eyed, red-haired little man who is the largest farmer in the North, and counts his flocks by 40,000 or 50,000. The greatest agriculturalist in the North compares notes of his experience with the celebrated member of the Highland Society who is also an extensive farmer in the Lothians. That stout man who is talking with the Highland drover came North some thirty-eight years ago a common shepherd. He is now a great farmer and the owner of 12,000 or 15,000 sheep.'

But Angus Cameron, a fox-hunter from Stratherrick, saw no merit in these sheep-farmers. 'They are the worst of all. It would hardly be considered a reason for grief if they were all to die. The lairds are so discontented they won't take their pleasures in reason. Their pride makes them seek pleasures painful to us, demanding exceptional rents, and causing hardship to the tenantry. They go to spend them in London and Edinburgh. Some go even further to the ports of France.'

The resistance and riot feared by the proprietors of Easter Ross came from the tenantry of Hugh Munro, the young and rakish laird of Novar. At the beginning of 1820 he made it known that he proposed to clear his estates at Culrain and to place the land under sheep. 'This Grazing,' announced his factor, James Aird, 'is very compact and well-adapted from its low and sheltered situation for a wintering to a larger farm. . . .' It was beautiful, too, a green valley floor watered by the black run of the River Oykel, rich pastures rising in gentle slopes to the south. The townships to be cleared lay on the west bank of the Kyle of Sutherland at Culrain, where John Munro was the principal tenant-at-will, and northward up Strath Oykel by the holdings of Duncan Kennedy at Achnagart and John Ross at Kilmachalmack. With these and other tenants, their relatives and dependants, between five and six hundred people were to be evicted, and according to their minister a hundred of them were aged and bedridden. The rents of Strath Oykel had been steadily increasing. One township of three farms, for example, supporting nine tenants and sharing a hundred acres of meadow by the river with muir-pasture to the west, had once paid a total annual rent of £9 sterling. This had been increased to £30. When the tenants first heard that their laird proposed to evict them they offered to pay five per cent more, hoping that this and the fact that they had never been in arrears would persuade him to change his mind. But Major Forbes of Melness, who wished to lease part of Strath Oykel for a sheep-walk, had offered £100, and young Novar, who had ambitions to be an art-collector, needed the money.

On 2 February 1820, the laird's law-agent, with the statutory Witnesses, arrived in the valley to serve Writs of Removal on all the tenants and their dependants, warning them to be ready to quit by Whitsunday. But this was the glen where the Men of Ross had gathered in 1792 before setting out on the great sheep drive. Alexander Mackay, taken prisoner afterwards and sentenced to banishment for life, had lived at Langwell on the upper braes of the Oykel. The memory of the Year of the Sheep was perhaps stronger in this strath than anywhere in Ross. The people had another reason for their pride, and for thinking that their laird and the Government were in their perpetual debt. During the Napoleonic Wars the county had supplied more than two thousand five hundred men for the three battalions of the 78th Regiment, Ross-shire Highlanders. Three-quarters of the third battalion raised had consisted of six hundred young men under the age of twenty,* many of whom later died in Calabria and Egypt. Strath Oykel had sent its youth with the rest of Ross, and those who had returned were in no mood to walk meekly from their homeland upon an order from an advocate of Novar. They may have remembered, too, the warning an old man had given the county thirty years before: 'Take care of yourselves, for the Law has reached Ross-shire!'

Law-agent and witnesses were met by a hostile crowd at Achnagart, driven through the snow and from the glen.

'They were maltreated and pillaged of their papers,' wrote Sheriff Macleod in his letter to the *Inverness Courier*, 'they were pursued off the bounds of the property, threatened that if they returned their lives would be taken and themselves thrown into the Kyle of Firth ... and one of the Witnesses, who had run away from the terror, was pursued and struck with stones to the danger of his life.'

The deforcement of the law-agent was no more than what the gentry had expected in their fear of resistance and riot, and on Novar's behalf they urged the Sheriff to come to their aid and to enforce the Writs. Macleod could remember the Year of the Sheep as well as any man in Ross. Nor did he need reminding of the contribution in blood which the county had made to the

---

*David Stewart of Garth, once of the 42nd, was later a Major in this battalion of the 78th. He said that the boys were 'healthy, vigorous and efficient, attached and obedient to their officers, temperate and regular ... possessing those principles of integrity and moral conduct which constitute a valuable soldier'.

78th. His son Patrick, a Lieutenant-Colonel of the young 3rd battalion, had been killed at El Hamet on the Nile when Albanian infantry and Arab horsemen had come down on his five companies of Highlanders and left only eleven of them on their feet. Class interests will interpret such things relatively, and the old Sheriff probably saw the bloody waste of life as a sacrifice to Law and Good Order, and he was conscious of no irony in the fact that he was now called upon to proceed in arms against the relations of the boys whose heads had been impaled on Arab lances with his son's.

He wrote to the Lord Advocate for military assistance (five hundred foot-soldiers and three cannon, so it was said in Dingwall). But the Lord Advocate seems to have thought the demand frivolous, or at best excessive, and no soldiers were sent from Fort George. Macleod had to be content with the army he could raise from the police, the militia and the gentry. This was substantial enough. On Thursday, 2 March he set out from Dingwall in his carriage to deliver the Writs himself, accompanied by forty constables, twenty-five sorry militiamen, and a large party of mounted gentlemen with their servants. The red-coats were the whole permanent staff of the Easter Ross Regiment of Militia, a corps which Macleod had himself founded and of which he was the proud Colonel, but there seems to have been some doubt about their efficiency or their loyalty today. Their black pouches were filled with blank cartridges only.

Macleod was seventy-six years of age, and in this cold Spring weather the journey must have been a great hardship, though he rode in the warmth of his carriage. For the first twelve miles the route of march followed the same road taken by his little army in 1792, then it climbed over the central hills of Easter Ross to the south shore of the Dornoch Firth. Northwards then through Ardgay to the Kyle of Sutherland, and at Culrain it was halted. Macleod put his head out of his carriage window.

Here, where the Orkneymen of the Great Marquess of Montrose had been defeated one hundred and seventy years before, Macleod saw a great crowd of people gathered on the road and on the braeside. There appeared to be more women than men, but the Sheriff always maintained that most of them were in fact men wearing their wives' or daughters' clothes. They had placed their battle order with instinctive rather than reasoned strategy, the women on the road and the men behind dry-stone walls on either side. There was a great deal of noise, the women shouting and crying, young boys blowing whistles* or horns to summon the laggards from the valley behind. Macleod said that some of the men had guns in their hands. 'There were also seen many running backward and forward from the shelter of a birch wood close by the scene. There were also observed many men running down the hill on the Sutherland side towards the Ferry, with the apparent desire of crossing to assist their neighbours.' This confirmed in the Sheriff's mind the ugly rumour that had been circulating in Dingwall since 2 February that a Sutherlander had been seen in Strath Oykel, warning the people of what had happened to him and his friends in Strathnaver, urging them to resist and promising them help.†

Old Macleod got down from his carriage, waving the Writs of Removal, and immediately the crowd pressed upon him and the wall of constables and militia. He shouted to them to disperse, but the women cried back desperately. They shouted. 'We must die anyway!' They said it would be better to die here than in America or on the Cape of Good Hope. '*We don't care for our lives!*'

The first blow was struck by a woman with a stick, and then a nasty struggle began, along the road and across the walls. The constables struck back with their ash-sticks, the gentry leant out of the saddle and beat at the women's heads with their crops. The militia fired one blank volley and then gathered about their Colonel with the butts of their muskets swinging. But among them was 'a disreputable young man', a drummer whose pride had been offended by that humiliating issue of blank cartridges,

---

*It is still said in the Highlands that gipsies made these whistles, selling them to the people for use as warnings when the evictors came.

† If this Sutherlander really existed, and was not just a creation of the guilt men felt about Strathnaver, one would like to think he was Donald Macleod, the stonemason.

and he had secretly loaded his piece with ball. The shot struck a woman in the chest, wounding her mortally.

Old, and too infirm for this kind of brawling, the Sheriff was saved from injury only by the passionate desire of his militia to get as far away as possible from the maddened women. They carried him away quickly down the Ardgay road. He left his carriage behind, the Strath Oykel people overturned it, kicking in its panels and scattering it with the torn Writs of Removal. Then – men, boys and bloodstained women – they chased the gentry and constables four miles down the bank of the Kyle to Ardgay, where the forces of Law then barricaded themselves in the inn. The people threw stones at the windows, shouted taunts, and at last went home in triumph.

Macleod made Ardgay his headquarters for a week, unwilling to return to Dingwall without issuing the Writs, but reluctant to advance once more upon Strath Oykel. He snatched at any reason to justify what had happened. 'We were joined by a man well-known to most of us,' he said, 'who had come through the body of men and who distinctly reported to us that many of them were armed with double-barrelled guns and wished to stop him. He was fired at by one of them whom he knew to be a man from Strathnaver.' But the only firing at Culrain had come from the muskets of his militia, and the only ammunition of the people had been the stones which the women had brought in their aprons.

He waited for the mob to storm the inn, but the little revolt was over. The old weaknesses of the Highlanders had ended it – their lack of leadership, their childish faith in the laird, who must now surely change his mind, and, most insidious of all, their melancholy belief that they had been a doomed race since Culloden. Their comfort came in the stirring sadness of their own destruction.

There was also the stern disapproval of the Church. The Reverend Alexander Macbean, in whose parish of Kincardine Strath Oykel was, had no sympathy with his parishioners in their scandalous defiance of the laws of God and man, and he threatened them with certain damnation if they continued. But on the other hand he was sincerely outraged by their bloody treatment at the hands of police, militia and gentry. In the next few weeks, by the letters he wrote to the *Inverness Courier* and to the Ministerial *Evening Courier* in London, he attacked the Sheriff for proceeding against the people as if they had been an invading army, and he derided Macleod's absurd habit of calling for soldiers at the first prompting ('There is no need for a body of 500 men and 3 fieldpieces to come amongst us!'). Goaded into the undignified necessity of defending himself in the Press, Macleod asked where the Minister had been *before* and *during* the affray at Culrain. 'It does not appear that he exerted his boasted influence with these tenants. . . .'

'I employed my catechist Donald Matheson to go among them,' replied Macbean, 'and to exhort them in my name to obedience; and from the reports he gave me from time to time I had no reason to anticipate the opposition given to the constituted authorities on the day of the riot.' And as to why he had not ridden with the Law to give it God's approval, he answered that boldly : 'To go to my people at the head of an armed force, that I would never do !'

But in the days following the riot he rode from one end of the valley to the other, quoting the Scriptures with terrifying skill and 'pointing out the madness and inutility of violence and the destructive consequences that must inevitably ensue' if the people did not surrender to the Writs of Removal. Unfortunately, one other man rode to Strath Oykel that week, and with quite different intent. This was Thomas Dudgeon, who had witnessed the advance of the Sheriff's army from his doorstep at Fearn, two miles down the Firth from Ardgay. 'He convened the people,' said the *Inverness Courier*, delighted with another opportunity of showing what a rascal Mr Dudgeon was, 'and as might be expected, sent them home with their minds more inflamed and hardened than ever.' He told the people that while they had certainly violated the Law by their opposition to the authorities, the Sheriff had outraged it by not reading the Riot Act, a nice point of procedure (not to say semantics) that may have had no significance for the confused tenantry.

'He said a great deal about the Stafford family,' reported the *Courier*, 'and about a train being laid for the extermination of all Highlanders. To prove his sincerity, he said, he would stand by them while he had a drop of blood within him, and whenever they discovered him to be faithless or deserting their cause, he bade them come down and put fire to all of his stacks, and after making this grand bonfire in honour of the occasion, to cut off his head.'

The Strath Oykel people may not have understood all that Dudgeon said (he having no Gaelic), and Sheriff Macleod soon drove the troublesome fellow away, but the fact that a gentleman had urged them to resistance prolonged their stubborn inaction. It took Mr Macbean another forty-eight hours, during which he described for them the fires of Hell, before their will broke. Humbly and sorrowfully seven of the principal tenants, led by Kennedy of Achnagart and Ross of Kilmachalmack, signed a letter which Macbean had probably written. It asked James Aird, the Ground Agent of Novar, to meet them at the inn of Ardgay with new Writs of Removal. And on 14 March they went with their Minister to the inn, and there accepted the papers. Later the Sheriff-Officers went among the rest of the tenants, and 'were received with the greatest of hospitality', said Mr Macbean.

The gentry were delighted. The Easter Ross Militia displayed their bruises in Dingwall as if they had been wounds received at Quatre Bras. Men said that Sheriff Macleod had shown the same strength of character and political courage as that needed the year before to suppress the Manchester mob. But the *Inverness Courier*, though its sympathies lay with the proprietors, warned them against a comparison of Culrain with Peterloo. 'There is no feeling of a political nature among the Ross-shire people further than somewhat of that lamentable alienation of the poor from the rich, which more or less pervades every disturbed portion of the Empire, nor do we believe that there was anything like a mutual understanding or concerted action between this people and the inhabitants of other districts. A population in this state is like a maniac, whose fury requires coercion to prevent dangers to his neighbours and to save himself from injury.' Which was another way of saying, perhaps, that the women of Strath Oykel had been beaten on the head and shot for their own good.

But if the gentry thought that Culrain had taught the tenantry a lesson, they were mistaken. A year later the terrible shadow of Riot and Anarchy again disturbed their digestions. 'It is with great concern that we have to advert to such violent proceedings on that part of the tenants on the Estates of Sutherland ...' reported the *Courier*.

This time the trouble was at Gruids, a warm saucer of high ground three hundred feet above the River Shin, and five miles to the north of Culrain on the road to Lairg. In April 1821, Sheriff-Officers who came with Writs of Removal on behalf of Lord Stafford 'were literally stripped of their clothes, deprived of their Papers, and switched off the bounds of the Property'. This time the Lord Advocate did not haver when Robert Nimmo asked for soldiers, and the 41st Regiment was put on the road at once from Fort George. Though they had followed the example of their southern neighbours in deforcing the officers, the people of Gruids did not stay to fight. They took to the hills, but after a day and a night of watching the redcoats below, and listening to the beating of drums, they surrendered to the Writs and walked from their homes to the mine and the fishery at Brora.

Thereafter, all attempts at 'Mobbing, Rioting and Deforcing Sheriff Officers' were ruthlessly punished before the Courts. Three tenants in Farr, for example – John Matheson, John Sutherland and Anne Macdonald – were sent to Dornoch jail for six months. In the parish of Wick, Caithness, two women and three men received the same sentence for 'Deforcing, Obstructing and Assaulting Alexander Farquhar, Messenger at Arms, who had proceeded there to eject them'. And in this way the little flames of resistance were extinguished, for a while.

The *Courier* had no doubt that the simple people had acted in good faith, however stupidly. 'Unhappily, their weak side was found out and their credulity worked upon until they were impressed by the belief that they were barbarously treated, and that they should walk in THE GOOD OLD WAY, that is – retain possession of their ancient settlements, which it was not possible for them to do without violating the laws of the country and bringing misery and destruction upon their own heads. Hence has arisen all the shameful riots and illegal acts committed in these parts during these two years past.'

'They want fine fields, what care they for men?'

THE land had once belonged to the people, and their tribal society had been patriarchal. The chief was *Ceann-cinnidh*, the founder of the tribe or head of the clan, and he and it were one in a mystic unity of blood. In time, and with the authority of Law, the chief made the land his, but because they were closer to the past than he the people always spoke of the earth as 'our land'. When they walked from it to the emigrant ships it was not always the chief's rights in Law that they were obeying, but his ancient authority as *Ceann-cinnidh*. And when they defied him it was because they felt he had betrayed the trust of his *clanna*, his children. This refusal of the people to look the nineteenth century in the face was to frustrate both their friends and their enemies, but it did not worry the chiefs for long. 'They,' said Thomas Maclauchlan, Presbyterian divine and Gaelic scholar, 'can ride out of a forenoon with their visitors and point out to them the splendid enclosures, the extensive sheep-walks or the well-stocked deer-forest as they pass along, without once alluding to the amount of human suffering by which the whole was purchased. They want fine fields and fine forests; what care they for men?'

Of all Highland chiefs none dispersed their people more thoroughly than the Macdonells of Glengarry or The Chisholms of Strathglass. Nor clung to so much of their pride afterwards.

By the end of the eighteenth century, and since the days when their Norman ancestors had come up from the Border, twenty-three chiefs of Clan Chisholm had held land in the black and green valley of Strathglass to the north and east of Loch Ness.

It was their odd boast that The Chisholm shared with The Pope and The King the exclusive right to a definite article in his title (a small distinction which several others were ready to dispute). Alexander the twenty-third chief, known as *An Siosal Ban*, The Fair-haired Chisholm, was the last to have any genuine feeling for his people. 'To his honour as a chief and a generous landlord,' it was written of him,* 'he did not suffer himself to be infected with the mania for sheep-farming which has proved so lamentable a scourge to a deserving and unobtrusive race.... The southland shepherds could not tempt him with their golden offers.'

But the temptation was strong, and the Fair-haired One would have weakened like other chiefs had it not been for his people. Or such was the story they told. Thomas Gillespie, the Lowland grazier, made the golden offer. He was in the Highlands with three partners, prospecting the land of bankrupt chiefs, and he came to Strathglass with a hearty recommendation from Grant of Corriemony, who, having leased most of his land to Gillespie, did not see why his neighbour, The Chisholm, should not have an opportunity of doing the same.

The sheep-farmers stayed the night at Comar House as The Chisholm's guests. They had ridden the length of Strathglass on their way from Corriemony, and they offered the old man a fortune if he would get rid of his people and let in their sheep. When the offer was made, the chief's daughter, Mary, his only child by his Lowland wife, angrily protested and was sent from the room. The Chisholm listened to the graziers for most of the night, but in the morning a thousand men of his clan gathered outside the house. They called upon him to protect them, and said that sheepmen were worse than any enemy who had once come to Strathglass with a broadsword in his hand. Gillespie and his partners did not wait for the old man's decision, but mounted their horses and rode away. At the ridge of Maol Bhuidhe, between Strathglass and Corriemony, they paused and looked back. The Chisholm was being carried on the shoulders

---

*By James Logan, author of *The Scottish Gael*, in a manuscript note quoted by Alexander Mackenzie in his *History of the Chisholms*.

of his clansmen, and his Piper was playing a rant of triumph.

The Fair-haired One died in 1793, and his title and most of his land passed to his half-brother, William, a man with no burdensome feelings of responsibility to anybody but his wife and his banker. In his will Alexander had offered his widow the choice between an annuity and the rents of a few townships which, upon her death, would return to the chief. She chose the townships, and for the rest of her life she and her spirited daughter stood between The Chisholm and the eviction of the people there.

With William, The Twenty-fourth Chisholm, there began the total dispersal of the clan. It was to be continued and finished by the sons who succeeded him. He was a sickly man, glad to leave the management of his estates to his energetic wife, Elizabeth. In her youth she had received excellent instruction in this business of eviction and clearance. Her mother, wife to a Glengarry chief, had evicted five hundred people from her husband's estate at Glenquoich and leased it to one southland sheep-farmer. As if she wished to improve upon this maternal example, Elizabeth Chisholm invited Thomas Gillespie back to Strathglass. He came with his pot of gold. The Chisholm clansmen, having no illusions about their wife-ridden chief, wasted no time in lobbying Comar House again. Some of the young men went off to join the Army, but most of the people waited with dull resignation.

In 1801 The Chisholm's factor cut a broad swathe down the glen, evicting almost half the clan. During that year, and the two years following, five thousand emigrants left Fort William for Antigonish in Nova Scotia and for Upper Canada, and almost a thousand of them, perhaps, were Chisholms from Strathglass. Fifty-three people died of fever aboard one of the ships before it made landfall. Donald Chisholm – Donald the Blacksmith from Glen Affric – was one of those driven out in this clearance, and since he was also a poet custom demanded that he record the event in verse. He was old and frail, and he had no wish to die in Canada, but he tried to encourage his companions with a hopeful picture of the life awaiting them there. More convincing was his bitter disavowal of The Chisholm. 'Our chief is losing his kin! He prefers sheep in his glens, and his young men away in the camp of the Army!'

In 1809 there was another great clearance in Strathglass. Five lots 'calculated to keep from a 1,000 to 5,000 or 6,000 Sheep each' were advertised for sale by The Chisholm's law-agents, Mackenzie and Moneypenny, W.S., of Edinburgh:

These Grazings have been lotted out in separate Sheep Walks by the most skilful, intelligent and eminent Store-master that could be found in the Highlands of Scotland, and after his favourable report it would be quite unnecessary to enlarge upon the quality of these Lots. The name of Mr Thomas Gillespie, who has brought the Sheep Stock of Glenquoich to unrivalled excellence, supersedes any comment that could be added in the way of advertisement.

It might also have been said that Mr Gillespie was once more bringing the human stock of Nova Scotia to unrivalled excellence, for that is where more of the people went the next year. The Chisholm was wasting no thoughts on resettlement, like Lord Stafford. He had not the land for it, in any case. This year he made strong efforts to persuade his sister-in-law to release to him the property his brother had left her. These townships were now crowded with hungry refugees from his estates. She made them welcome, but supporting them was not easy, and her kinsman, Bishop Aeneas Chisholm, told her that soon the people under her care would be double the number left on The Chisholm's estates. 'Allan Chisholm and his brother Duncan are driven from their place by a vile fellow, and sixteen good fellows driven out of their places.... Oh! madam, you would really feel if you only heard the pangs and saw the oozing tears by which I am surrounded in this once happy but now devastated valley of Strathglass, looking out all anxiously for a home without forsaking their dear valley; but it will not do, they must emigrate!"

Old and growing simple in the mind, the Dowager Mrs Chisholm was no match for Mr William Mackenzie, the law-agent. He called again and again, urging her to sell the townships to the chief. Her daughter, Mary, refused him entry to the house, but once she went into her mother's room and found the lawyer forcing a pen into the old woman's hand. She scolded him from the estate like a fish-wife, shouting, 'If ever you come here again, I'll make Edinburgh too hot to hold you!' The memory of Mary Chisholm in Strathglass was to live longer than that of her uncle or his lawyers.

The Twenty-fourth Chisholm died in 1817, leaving the title to his son, Alexander, a minor, and the immediate future of what remained of his clansmen to his wife. She evicted some of them, leased their land to a sheepman from Peebles, and with the money received sent her boy to Cambridge for three years. When he came of age in 1831 he returned to the Highlands full of plans (so his friends said) 'for ameliorating the condition of the people on his property'. Old Alexander Chisholm's widow had been dead for five years, and her holdings were now the new chief's. Mary Chisholm was the wife of a London merchant called Gooden, with nothing to offer her father's people but her sympathy.

The Twenty-fifth Chisholm's plans for his people turned out to be nothing that might have shamed his mother. In the spring of the year his factor told all the men in Strathglass to gather at the Inn of Cannich, where their chief would meet them and explain what was to happen to them now that all the leases in the valley were about to expire. The men came, and waited. 'After some hours,' remembered Colin Chisholm, who was there, 'a gig was seen at a distance, driving toward the tenants. This was the signal for a momentary ray of hope. But on the arrival of the vehicle it was discovered that it contained only the "sense-carrier" of the proprietor, viz., the factor, who told the men that The Chisholm was not coming to the meeting, and that, as factor, he had no instructions to enter into any arrangement with them. Imagine the bitter grief and disappointment of the men ... who had to tell their families and dependants in the evening that there was no alternative before them but the emigrant ship. In a short time after this meeting it transpired that the best farms and the best grazing lands in Strathglass were let quite silently, without the knowledge of the men in possession, to shepherds from other countries, leaving half the number of the native population without house or home.'

Some of the people went over their northern wall of hills to Glenstrathfarrar on Lord Lovat's land, and there the Chief of the Frasers gave them work and shelter on a sheep-farm. In time, said Colin Chisholm, he too 'informed the evicted men of Strathglass that he required their new holdings for the purpose of enlarging his deer forest and they were again removed'. A number went to other parts of Lovat's estates, but many, trusting no Highland laird now perhaps, went away to Antigonish and the timberlands of Upper Canada.

It was the evicted, exiled people of Clan Chisholm who gave the best example of the complex and intimate relationships that had existed between clan and chief. In 1832 the exiles in Canada sent the graduate of Trinity (who had just ejected half of his remaining clansmen) an address of loyalty on his majority, acknowledging him as their chief and affirming their allegiance to him though they no longer lived in their homeland. This admirable if naïve gesture has been offered as proof that Clan Chisholm went willingly, even gratefully, to the emigrant ships and bore the chief no grudge, but the truth of it was probably more moving. Though the men who held the rank had betrayed its trust, the people still held to the noble ideal of the *Ceanncinnidh* and the unity of his children. And perhaps some of those who signed the loyal address hoped that it would awaken a proper sense of shame in The Twenty-fifth Chisholm.

If so, they were mistaken. He and his brother Duncan, who succeeded him, continued to empty Strathglass from the beautiful vale of Affric to the Beauly River. As their factor they now had Donald Robertson from Atholl, a hard and canny fellow who followed the profitable example of Patrick Sellar, taking for himself some of the land from which he evicted his employer's people. It was he who leased much of Strathglass to James Laidlaw, the *Sasunnach Mor*, one of the greatest sheep-farmers in the Highlands. Laidlaw was a tall, impressive man with a good share of that solemn rectitude that made Improvement sometimes appear to be the executive branch of the Almighty. He was a Lowlander of the peasant stock that produced native poets and natural businessmen with prodigal profusion at the beginning of the last century. He had learnt his letters from his father's shepherd, James Hogg the Ettrick verse-maker who was the friend of Byron, Wordsworth, Southey and Scott. Laidlaw, too, was Sir Walter's 'dear friend', and he was known to be a liberal man and kind, but the Chisholms were driven from the land so that he might pasture his sheep.*

Laidlaw's shepherds and Donald Robertson were attacked in one of the most bitter poems ever written in the Gaelic. It was the work of a Chisholm bard *Donnachadh Buidhe*, Yellow-haired Duncan, and the part of it which follows is an inadequate prose translation only:

Destruction to the sheep from all corners of Europe! Scab, wasting, pining, tumours on the stomach and on the hide! Foxes and eagles for the lambs! Nothing more to be seen of them but fleshless hides and the grey shepherds leaving the country without laces in their shoes. I have overlooked someone, the Factor! May he be bound by tight thongs, wearing nothing but his trousers, and be beaten with rods from head to foot. May he be placed on a bed of brambles and covered with thistles. Thus may this stray cur be driven back to Atholl!

For the Twenty-fifth Chief this same bard had nothing but pitying contempt: 'He is a man without power, under the control of *gentlemen* who misdirect him. He desires nothing so much in the world as sheep on his meadows, in place of his people, his family from the beginning of time!'

But so far as the gentry, the county authorities and the Government were concerned, the emptying of Strathglass was long overdue. It was, in their opinion, a most unsavoury spot, with more illicit stills to the square mile than could be found anywhere else in the Highlands, including Sutherland (and that was bad enough). Not only did the Chisholms make so much of their

---

* Two men of Kintail tried to kill Laidlaw, firing a shot through his bedroom window at Lienassie House. They had planned to shoot him as he rode through the pass from Glen Affric, but lost their nerve for so open an act of retribution. It is said that their names are still known in Kintail, but are kept as secret as the identity of the Appin murderer.

raw whisky, they also offered shelter and protection to the smugglers of it. Now and then the King's officers were forced to make armed forays into Strathglass, with considerable risk. In April 1827, for example, a Revenue party under a Mr Macniven marched into the glen, destroyed some stills, and then retired to the Inn at Comar. There the officers remained under siege until Mr Macniven pricked their courage to a sortie.

'About two miles beyond the public-house,' said the *Inverness Courier*, 'a smart fire commenced from the upper grounds, and on arriving in a narrow pass of the road, Mr Macniven's further progress was opposed by about twenty men, armed with muskets and arrayed within gunshot. The Revenue Party, consisting of ten men, and being armed only with pistols and short cutlasses, had no alternative but to retreat from the determined purpose of slaughter shown by the smugglers, and retired accordingly from the unequal contest; nor is it of any avail for the Revenue Officers to attempt a seizure in that quarter until powerfully reinforced and efficiently armed.'

As late as 1835, when most of the Chisholms had gone, the survivors were still making whisky and entertaining smugglers. A detachment from the revenue cutter *Atlanta* was attacked in Strathglass by fourteen armed men 'and driven back with great violence'. Beyond any other consideration of their value, sheep were infinitely preferable to such unruly people.

When he became the Twenty-sixth Chief, Duncan Chisholm went south to London to enjoy his rents and to nurse the chronic ill-health which he had inherited from his father. He did not live long, and the old bard of Glen Affric got an answer to the passionate cry he had uttered as he stepped aboard an emigrant ship: 'May a shroud be spun for the chief who runs after money!' He was the last chief of the direct line, and when he died in 1858 the title of *An Siosalach*, for what it was now worth, passed to Mary Chisholm's descendants (who dropped the Gooden and became Chisholms). It was said that in the year of his death he would have been unable to muster more than six tenants of his own name in the whole of Strathglass. In 1878 there was one only, Colin Chisholm, who had waited by the Inn

at Cannich forty-five years before, said of this single survivor:
'He is paying rent as a middle-class farmer to the present Chisholm
for nearly twenty years, and paid rent in the same farm to the
two preceding Chisholms. This far he has satisfied the demands
of four proprietors and seven successive factors on the same estate.... He is obeying the spiritual decrees of the fifth Pope, protected by the humane laws of the fourth Sovereign, and living
under the well-meaning but absent fourth chief.'

To the west of Strathglass were the wide lands of the Macdonells of Glengarry, and here the bitter story of eviction and
emigration had begun thirty years before the Year of the Sheep.
It continued for almost a century, and when it was over there
were twenty thousand Macdonells in Upper Canada and next to
none in Glengarry. In the years immediately following Culloden
this Macdonell country was still one of the largest estates in the
Highlands, ranging westward from Loch Lochy to the broken
coast and white sands of Knoydart. A thousand young men
were its warrior rent-roll, but the contribution in coin to their
chief's purse was little more than £300 a year. Under the pressure
of increased rents or unrenewed leases, Macdonell tacksmen began to take their sub-tenants to British North America soon
after Culloden. Like the Chisholms, they were Catholics, and a
stubborn adherence to their faith was a contributory cause of
their exile. Year by year the small ships that sailed down Loch
Linnhe from Fort William took a dozen, a score, and sometimes
a hundred Macdonells in their poisonous holds.

In 1782 Thomas Gillespie came to Glengarry with his partner,
Henry Gibson. They came, as seems to have been the way with
them, at the invitation of a woman, Marjorie, the wife of Duncan
Macdonell of Glengarry. She was the mother of Elizabeth Chisholm, and although she was known as *Marsailidh Bhinneach*,
Light-headed Marjorie, she was a shrewd and ambitious social
climber. Three hundred pounds a year in rents may have
seemed little reward for the £2,000 she brought her husband in
her dowry. She gladly accepted, on her weakling consort's behalf,
Gillespie's handsome offer for the lease of a sheep-walk along
Loch Quoich, provided the five hundred people living there were

removed. The contract was concluded quickly, though not quickly enough for the impatient Gillespie, who was soon writing to Glengarry 'begging of him to write us as soon as he receives our letter, that we may take the proper measures for building houses for the reception of our herds'.

The evicted tenants left for Canada aboard the ship *Macdonald* in the summer of 1785, and although the nineteen cabin passengers (tacksmen and their families) may have enjoyed the voyage, it must have been a sickening hell for the five hundred and twenty sub-tenants and cotters crammed below decks. They were leaving one Glengarry for another, for this was the name given to a Canadian settlement made by earlier Macdonell exiles who had left the United States at the end of the American Revolution. Travelling in the *Macdonald* with his parish was the Reverend Alexander Macdonell, an iron and devoted man in the tradition of those Catholic priests who had stood in line with the clansmen at Culloden. He built his own church of Canadian timber, called it the Blue Chapel, preached and prayed in the Gaelic, and stayed with the exiles until he died.

Light-headed Marjorie evicted more tenants in 1785, and more in 1787, and more still in 1788, when her husband died on his way to take the waters at Peterhead, too late to discover whether they would cure him of whatever it was that ailed him. There was little weeping among his people at his death, although there was great drunkenness as custom demanded. There was even less approval when Marjorie Macdonell went to great expense to erect a tasteless mausoleum over his corpse. For the next four years, until her own death, she concerned herself with spoiling the already overspoilt heir to the title and lands of Glengarry.

This was Alistair Ranaldson Macdonell. Freed from the control of his mother, as much by his majority as by her subsequent death, he shot into the air like a bright rocket that illuminates nothing while it entertains all. He was an absurd, heroic, impossible man who seems about to strut from the superb portrait which Raeburn painted of him. While other young men of his age were thinking of steam-engines, roads, canals, consols, the cultivation of turnips or seats at Westminster, Alistair Ranaldson behaved as if the world had received an order to mark time in 1745 and had not yet taken a forward pace. He was the rich inspiration of Fergus MacIvor in Scott's *Waverley*, the young Highland chieftain, but if other chiefs of his time were abandoning the role of *Ceann-cinnidh*, Glengarry overplayed it. He lived and behaved like his ancestors, was as proud and as sensitive about his honour as he believed them to have been. He challenged Flora Macdonald's grandson to a duel, killed him, and was more offended by the impertinence of his trial for manslaughter than he was relieved by his acquittal. He wore nothing but Highland dress, kilt, plaid and bonnet, strapped himself with barbaric arms at every opportunity, and went nowhere without a chief's ancient tail of henchman, bard, piper and gillies. When the Highland chiefs held a theatrical gathering of their clans to celebrate the visit of a fat and tartaned George IV to Edinburgh in 1822, the city's cobbles seemed covered by a great contingent of Glengarry Macdonells. They made the wretched handful of Sutherlanders whom James Loch had reluctantly sent look like a band of gipsies.*

Though his preoccupation with the martial glories of his race was constant, Glengarry never put it to present use by raising a line regiment from his people, or by going on arduous campaigns himself. His brother James did the actual fighting for the family. But Alistair Ranaldson did muster the Glengarry Fencibles in 1794, making himself their Colonel, clothing them in his tartan and in a bonnet which is about all the British Army now remembers of him. The men were raised in the old way, of course. Every township on Glengarry lands was told the number of young men the chief expected it to supply. Parents who were reluctant

---

*Donald Macleod, who expected no more from Loch, said: 'The Sutherland turn-out was contemptible. Some two or three dozen squalid-looking, ill-dressed and ill-appointed men were all. So inferior, indeed, was their appearance that those who had the management refused to allow them to walk in the procession and employed them in some duty out of public view. They were huddled in an old, empty house, sleeping on straw and fed with the coarsest fare while the other clans were living in comparative luxury.'

to release their sons were threatened with eviction. Some young men, lacking Glengarry's passion for this military play-acting, took to the hills and remained there. Glengarry was not particular where he got his recruits, and was inclined to think that he had rights of enlistment on other men's lands. The Widow Kennedy, for example, though she was a tenant of Cameron of Lochiel, found Macdonell's recruiters at her door one day, gave them one son, and was only saved from parting with another later by the intervention of a Cameron tacksman.

When the Fencibles were disbanded in 1802, more evictions began again in Glengarry, and there was another great emigration to Canada. This time the holds of three ships that sailed from Fort William were for the most part filled with disgruntled young men who had come home from service with the Fencibles to find that Alistair Ranaldson was busy removing their parents. Glengarry had little choice; his debts were mounting toward the astronomical figure of £80,000 which they would reach before his death, and although his rent-roll was far greater than his father's had been, it was still only £5,090 a year, and this scarcely supported his dignity, let alone his dreams. Yet such was the paradox of the man that, although he was evicting his tenants, he was angered by their decision to emigrate, though he did not say where else they might go. He tried to stop them, and was promptly denounced by Burns, who called him a tyrant for preventing the escape of his people from slavery. Alistair Ranaldson probably thought the opinion of a Lowland ploughman beneath his attention, but it does show that even Burns could be wrong where Highland commonality were concerned, and could believe with the gentry that the people were going willingly and happily to the other side of the world.

Glengarry could have told him that eviction was not always as easy as it appeared, that his people sometimes showed a fierce attachment to their land, slavery or no. When his factor tried to evict Archibald Dhu Macdonell from his holding at Kinlochnevis, and to impound his stock against some debt, the old man called up his seven stalwart sons, armed himself with a broadsword which his grandfather had carried at Culloden, and defied both the Law and his Chief. That one of his own people should 'so maintain illegal and unwarrantable possession of *my* property by violence' was not something Glengarry could stomach for long. By 1817 he had found a way to clear Kinlochnevis of Archibald Dhu, his seven sons and his broadsword, and to put a Lowland sheepman in their place.

Not that Alistair Ranaldson liked sheep-farmers. He quarrelled with all of them, and tried to stop them from burning pastures in the spring, saying, with some justice, that they were killing the birch and oak that had cloaked the hills in his youth. He took their rents, but saw no reason to accept them socially. One of them who addressed him on equal terms was icily reminded of the fact that when he had come to Glengarry he had been barefooted, that he had lived for three years with a common foxhunter, 'taking his porridge out of the same cog'.

Alistair Ranaldson also hated the Caledonian Canal, and made its promoters pay handsomely for that part of his land they cut. Since he lived in the past, he thought that the Canal's saw-pits, timber-piles and brick stocks were his to raid when he chose, and took delight in leading his men on forays against them. When the Canal Commissioners challenged him with theft, he plucked justification from the past and said: 'I would be exceedingly sorry to deprive the complainers or any person of their property, but it is a well-attested fact that a Highlandman is not accustomed in practice to such refined notions of property as to lead him to suppose that he is committing a crime of theft when he finds a stick of little value seemingly neglected by everybody.'

The Commissioners abandoned the complaint in bewildered disgust, but they were less tolerant the next time Glengarry made an assault on their works, accompanied, so their complaint alleged, 'by several persons all armed with fire-arms, saws, hatchets or axes'. Alistair Ranaldson threatened the workmen with their lives if they continued to cut the Canal through one of his lochs, and then carried a boat off to Invergarry House in triumph. The case cost him a great deal before it was settled, and Thomas Telford, bitter and angry at being fleeced and badgered by men like Glengarry, said that Highland landlords were the most rapacious in Europe. Alistair Ranaldson saw the situation in quite another light. 'A Highlander,' he said, 'is naturally generous as well as brave, and an enemy to anything wearing the semblance of oppression.' By oppression he meant the cutting of canals through a man's land, not the eviction of people from it.

When he was approaching fifty, he was not only able to make a reality out of his fanciful dreams of romantic Gaeldom, but managed to persuade others to believe in them too. On 23 June 1815, the *Inverness Journal* reported that at a meeting by Inverlochy earlier that month a number of Highland gentlemen had formed themselves into 'a pure Highland Society in support of the Dress, Language, Music and Characteristics of our illustrious and ancient race in the Highlands and Isles of Scotland, with their genuine descendants wherever they may be'. Membership of the Society would not have included the men and women of Kildonan who took ship for Canada that same month, nor the hundreds of common tenants who had been leaving Glengarry's lands since the days of his grandfather. This was an exclusive organization for the *duine-uasal* and *bean-uasal*, the Highland gentleman and lady, thoroughly anglicized now, but happy to play-act their ancestors while the summer sun lasted.

To Alistair Ranaldson, however, it was all a serious dream. It was he who had brought the ninety-seven gentlemen of birth and property to Inverlochy, to a green grass field where the Highlanders of Montrose had broken the regiments of Clan Campbell in a bloody battle one hundred and seventy years before. And it was he, no doubt, who formulated most of its rules: that all real chiefs were to be hereditary, that the Society's President was to be chosen annually from among the vice-presidents 'be he in or out of the peerage', that all proceedings were to be conducted in Gaelic (which must have been a hardship for some of the members). Absent from the acclamations and the speeches, the gossip over the cold collations, was the voice of Alan MacDougal, *Ailean Dall* the blind bard of Glengarry. 'Thàinig oirnn do dh' Albainn crois ...'

A cross has been placed upon us in Scotland.
Poor men are naked beneath it.
Without food, without money, without pasture,
the North is utterly destroyed.*

The Society of True Highlanders flourished for some years, as long as Alistair Ranaldson could give movement to its sawdust limbs. *Waverley* had been published the year before its birth, and Walter Scott continued to feed its members with pictures of a never-never Highland past, peopled with proud and noble gentlemen, and an amusing and simple peasantry that gave its betters the right amount of service and devotion. Glengarry was *Ceann-suidhe*, the chairman of the Society's meetings at Fort William, and the gentlemen would drink toasts with their feet on the table, flirt with Jacobite thoughts, boast of the Highland dead which their levies had left in Spanish valleys and French ditches. The appearance of Alistair Ranaldson at these meetings, in full Highland dress, always accompanied by his piper and bard, and sometimes by his brother James, the hero of Hougomont, was greeted with shouts of '*Slainte!*' and a hammering of dirk-hilts on the board.

With their glens emptied and their land under sheep, the lairds had time and money to spend on the Society's theatricals. They held grand balls, at one of which, said the *Inverness Journal*, David Stewart of Garth 'wore large round Cairngorm buttons richly set; others had the globular silver buttons of their ancestry, and the highly-finished pistols, dirks and powder-horns, and other paraphernalia, gave an air of magnificence to the whole scene'. They revived the Ancient Caledonian Hunt, calling it The True Highlanders' Fête, three days of bucolic delight during which the ladies and gentlemen danced on the heather and dined on roe-deer brought down from the hills. The lesser gentry were

---

Ailean Dall spoke no criticism of Glengarry in his verse, but the words he chose were significant. By *crois* he meant more than cross, something terribly close to the sins of Sodom and Gomorrah. And the Gaelic word for pasture meant not only meadowland, but the abstract idea of peace, happiness and tranquillity.

overcome by the presence of the greater. 'Such was the enthusiastic feeling abroad,' said the *Journal*, 'that a gentleman named Macintyre took a silver dirk from his own side and presented it to the young heir of Glengarry, and when the boy refused, the gentleman sent it on to Glengarry, begging him to accept it on behalf of his son, as the Macintyres claimed the chief of the Macdonells as the chief of their blood likewise, and the author of their race.'

Alistair Ranaldson's Highland Games were always barbaric. At one three cows were torn to pieces, after they had been felled by a hammer. The *Inverness Courier*, less awed by Glengarry than the *Journal*, found this highly amusing. 'Even the most expert of the operators took from four to five hours in rugging and riving, tooth and nail, before they brought off the limbs of one cow. This achievement was paid at the rate of five guineas per joint, so we hope this rise in the value of black cattle will make the Glengarry men some small amends for the fall of ewes and wedders at Falkirk Tryst, lately noticed by their chief.'

If Walter Scott thought Alistair Ranaldson was a 'treasure', Robert Burns despised him for his arrogance and his indifference to the true condition of the people. Yet it is the myth created by Glengarry and by Scott that inspires many of those who drink to the poet's immortal memory every January.

Towards the end of his life Macdonell took on another complicated law suit, this time to prove that he was the lawful heir in blood of the line of Clanranald. The case floundered in charges and counter-charges of bastardy, and left Glengarry more in debt than ever. His death was a spectacular irony. When leaping from the wreck of one of the canal steamers he despised, he fell and killed himself.

He was buried in a thunder-storm and a double coffin of lead and wood, escorted to his grave by four Highlanders with flaming torches. 'Blessed the corpse that the rain falls upon!' sang his blind bard. One hundred and fifty members of his True Society sat down in his house to enjoy his funeral meats, below candles stuck in the white skulls of the stags he had killed. His young son, with an eagle feather and crepe in his bonnet, stood beneath the yellow banner of the clan and shouted its slogan, 'Creagan-an-Fhithich'. Outside in the rain fifteen hundred of the commonality were given bread, cheese, and whisky. The *Inverness Courier* was happy to report that the solemn occasion had not been marred by the riot and drunkenness which customarily launched a Highland chief into Valhalla. This was no doubt due 'to the better sense of propriety which begins to prevail in the Highlands'.

The evictions would continue. Within thirty years no descendant of Alistair Ranaldson would hold land in Glengarry, and few clansmen of his name would be left between Loch Oich and the sea.

'Is it possible that there are people living yonder?'

FOR twenty years after Strathnaver and Culrain there were no more great Clearances. Within the span of one man's youth and middle age from one-half to two-thirds of the Highland people in Caithness, Sutherland, Ross and Inverness had been uprooted and dispersed. The proportion may have been more; no one can now calculate it. In 1831 the population of the parish of Kildonan was one-fifth of what it had been in 1801, and although the figures for other parishes show a slight increase (of a score, fifty or a hundred), this increase was far, far below the national figure and does not explain that the people were now crowded into small coastal townships and that the glens they had once occupied were filled with half a million sheep. For twenty years the mountains rested after the great disturbance, and the evictions that continued to take place were small erosions as the small lairds aped their superiors, leased their land to sheepmen and took their gentility southward to the terraces of Edinburgh or the squares of London. The Lowland shepherd, the 'grey shepherd' despised by *Donnachadh Buidhe*, became the new Highlander, picturesquely posed against a Gothic landscape by Edwin Landseer. His image was fixed for ever in the minds of Lowland Scots and English, balancing humble and industrious virtues against that other dramatic irony, the loyal Highland soldier.

The Highlands became Britain's Alps, a stage for romanticism and healthy sport. When Lord Brougham introduced the fashion of tartan trousers to London, ordering bolts of every sett from Mr Macdougall the draper at Inverness, English Society went *à L'Ecosse* in a fanatic way that lasted until the death of Victoria seventy years later. Those picaresque confidence tricksters, John and Charles Sobieski Stuart, charmed everybody with their claim to be the grandsons of Bonnie Prince Charlie, by a legitimate son no less. They handsomely refused to press their right to the Throne, grew their black hair down to their shoulders, painted their own portraits in Highland dress, lived with musical-comedy splendour on an island given them by Lord Lovat, and fed public credulity with their *Vestiarium Scoticum*, a treatise on the tartan based on three ancient manuscripts which they said they possessed, but which nobody else ever saw.

Although wool and mutton continued to pay for the gentry's expensive preoccupation with what tartan they ought to be wearing, and with the colourful advantage they had over English landowners, fluctuations in prices led most of them to buttress their income with the letting of shooting-rights on their emptied estates. Some of them found this more profitable than sheep, though the Marquess of Breadalbane never succeeded in introducing the capercailzie to an estate from which many of his Campbells and the whole of Clan MacNab, with its testy tyrant chief, had been removed. He spent a small fortune on the effort, however. Rents for shootings were fixed on the grouse as a unit of value, a brace being worth 5s. One red deer was held to be the equal of a hundred brace of birds, a roe-deer or a salmon equal to twenty. A man could shoot a hare, if he had the taste for it, for the price of one brace. English sportsmen rented the shootings in syndicates of four or six. By 1841, ninety Highland estates had shooting tenants paying £125 a month (more if the accommodation was good). Fifteen years' purchase was considered the average value of game on an estate. 'This new branch of trade or commerce,' said the *Inverness Courier*, rightly seeing it as something more than a sport, 'has added greatly to the rental of many estates. Instances are not rare of the shooting letting as high as the grazing of a mountain district.' Some lairds, with a perspicacity rare among their kind, were beginning to abandon sheep-walks and to turn their lands into deer-forests.*

One of the most popular districts for English guns was Lochaber, easily and pleasantly reached by the Caledonian Canal. Here was Cameron country, or, to be exact, here had been their country. Sheep had scattered more of this honour-obsessed clan than Barrell's Regiment had been able to slaughter with bayonet and musketry at Culloden. The estates of the chief, Donald Cameron of Lochiel, had been forfeited after the last Jacobite Rebellion, but in 1784 they were returned to the family, to a weak boy of fifteen also called Donald. He was extravagant and selfish, and since he had been educated abroad he felt little kinship with his people and no great concern for their future, provided he survived. Before he reached his majority, and before he first came to the land of his ancestors, he was already burdened with debts, his own or those he had inherited. His estate, stretching southward across the Great Glen from Loch Arkaig to Loch Leven, was divided among one hundred and twenty-nine tacksmen, but produced less than £1,200 a year in rents. Like his neighbour in Glengarry to the north, the young man began to increase some of the rents, withdraw some of the tacks, and offer the vacant hills for sheep-walks.

These Cameron tacksmen were sharper than most of their rank in the Highlands. Many of them bid for their own property and regained it, clearing out their people and bringing in the Great Cheviot. For a while they did well, and the most successful among them were the two brothers who bought land in Ross and became the immediate cause of the Great Sheep Riot there. The evicted people endured all this as best they could. Having no

---

*In 1872 a Parliamentary Select Committee was appointed to inquire into the laws for the protection of deer and to discover, by the way, if people had been evicted to make way for the animals. It found no proof of eviction. Nor was there any reason why it should. The people had long since gone to make way for sheep, which were now being replaced by deer.

taste for emigration, many of them became navvies on the Caledonian Canal, or went south to Glasgow. There was also the
Army. The Great Cheviot Sheep won more battles in the Napoleonic wars than regimental historians have acknowledged. A
thousand young men of Lochaber joined the 79th Regiment
when it was raised by Alan Cameron of Erracht in 1793, at his
own and his officers' expense. They fought from Bergen to
Aboukir, Nivelle, Toulouse, Quatre Bras and Waterloo, and
transfusions from Lochaber restored the blood lost at each. Yet
perhaps these 'aspiring young men', whose grandfathers had
marched to Derby and Culloden in the '45, had gone willingly to
the 79th. Less willing were the recruits for the Lochaber Fencibles
whom young Lochiel raised in 1799 by the customary method
of threatening to evict their parents.

He never did escape from his debts, though he doubled, trebled
and quadrupled the rents of his tacksmen until he got rid of
them entirely and gave the land to Lowlanders. Glen Pean, Glen-
dessary and Glenkingle were cleared, the people driven to
wretched hovels on the moss at Corpach. When this Lochiel died
in 1832 he left debts of £33,000, a half-finished house at Achna-
carry (which was to have been a replacement of the one burnt
by Cumberland in 1746), a hopeless claim against the Canal
Commissioners, and some timberland which had only been saved
from the axe by his kinsman of Fassifern. His son held a banquet
to celebrate his accession to the title, but could not find a single
tenant of his own name on Locharkaigside to attend it.

And the 79th was looking for recruits in Glasgow.

One common man of Lochaber stood up against sheep, tacksman, factor and chief, and so closely resembled a character from
Walter Scott that his unseen presence in the hills would have
been worth another £25 on the shooting rental, had he not been
a sheep-stealer as well. He was Ewen MacPhee, the 'Outlaw of
Loch Quoich', a goatherder who believed that since the Almighty
had made both land and goats, the one was intended to graze
unhindered upon the other. Among the ordinary people he was
highly esteemed as an unorthodox veterinarian, possessing a
number of charms for curing the diseases of their stock. He could

also neutralize the harmful effects of the Evil Eye, should that bother them also. 'He exacts an annual tribute according to the circumstances of the parties,' said the *Inverness Courier*, tempted to list the report under the heading of *Antiquarian Notes*, 'and although it may appear strange, he has a very extensive practice.' He had also a terrifying wife, a wild woman with the bearing of Helen Macgregor, and the courage to match.

Unfortunately, the land on which MacPhee chose to graze his goats belonged to John Cameron of Corriechoillie, an industrious fellow who had begun by renting a sheep-walk from Lochiel in 1824 for £70 a year, and had so increased the holding in ten years that he was now paying £1,430. It was his mutton on which the MacPhee family dined so often and so liberally. This was galling enough for Corriechoillie, but when MacPhee threatened to shoot him Cameron asked Lochiel to intervene. Lochiel sent a message to MacPhee, saying that he hoped that he 'had better principles than Rob Roy'. The old rogue took this as an insult and a challenge, retired to an island on Loch Quoich with his family and goats, and declared that he was now under the protection of the Macdonells of Glengarry, a claim which nobody supported (certainly not the Macdonells, who had troubles enough).

Finally Corriechoillie decided to get rid of him. When MacPhee was away from home ('on one of his *professional* excursions', said the *Courier*), fifteen of Cameron's shepherds armed with guns and clubs called on Mrs MacPhee. She kept them at bay with her husband's flintlock, but in the end they overran her. The goats were driven to Inverlochy, and there sold. Under sentence of outlawry for past offence, MacPhee could not ask the Law for help. Lochiel is said to have persuaded Corriechoillie to pay for the animals, and perhaps he did, but nothing more was heard from Ewen MacPhee the Outlaw.

He had been an exception. The effect which eviction and its accompanying destitution was now having on the Highland people was less colourful. There was little sympathy for them yet. Society still believed that whether a man starved or not was entirely his own responsibility. When visitors were faced with

the appalling degradation of the Highlanders, and were unable
to see what could or should be done about it, they decided that
it was no more than the sufferers deserved. This made for an easy
conscience and an unbuttoned purse. Such a visitor was John
MacCulloch, Doctor of Medicine, Fellow of the Royal Society,
who made a series of annual journeys through the Highlands
over a period of ten years, and later crammed all that he saw and
felt into four tight volumes. They resembled the mezzo-tints and
water-colours, the preposterous scenes of alpine grandeur that
were spreading across the walls of southern drawing-rooms. And
when he came across people, other than the gentry whose grateful guest he was, he seemed to regard them as an offence to the
noble landscapes he wished to enjoy.

On the shores of Loch Kishorn one evening ('Our vessel lay
in a beautiful rocky creek, over which rose a picturesque and
wooded hill') he met with something that spoiled the whole
pleasure of the walk he was taking and the sentences he was no
doubt composing. By the water was some flotsam of the evictions,
a dirty, haggard woman and her children, cooking shell-fish. In
a shelter of branches lay a husband, sick with fever. Except for
one blanket and the cooking-pot, the family possessed nothing
but their clothes. They made no complaint to MacCulloch, and
he put this down to insensibility rather than pride. His account
of his emotions at that moment is more concerned with syntax
than with sincerity, but in a burst of extraordinary honesty he
said that in his opinion while such a scene would have been
remarkable in England, in the Highlands it was commonplace.
'The condition of these poor people is not so widely different as
it seems to be from that which, however miserable to the stranger, is in this country the usual state of life.'

In Sutherland he saw the black ruins of emptied townships,
'the former hamlets of the idle and useless population', and
while his heart stirred with compassion for the evicted (not for
being evicted, but for the degrading nature of their life before
removal) he was impatient with them, and with their attachment to the land they had once occupied.

'The attachment of the wretched creatures in question was a

habit; the habit of indolence and inexperience, the attachment of an animal little differing in feeling from his own horned animals. Had it been even more, they were children, unable to judge for themselves, and knowing nothing beyond the narrow circle of their birth. As children, it was the duty of their superiors to judge for them, and to compel them for their own advantage.'

An interesting example of this compulsion occurred in 1827, three years after the publication of Dr MacCulloch's book. Lady Stafford made one of her infrequent visits to Dunrobin, in some discomfort since most of her teeth had just been removed by a London dentist. Her factors and ministers made her feel welcome by presenting her with a set of ornaments 'in the name of the tenantry'. Donald Macleod said that the money for these had been collected from all the people 'on the moors and the barren cliffs'. He said: 'They were told that those who would subscribe would thereby secure her ladyship's favour and her factor's, and those who could not or would not, were given to understand very significantly what they had to expect by plenty of menacing looks and an ominous shaking of the head.' The gift was presented at a great entertainment in the Castle, 'but, of course, none of the poor victims were present, and no compliments were paid to them'.

Three years later, at the age of sixty-five, she came again to Sutherland, and this time she toured the northern parishes. Her husband had just purchased Lord Reay's estate for £300,000, and Mr Loch (shortly to be returned unopposed as M.P. for the Northern Burghs) was busy with plans for its resettlement and its transformation into sheep-walks. The coastal towns were still being built under the direction of southern masons. 'Even female labour could not be dispensed with,' said Macleod, 'the strong as well as the weak, the delicate and the sickly, and (shame to their oppressors) even the pregnant. . . . In one instance I saw the husband quarrying stones and the wife and children dragging them along in an old cart to the building. The timber for their houses was furnished by the factors, and charged about a third higher than it could be purchased in any of the neighbouring seaports.'

The sight of her northern lands and northern people, for the first time, was unnerving for the Marchioness. 'At one place she stood upon an eminence,' said Macleod, 'where she had about a hundred of those wretched dwellings in view. She turned to the parish minister in the utmost astonishment and asked, "Is it possible that there are people living in yonder places?" – "Oh yes, my lady!" was the reply. "And are they quite comfortable?" – "Quite comfortable, my lady."' But, says Macleod, Mackenzie the minister knew that some of his parishioners were at that moment begging in Caithness, carrying his own certificates attesting that they were objects of charity.

Lady Stafford was no fool. She drove down in her carriage, alighted among the people and asked them how her factors were treating them. But she had no Gaelic and they little English, and since the interpreter was Mr Mackenzie the answers she received no doubt relieved her mind. She went back to Dunrobin, leaving behind gifts of clothes for the needy. 'But as usual,' said Macleod, 'all was entrusted to the ministers and factors, and they managed the business with the same selfishness, injustice and partiality that had marked their conduct on former occasions.'

This was the year in which the stonemason was finally driven from Sutherland by the persecution of factors and ministers. Though he worked outside the county, in Wick and sometimes as far south as Edinburgh, his wife and children lived in Sutherland, at Armadale eight miles to the east of the manse of Farr. Since the last evictions from Strathnaver he had refused to close his mouth, but spoke his mind clearly and directly against what he had seen and what he had heard. 'Had I possessed a less independent mind and a more crouching disposition I might perhaps have remained, but stung with the oppression and injustice prevailing around me, and seeing the contrast my country exhibited to the state of the Lowlands, I could not always hold my peace.'

In 1827 he was summoned for debt, for £5 8s. which the factor in Strathnaver claimed was owing to him, though Macleod produced receipts of payment. It was an odd trial, for the complainant was prosecutor and judge also. No attention was paid to the receipts. 'All went for nothing,' said Macleod, 'The factor, pursuer and judge commenced the following dialogue:

JUDGE: Well, Donald, do you owe this money?

DONALD: I would like to see the pursuer before I enter into any defences.

JUDGE: I'll pursue you.

DONALD: I thought you were my judge, sir.

JUDGE: I'll both pursue and judge you. Did you not promise me on a former occasion that you would pay this debt?

DONALD: No, sir.

JUDGE: John Mackay (constable) seize the defender.

I was accordingly collared like a criminal and kept a prisoner in an adjoining room for some hours, and afterwards placed against the bar, when the conversation continued.

JUDGE: Well Donald, what have you got to say now, will you pay the money?

DONALD: Just the same, sir, as before you imprisoned me, I deny the debt.

JUDGE: Well Donald, you are one of the damnedest rascals in existence, but if you have the sum pursued for between heaven and hell, I'll make you pay it whatever receipts you may hold, and I'll get you removed from this estate.

DONALD: Mind, sir, you are in a magisterial capacity.

JUDGE: I'll let you know that (with another volley of execrations).

DONALD: Sir, your conduct disqualifies you from your office, and under the protection of the law of the land and in the presence of this court I put you to defiance.'

This report, as he published it years later, shows signs of polishing for dramatic effect, but his defiance was probably real enough. He was ordered from the bar and the case was declared undecided, but shortly afterwards he was issued with a writ of removal. He continued to fight, petitioning the Staffords for an investigation. They showed fairness in ordering that he be allowed to remain in possession of his house, but a complete lack of understanding by asking Loch to look into the matter when next he was in Sutherland. Macleod prepared for the investigation in the manner he knew would be expected of him. He asked the Reverend Mr Mackenzie for a certificate of good character, without which Loch would waste no time on him. 'Some days after I waited on the Rev. gentleman. . . . His manner was contemptuous and forbidding. At last he told me that he could not give me a certificate as I was at variance with the factor, that my conduct was unscriptural, as I obeyed not those set in authority over me.'

Macleod prepared his own certificate, and persuaded some of the elders and parishioners to sign it, which says much for their courage. When Loch came he treated Macleod with good humour, but without the minister's signature on the certificate would do nothing. And when Macleod asked that Mackenzie be examined on oath, Loch shook his head. 'By no means. We must believe the minister.'

And after that it was not long before the Sutherland Estate got rid of the bold stonemason. On 20 October 1830, when he was working forty miles away in Caithness, a party of eight men threw his wife and children out of his house. Furniture and bedding were tossed out after them, the hearth-fire was extinguished, doors and windows were nailed up, and the neighbourhood was warned to give no shelter to Mrs Macleod or her children. In the night she made a little wall of her furniture, placed her children by it under the care of the eldest, a boy of seven, and then set out to meet her husband.

Her spirit and strength gave out before she had gone far, and she was given shelter by William Innes, tacksman of Sandside, a man of integrity and compassion who was protected by his lease from any action the Sutherland factors might take against him. In his house, a day later, Macleod found his wife. He then went to look for the children, but found that they had left the protection Mrs Macleod had built them. The seven-years' old boy had his father's courage. 'He took the infant on his back,' said Macleod with pride, 'and the other two took hold of him by the kilt, and in this way they travelled in darkness, through rough and smooth, bog and mire, till they arrived at a great-aunt's house.' The man of this house left it immediately, saying that though he could not turn the children out he was afraid of what might happen if it were thought he had taken them in.

He stayed two miles off until they were gone with their father.

The Macleods were safe on the land of William Innes for a year or more, during which time Macleod was often away. He was in Edinburgh when his wife, frightened by the visits of a factor who told her that 'he would take steps that would astonish her', left Sandside and went to Macleod's mother in Bettyhill at the mouth of the Naver. Under no protection now, she was once more evicted. With her children she walked thirty miles to Thurso in two days, and the bitter journey, with all that had preceded it, drove her out of her mind. 'Instead of the cheerful and active helpmate she was formerly,' wrote Macleod sadly, 'she is now, except at short intervals, a burden to herself, with little or no hopes of recovery.'

They went south to Edinburgh, but Macleod returned frequently to the north for his work, and often to Sutherland. He kept in correspondence with the people there. The presence of his demented wife stiffened his resolve to publish the truth about James Loch's Improvements. Each time he visited Sutherland the changes saddened him. In Assynt, for example, where once there had been hundreds of small tenants there were eleven families only, and these belonging to shepherds on a sheepwalk of 30,000 acres. New factors had taken the place of Young and Sellar long since, but only their faces seemed different. There was George Taylor and George Gunn at Golspie, and Robert Horsburgh at Tongue. Taylor was as harsh and as demanding on his employer's behalf as ever Young had been, though he had literary pretensions that charmed the Marchioness. He had written a history of Montrose's wars, articles on deer-stalking for *Knight's Cyclopaedia*, and was now planning a great history of the Rebellion of 1715, illustrated by material from the archives at Dunrobin.

With Loch's approval, the factors were now increasing rents in the fishing-villages when a son succeeded a father. The legality of this was never clear, but nobody ever successfully disputed it. The rent-roll of the Sutherland Estate was three times what it had been when it had come to Stafford as a dowry, but it still brought him no profit. More bitter for the people to endure than rent-increases was Loch's order that though a small tenant might keep his children on his croft whatever their age, should one of them marry then he or she must leave. This amounted to marriage-by-permission, for unless the factor agreed to it, and found the pair a cottage and half-acre of land, they had nowhere to go. Those who married without permission were forced to leave the county. 'They may travel the length and breadth of Sutherlandshire,' reported a *Times* commissioner some years later when the practice was still continuing, 'but not a cottage will they find, or a place where they will be suffered to remain.' James Loch, who had two houses in Scotland and one in England, sincerely believed that he was in this way preventing over-crowding, over-population and over-indulgence.

On one of his last visits to Strathnaver before he left the north for Edinburgh, Donald Macleod went to a service in its 'parish church' (probably the mission-house at Altnaharra). A deeply religious man, though fiercely anti-clerical, he was shocked by the experience, and his description of it vividly illustrated the changes that had taken place since Donald Sage preached his first sermon to three hundred people at the foot of Rowan Tree Hill.

'The parish church was now reduced to the size and appearance of a dove-cot. The whole congregation consisted of eight shepherds with their dogs to the amount of 20 or 30, the minister, three of his family, and myself. I came in after the first singing, but, at the conclusion, the 120th Psalm was given out and struck up to the famous tune *Bangor*, when the four-footed hearers became excited and raised a most infernal chorus of howling. Their masters attacked them with their crooks, which only made matters worse, the yelping and howling continued till the end of the service.'

'There will be no weeping of children . . .'

JUST before nine o'clock one evening in August 1832, the southbound coach from Tain drove into Inverness with Mr Morrison the guard ill on his box. He delivered his mailbags, stumbled to his home, and was dead within four hours. The Board of Health ordered an immediate meeting of all the doctors in the burgh. Cholera had come to the north-east.

Its coming had been feared since January when it had reached the Lowlands from England. The Inverness Board of Health and similar boards in all the Highland counties had much to worry them. Poverty, destitution and over-crowding, for which the clearances were largely responsible, had made an epidemic inevitable once the disease arrived. Pigs rooted in dunghills that were placed by cottage doors. The poor slept on dirty straw in hovels where the windows, if they existed at all, were without sashes or hinges. In Inverness the poor quarter had an open slaughterhouse on every street. Public subscriptions were raised to provide manure stances, lime-washing, food and clothing (and a cholera hospital if the money would run to it). Agents of the Sutherland Estate visited every township and herring-village on the coast, ordering dunghills to be removed thirty yards from each cottage, but nothing could be done about the pigs which spent their days on the heaps and their nights in the cottages. In February, when the epidemic reached the Lothians, the rates of Inverness were increased by a penny per pound Scots to raise a fund of £300 to fight the disease. And in March, by Royal Proclamation, the Government ordered a General Fast in Scotland, which showed interest, if little effect.

Men began to look for scapegoats, and these were found in the beggars; men, women and children who had been wandering from county to county since eviction. By tuck of drum, the Sheriff of Inverness prohibited all inhabitants from harbouring vagrants, and posted constables to see that they did not enter the town. The panic increased in the Spring, and even the successful second reading of the Reform Bill was less a talking-point than the northward tide of cholera. The disease now had a strong hold on Edinburgh, Glasgow and Perth, but when it did reach Inverness it came not from the south but the north.

In the July of that hot and sinister summer a Lowland herring-boat called at Helmsdale from Prestonpans. It brought the cholera. The disease ravaged Sutherland and Easter Ross, burning with particular intensity in the villages about Tain. At the village of Inver only half the people survived. Whole families were found dead on the rotten straw of their beds. 'In one instance,' said the *Inverness Courier*, 'an infant, the only survivor, lay grovelling on the body of its mother, sole mourner in the charnel-house of the pestilence. . . . Many survivors fled, leaving behind them the dead and the dying, and took shelter, some in the woods and some among the hollows of an extensive track of sandhills. But the pest followed them to their hiding-place, and they expired in the open air.' Children buried their parents without shrouds, in common pits, shunned by their neighbours. So great was the poverty in most of the afflicted townships that many of the cottages were without candles, and men and women fought the first terrible attack of the disease in total darkness.

There were three hundred cases in the poor quarter of Inverness, and eighty deaths already, when the gentlemen of the county and neighbouring shires met in the town for a 'great procession of trades to celebrate the passing of the Reform Bill' with flags, banners and triumphal arches. When they returned to their own towns they were refused entry unless they were first washed with chloride of lime, and 'smoked' in a hut full of fumes of sulphur.

And then, in September, the epidemic began to recede. By November it had passed. Its effects were to be felt for years, particularly in the famine of 1836, and while everybody saw that poverty and squalor had contributed to its ferocity, none remarked that the creation of a landless poor by three decades of eviction may have had something to do with it too.

In July 1833, one single death was reported in the Highlands with more column-inches of mourning than any of the cholera victims had received the year before. George Granville Leveson-Gower died a Duke, not a Marquess, though he enjoyed the title for six months only. His elevation to the rank he coveted had been publicly announced in the pleasantest fashion possible, at a dinner party held by William IV. The King had proposed the health of 'The Duke and Duchess of Sutherland'. The news was said to have been received with great happiness in that county.

He died in the castle of Dunrobin, during the Annual Wool and Sheep Fair at Inverness. The price of wool per stone of 48 lb. had risen six shillings above its unhappy fall during the epidemic. Cheviot wedders from Sutherland were selling at thirty shillings, ewes at twenty, and lambs at eleven. When the Fair ended (before his Grace's interment) business transacted had amounted to £100,000 in sheep and £80,000 in wool. These handsome figures alone would have been sufficient valediction for the Duke, but a better was being prepared by James Loch, though he had stated his own preference in his will: 'I coincide with Tacitus in his opinion so beautifully expressed in the account of the death of Germanicus. I wish it to be without parade or absurd expense.'

He was buried in the ancient cathedral at Dornoch, where the Earls of Sutherland had been laid since 1248. 'The day was uncommonly fine,' wrote James Loch in a tasteful memorial he prepared for the Duchess-Countess, 'lighting up the Alpine scenery of Sutherland, its rocks, glens and bays, with a grace and splendour that only rendered the presence of death more mournful and impressive.' All shops in the county were shut ('spontaneously', he said), all work abandoned. Ten thousand people came to Dornoch and Dunrobin at their own request. They were brought, in some cases as far as eighty miles, by their ministers and elders, and were stationed along the road from Dunrobin to Dornoch in order of their parishes: Golspie, Loth, Kildonan, Reay, Clyne, Rogart, Lairg, Assynt .. seventeen in all, including three in Ross-shire. 'Ample refreshments in bread, meat and ale were provided for the whole, all whisky and ardent spirits were excluded.' Mr Loch was permitting nothing of the disgusting bacchanal that usually followed the committal of a Highland laird. His Grace was to be dispatched with the dignity of an English gentleman.

Donald Macleod had another memory. 'The day of the funeral was ordered to be kept as a fast day by all the tenantry, under penalty of the highest displeasure of those in authority, though it was just then the herring-fishing season when much depended on a day. Still this was a minor hardship. . . .'

A hundred superior tenants and gentry gathered in Dunrobin Castle at ten o'clock in the morning, listened to some prayers from the Minister of Dornoch, and then fortified themselves with wine and cake until his Grace was brought into the courtyard in a coffin made by his carpenters, and in a shroud sewn by the women of his family and the daughters of his principal tenants. The coffin was attended by his son the new Duke, by his son-in-law the Earl of Surrey, his grandson Lord Edward Howard, his nephew the Honourable Mr Howard, his physician Doctor Dunbar, two of his law-agents from Edinburgh (one of whom was William Mackenzie, the lawyer of Strathglass), and 'Mr Loch his confidential friend'.

Also present to claim an ancient privilege of leading the funeral processions of the Earls of Sutherland was the Chief Factor of the Estate, George Gunn, who was also head of whatever the evictions had left of his clan in Kildonan.

The procession left for Dornoch shortly after ten-thirty: five mourning-coaches, forty carriages and gigs full of sheep-farming tenants, and a hundred mounted gentlemen riding two by two. George Gunn, *Mac-Sheumais-Chataich* the Chief for this day, was in the van, followed by the factors of Tongue and Scourie, followed by William Lewis the agent of the English estates, followed by John Mackenzie, Clerk to the County, followed by eight gentlemen riding in pairs, overseers, wood-rangers and surveyors of the Sutherland lands. Then the hearse drawn by six black horses. Then 'his Grace's chariot, empty, and drawn by six horses with servants on the dicky'.

Finally, but before all the other carriages, gigs and horsemen, the new Duke rode in his carriage alone. 'The road from the avenue to the further extremity of Rhives plantation,' he wrote to his young wife Harriet that evening, 'was lined on the right hand by a row of men of the common people, all from Kildonan and Loth, their heads uncovered, and with their hats before their faces while the cortege passed, as if they were each of them praying.' As indeed they were, led by their ministers. At Kirkton, where Robert MacKid had once lived, another line began, people from Rogart and Assynt, Tongue and the Reay country. A mile from Dornoch the line stretched on both sides of the road. 'One felt sorry not to be able to give something to each as one passed, and one would have wished to have been a Pope to have given them a blessing.'

At the boundary of Dornoch, the procession, which was in one sense an assembly of all the prophets and profiteers of Improvement in Sutherland, was met by the magistrates of that burgh and, said Loch, by 'three hundred and sixty of the most respectable persons of the burgh of Tain'. These gentlemen had been spending some weeks on the preparation of An Address of Thanks to the Duke for extending his interests to the County of Ross by the purchase of their town. Now that he was dead they did the next best thing and came to his funeral.

From the town boundary the magistrates led the cortège to the cathedral. Following a funeral service conducted in the manner of the Church of England by the Reverend Edward Ramsay of St John's Chapel, Edinburgh, the Duke's coffin was lowered into a tomb at the south end of the south transept. The last member of the family of the Earls of Sutherland to be buried there, in 1766, had been the elder sister of the Duchess-Countess, aged two years. The new Duke stayed in the cathedral until two large flagstones, fixed with brick and stucco, had been placed over the tomb, and then he rode back to Dunrobin by way of Embo and Skelbo to avoid the crowds. From the window of his carriage he could see 'the good people returning quietly home in bodies across the moor'.

There was time that late afternoon in his room at Dunrobin, with the sun still hot on the sunken gardens and on the sea beyond, for the new lord of Sutherland and Stafford to reflect upon his father's work and upon the obligations now laid on him. 'One must do all the good one can,' he told his wife. 'We come to our wealth, etc., certainly at a time that disposes us to such thoughts, and it is better for ourselves that we do so than if we had been younger, and perhaps too much occupied with the thoughts of enjoying all this.' Then he seems to have remembered that though he was forty-seven, his pleasure-loving and ambitious wife was twenty years younger. So he finished the letter with a reassurance. 'There is no reason, I think, why we should not enjoy it all very much too. In short, dearest love, I hope and trust that you will have much enjoyment, and of the purest sort.'

In the months that followed, while the Duke's widow planned to restore Dornoch Cathedral in his honour 'under the direction of Mr Burn of Edinburgh and to adorn it with a statue from the talents of Chantrey', Mr Loch was preparing to resurrect him in stone and place him above the heads of all men at Trentham in Staffordshire. Lilleshall in Shropshire, and on Ben Bhraggie in Sutherland. The cost was to be borne by the Duke's grieving tenantry on all three estates. Sir Francis Chantrey designed the model for the Ben Bhraggie statue, entrusting its final execution to Joseph Theakston, a journeyman who usually carved the drapery and accessories of his work. 'Although the model is only four feet in height,' said the *Inverness Courier*, 'and the final statue will be thirty, every line and feature can be pre-served by the most exact measurements, and by mechanical pro-cesses which impose a check on each and secure certainty to the whole.'

James Loch made personal contributions to each monument: ten pounds for Lilleshall, ten guineas for Trentham, and forty pounds for Ben Bhraggie. Collections were taken from two thou-sand people in Sutherland, and Donald Macleod, remembering how they had been asked to pay for Lady Stafford's set of orna-ments, said: 'Exactly similar measures were resorted to to make the small tenantry subscribe, in the midst of all their distress and with similar results. All who could raise a shilling gave it, and those who could not awaited in terror for the consequences of their default. No doubt the Duke deserved the highest post-humous honours from a portion of his tenantry – those who had benefited by the large sums he and the Duchess had lavished for their accommodation – but the poor, small tenantry, what had been done for them?'

Of the £1,430 16s. 8d. raised for the statue on Ben Bhraggie (£1,858 was collected for the monuments in England), little came from the parishes of Assynt and Farr where evictions had been so bitter. There, five hundred people gave no more than £111, and in lonely Kildonan Mr Loch's agents could get £18 only. From the Ross-shire parish where the Sutherland Estate was a new landlord came £3, one from the minister and two from the innkeeper at Ardgay.

The restoration of the cathedral was still unfinished, and the statues uncompleted when the harvest failure of 1836 brought a terrible famine to the Highlands. There was hunger all over the British Isles, from the Channel to the Orkneys, but in the mountains of Scotland it was worse than even they had ever known (or were to know until ten years later). Half the population of Skye, for example, was destitute and starving. Bad weather had destroyed peat stocks, and people burnt the divots of their roofs to keep warm. Each week the men of some villages met and drew lots to decide whose house should next be taken down for fuel. Destitution had followed eviction, and now famine made the trinity.

Government and proprietors were ill-equipped to face the emergency. The former had allowed the latter the rape of the Highlands, it had abolished the fishery bounties, and it had lent its soldiers for the clearing of the hills. It had no real power to control the poor-law authorities, its public works had been in-effectual in stopping the growth of unemployment and poverty. Still following the logic of its political philosophy, it left the work of relief to the charity of the public in general, and of the new proprietors in particular.

(And, be it noted, there was sold at this time for £59,000 the estate of one of the most successful of these proprietors – Donald Macleod Esquire of Geanies, late Sheriff of Ross, who had died in his eighty-ninth year.)

The response of the nation was generous, though still not adequate. More than £70,000 was collected to buy oatmeal, pota-toes and clothing. Three times the amount would not have been enough to stop the famine, but, even so, a Select Committee rightly declared later that but for this money thousands would have died of starvation in the Isles, Inverness, Argyll, Ross, Sutherland and Caithness. On a handful of meal, a few potatoes, men were able to survive. Middle-class women of England and the Lowlands, who had recently had their emotions aroused by the abolition of slavery in the colonies, and by Lord Ashley's campaign for humane factory legislation, now gave their support (with decency and discretion) to meetings appealing for funds. Speakers from the Highlands were welcomed to London, and one of the most popular was the handsome, white-haired Moderator of the Church of Scotland, Norman Macleod.

He was a Highlander with a rich and musical voice that charmed more guineas from the purses and reticules of his audiences than the sense of what he said. He was one of the few ministers of his church who was beloved in the Highlands. He liked to roam Morven in a kilt of his tartan, talk in the Gaelic of old days and old ways, but at the London Mansion House in March 1837, he was dressed in the black of his cloth. He told the Lord Mayor and a great audience that when he had been a boy rent had been of secondary importance to men, but that sheep had changed all this with fearful consequences. He was inclined to exonerate the old lairds, which was more than they deserved, but in his description of the present famine he was passionate and angry.

'There are many parishes without meal, and having no more potatoes than sufficient to keep the people in existence for a few weeks, while a fearful portion of them are without peat to burn, or an article of food to maintain life except the miserable subsistence obtained from shellfish and sea-weed. ... The means of emigration they do not possess, and from their ignorance of the English language they cannot now compete with the myriads of Irish labourers who flock for employment to the Lowlands from whence the Highlanders now find themselves almost excluded. Heaven forbid, my lord, that I should dare to make one statement which I do not believe to be true !'

Donald Macleod said that the Moderator, for all his zeal, had not visited Sutherland in his tour of the Highlands, and this because he had been assured by the Duke's factors that all was well and the people well cared for. This was a lie, said the stonemason. The relief which Sutherland received arrived two months later than that of other counties. 'Of the whole seventeen parish ministers not one could be moved by the supplications and cries of the famishing wretches. ... They answered all entreaties with a cold refusal, alleging that the proprietors would, in their own good time, send the necessary relief; but so far as I could ever learn, they took no means to hasten that relief. They said in their sermons "that the Lord had a controversy with the land for the people's wickedness, and that in his providence and even in his mercy he had sent this scourge to bring them to repentance".'

In April relief supplies of meal, barley, potatoes and seed-oats reached Sutherland, and the people were informed that it would be distributed at Tongue and other points. Great crowds came to Tongue from all over the northern part of the county, and were told that they could be given nothing without production of a certificate from their minister, proving that they were objects of charity. 'Many travelled fifty to a hundred miles back and forth after certificates and relief,' said Macleod. 'Then they got 7 to 28lb. of meal, and seed-oats and potatoes in the same proportion. In the field and about the dyke adjoining the places where these pittances were doled out, groups of famishing creatures might be seen lying in the mornings (many of them having travelled the whole day and night previous) waiting for the leisure of the factors or their clerks, and no attention was paid to them till those gentlemen had breakfasted and dressed, etc., by which time the day was far advanced.'

The Duchess-Countess came to Dunrobin from London in September. She was now seventy-two, almost toothless and chronically infirm. She was childishly pleased to be in her Ruritanian castle again, and to be close to her husband in the Cathedral that was fast becoming a neo-Gothic nightmare. But she was also genuinely concerned about the condition of the people. Her ministers reassured her. The Presbytery of Tongue, for example, headed by its Moderator, Hugh Mackenzie, sent her an address of joyous welcome. Mr Mackenzie had some personal reasons for joy unconnected with her visit. During the worst days of the famine he had exchanged part of his glebe for more extensive property. 'But in consenting to the change,' said Macleod, 'he made an express condition that the present occupiers, amounting to eight families, should be removed, and accordingly they were driven out in a body.'

The Presbytery of Tongue told the Duchess-Countess that the people of their parish had survived the hard times as a result of her bounty. 'When other districts were left to the precarious supplies of a distant benevolence, your Grace took on yourself the charge of supporting your people. By a constant supply of meal you not only saved them from famine but enabled them to live in comfort.' They hoped that the Almighty would bless her and long spare her for her people.

But within eighteen months she had gone to 'that inheritance which is incorruptible, undefiled, and that fadeth not away' (which is how the Presbytery described her inevitable death). She died at her house in Hamilton Place, London. Mr Loch made all the necessary arrangements, of course. Her coffin was taken to the steamer *City of Aberdeen* at Blackwall in a great hearse, which was draped with black Genoa velvet and emblazoned with the arms of Sutherland and Strathnaver. A mounted man, attended by two pages, carried her coronet on a crimson cushion. He was followed by a long carriage procession of dukes, marquesses, earls and barons. When the steamer arrived at Aberdeen, the coffin was carried by road to Dunrobin Castle where the Duchess-Countess lay in state for three days.

She was buried beside her husband on a bitterly cold day, and once more the people of the parishes were gathered by their ministers. There was undoubtedly genuine sorrow among them, a sense of loss at the passing of the *Ban mhorair Chataibh* rather than the anglicized wife of an English lord. Her son, the Duke, in one of those spontaneous acts of generosity that contrasted oddly with his more frequent indifference to what his agents were doing, remitted all arrears of rent among the small tenantry. Donald Macleod said that the factors added their own qualification to this – all future defaulters would be instantly removed. Macleod also gave the old woman his own valediction: 'That she had many great and good qualities, none will attempt to deny.... Her severity was felt, perhaps, far beyond her own intentions, while her benevolence was intercepted by the instruments she employed.'

The death of this last link with the last true Earl of Sutherland may have released some of the people from any strong sense of loyalty to the authority of Dunrobin Castle. Or it may be that in most of them, those below the age of forty, this feeling had no meaning now, for throughout the whole of their lives they had known nothing of that authority but writs of eviction, burnings, famine and emigration. As early as 1816, only the *Military Register* found it significant that soldiers finishing their term of service with the Sutherland Highlanders were refusing to re-enlist in that regiment, saying that they had been betrayed by the removals in Strathnaver, and asking to be re-mustered in the regiments of Ross or Argyll. And the people were no longer afraid of their ministers, seeing them now as creatures of the landlords. The Church was moving toward its great Disruption, and the threat of hell-fire from a churchman had little effect when men saw that while their land was taken from them his glebe was increased. Certainly, in the few years following the death of the Duchess-Countess, there were bitter acts of violence and resistance such as Sutherland had never before known. The greatest of these occurred at Durness in September 1841.

A Low Country man called James Anderson was the principal leaseholder of Keneabin and other farms in the area, which he sublet to a number of small tenants who had tiny crofts of land but whose principal source of living was herring and deep-sea fishing. According to Donald Macleod, Anderson had originally come to the district as a fish-curer, renting the sea to his sub-tenants as if it were land, 'furnishing boats and implements at an exorbitant price while he took their fish at his own price, and thus got them drowned in debt and consequent bondage'. In 1841 he decided to turn his attention to sheep for the more profitable exploitation of his leases. 'With which view,' said the *Inverness Courier* 'it became necessary for him to remove several of the Keneabin people who, besides, had fallen into arrears of their rents.' The reaction of the people was violent.

When a Sheriff-Officer called Campbell came with the writs

in August he was mobbed and his papers were burned. The Superintendent of Police at Dornoch, Philip Mackay, got the same welcome when he rode across to tell the people to behave. He was driven off with sticks and stones, and when he returned with constables they too were routed.

On Friday, 17 September, the Law came back to Keneabin in force, and far south in Edinburgh Castle the 53rd Regiment was put under marching orders in case it should be needed in the north. When Campbell and Mackay had come to Keneabin most of the men of the crofts had been away at sea, and the officers had been driven back by the women, but now men and women were waiting to resist the Sheriff-Substitute, the Procurator-Fiscal and their army of Sheriff-Officers and constables. According to reports there were three hundred people on the cliff road, the men with sticks, the women with aprons full of stones. 'They were all in a highly-excited state,' said the *Courier*, 'using the most threatening language and swearing vengeance against all who dared to lay hands on the rioters.'

With Superintendent Mackay at their head, constables and officers fought their way through the crowd which, at one moment, almost succeeded in tossing Mackay into the sea. Finally the Law reached the Inn of Durine where it decided to spend the night under siege. Doors and windows were barred. At ten o'clock, in the pale light of the northern night, the people launched an assault on the house. They tore up railings and used them to prise open the windows. They broke down the door with blocks of stone. After a furious, clubbing fight, they dragged out the constables and dispersed them over the hills. The Sheriff-Officers escaped through the back of the house, hid in a field of standing corn and in rocks by the shore until dawn, when they escaped toward Loch Erribol.

Having got rid of constables and officers, the people came back to the Inn for the Sheriff and Procurator-Fiscal who, with commendable courage, had stood their ground in their room. They were pulled out, and maintained what they could of their dignity while the people argued what should be done with them. 'Some proposed to destroy their horses and gigs,' said the *Courier*.

'while others suggested that they should be stripped naked and turned out to the rocks. At length they were compelled to retrace their steps to the nearest inn, about twenty miles distant, which they reached at five in the morning.' And the people of Keneabin went back to their crofts, jubilant.

But a few days later Hugh Lumsden, the Sheriff-Depute of Sutherland, came to Durness with his Clerk, the Procurator-Fiscal, and the threat of ordering the 53rd against Keneabin if it did not obey the Law. The people changed from angry lions to timorous sheep. Under direction from their minister, they wrote a letter to James Anderson and the Sheriff, 'stating their contrition and soliciting forgiveness, and promising to remove voluntarily the May next if permitted in the meantime to occupy their houses'. Anderson grudgingly allowed them to stay until spring, and by the following autumn he had their land under sheep.

In Assynt, two years later, John Macleod, a small tenant at Balchladdich, also stood up against the Duke of Sutherland's factor and refused to be evicted. 'He set his Grace and the managers at utter defiance,' reported the *Courier*, 'in violent and threatening letters which he addressed to them.' He was also a natural leader, a rarity in his race, for he gathered a small band of men and women willing to defend his holding with him. Together they drove the first party of Sheriff-Officers from Balchladdich with sticks and stones. But once again Hugh Lumsden came 'with a sufficient force to teach the deluded people that they would not be allowed again, as in Durness riot, to set the law at defiance'.

Thirty constables, armed with ash-sticks, came down on Balchladdich, led by Lumsden, the Vice-Lieutenant of the County, the Procurator-Fiscal and several Justices of the Peace. John Macleod was for making a heroic fight of it, but his little army drifted away in despair until he was left alone with his son and two other young men. They were arrested and carried in manacles to Dornoch Gaol, eighty miles away.

The Highland people believed that there must be a punishment for the inhumanity with which they were treated. They could not see it coming from the Law now, nor perhaps from God even, and in their own knowledge of the worst that could happen to a man they decided that surely there would be none to mourn the landlord at his death. Only a Highlander, who was capable of such deep and terrible grief at a graveside, could understand what a punishment that would be. ''S 'n air théid spaid de 'n ùir ort....' cried the bard John Maclachlan to all evictors.

> And when a spade of turf is thrown upon you
> the country will be clean again!

> Or nothing will be placed over you
> but the dung of cattle!

> There will be no weeping of children,
> nor the crying of women.

> There will be no widow or poor creature
> striking their palms.

4

THE WHITE-SAILED SHIPS

'Oh, send us something immediately ... many are dying!'

LITTLE that the people had endured in 1836 prepared them for
the great famine that came ten years later. In 1845 the potato
blight, which also destroyed crops in Belgium, Denmark, Sweden
and Canada, visited Ireland with such appalling effect that its
history and its economy were scarred for a century. Yet in the
Highlands the harvest of that year was one of the finest ever
known, and men wrote of the summer months with pride, as if
credit were theirs for its ripening sun and gentle rains. Blight
had of course afflicted potato-fields in the Lowlands, with a loss
of £50,000 along the Border, but this was far from the Isles and
the Highland Line. Even so, there were portents into which old
men and old women read a coming judgement. At the beginning
of September a fine white dust fell upon the Orkneys like a
shroud. Terrible storms broke upon the Caithness coast long
before winter, destroying boats and nets and leaving five hundred
men without employment. Summer lingered into October, a
sickening warmth and stillness in the air, and snow was very late
in coming to high ground. In November the *Inverness Courier*,
less confident now of Highland immunity as it reported the news
from Ireland, expressed the general uneasiness: 'We are sorry to
find that the potato murrain is gaining ground. The disease is
yet abroad, extending over three kingdoms, and no human
agency can yet forsee to what extent the pestilence may spread.'
It had not reached the seven northern counties except for one
trifling case recorded in Sutherland, but it was remembered that
to this same county and in this same stealthy fashion cholera
had come in 1832.

One half of the total population of Scotland lived on the potato for nine months of the year, and in the mountains the proportion was probably more than two-thirds. A chief of the Clanranald Macdonalds had brought it to the Highlands and Isles a century before, forcing its cultivation on his clan with some difficulty (the people of South Uist, for example, long resisted it). It was easy to grow and to store in a land that could produce no great harvests of grain, and when sheep destroyed the black cattle economy, and the lairds restricted the shooting of game to paying tenants from England, the potato became the staple diet of the Highlander. In the coastal townships of Sutherland it was almost all that would grow on the thin allotments. Nonetheless the south still believed that the mountain people were bred on oats and beef.

At the beginning of February 1846, the weather was mild and spring-like, bringing pear-trees to leaf in the gardens of Inverness. No one doubted now that the blight would come with the summer, if it had not already attacked the pits in which some of last year's harvest had been stored. As each pit was opened there was fear, and then relief at finding the potatoes pure and whole. They were sent south in shiploads from Inverness and The Aird, to collect high prices in the Lowlands and England, the farmers arguing in their own defence that the Corn Laws made profit on their grain impossible. At first the people of Inverness watched these shipments impotently, and then protested with a week of angry violence. A crowd of five thousand halted a convoy of wagons on its way to the quay. They unloaded the potatoes and rolled the wagons into the River Ness. Urged on by a screaming woman who led them from a cart, they fought for several days against two hundred special constables, conscripted navvies from the Caledonian Canal, and soldiers of the 87th Regiment from Fort George.

Twenty men and women were sent for trial. In the same week the contents of potato-pits opened in Lochcarron were found to be rotten and uneatable. It was soon the same in Kintail, Sutherland, Ross and the Isles. In the spring men planted what seed they had and waited with no hope.

The summer of 1846 was as quixotic as the preceding winter

had been. Fierce droughts sucked dry the streams and lochans, and men swore that they had seen salmon swimming in red dust only. The rainless weeks were followed by great storms that flooded all low ground and rotted the feet from the sheep. In July there was hope again. The potato-fields were rich and green and promising. And then, at the beginning of August, the airborne spores of fungus (about which nothing was known, or would be known until the next century) floated silently from Morayshire to the Isles, from Perth to Caithness. They were carried by the rain and mist, by the hands of men, the hair of animals, and the wheels of carts. Overnight the potato-plants withered and blackened, the leaves turning to slime as if struck by frost. When the earth was opened, the tubers wept and smelt of death.

'In every kind of soil and situation,' wrote a correspondent to the *Inverness Courier*, 'in land newly cultivated and planted for the first time, as on old fields, and with every kind of seed, the disease has been found to exist, nor has the remedy been discovered.' Crops that were sound and healthy on Friday were black and rotten by the Sabbath. 'A friend had a few days ago gone to Knoydart, Skye, Lochalsh and Kintail, and he tells me that in all that extensive district he had scarcely seen one field which was not affected. Unless a gracious Providence look upon our poor Highlanders in mercy there is every likelihood that starvation must be their portion.'

By autumn it was known that the whole potato crop of the Highlands had failed.

County and parish authorities met in desperate panic, demanding aid from the Government for the purchase of corn, and asking the proprietors to loosen their purse-strings, which most of them did with unexpected liberality. London promised to send a commissary officer as soon as possible, but meanwhile, seeing that ray of good cheer that is sometimes only visible to politicians, 'Her Majesty's Government has reason to believe that the crop of oats in the West of Scotland is this year generally abundant and the quality is excellent.' It took no steps, however, to see that this abundant crop (the adjective was its own) remained in the Highlands and was used for the relief of famine. Throughout the months of hunger ahead, merchants would continue to export grain and other foodstuffs from the Highlands to markets in the south where prices were much more agreeable.

Local authorities did their best in the absence of direct relief from the Government, proposing schemes of road-mending that would give employment to the tens of thousands of unemployed. The Government encouraged them, directing their attention to an Act of the previous year which authorized the advance of public money for drainage purposes. But no one could say where men might buy food with the money earned that way. A meeting of proprietors and others held at Fort William decided that South Uist and Barra would need eight thousand bolls of meal if the people there were to survive the winter. North Uist would need five thousand and the Isle of Harris five thousand. A meeting of the Inverness Farmers' Society (with some twinges of conscience, perhaps) discussed the possibility of substituting the potato economy with other vegetables, such as beans, peas, cabbages, carrots or artichokes. But since no one suggested a way of growing these crops overnight, the meeting was of no help to the situation.

Sir Edward Coffin, the intelligent and conscientious Commissary-General who had been knighted for his work during the Irish Famine, came north on the Government's instructions. He set off on a tour of inspection, and promised that revenue cutters would be put at the disposal of any authority wishing to send grain to the west coast and the Isles. The difficulty, however, was to get the meal. Ross-shire farmers, for example, produced twenty-thousand quarters of wheat every year, exporting half of it to London and selling the rest as flour. They were doing the same this year, and would sell the flour only at prices equal to those that could be received for it in England. Aware that the people might not appreciate the sound economics of this, they asked the Sheriff for an assurance that their wagons would be protected by constables and soldiers if necessary on their way to the ships.

A special reporter of the *Inverness Courier* who made a quick visit to the Black Isle, Easter Ross and the west coast of Inverness, reported two conclusions: 'First, that there is great destitution present and in prospect; and secondly that the proprietors on the whole are meeting the crisis well.' But from his report it is evident that only those people who could be classified within the law as paupers were receiving help. And any family that had at least one member at work did not come under this classification.

From Glenshiel, in October, another correspondent of the *Courier* reported: 'On the side of the lake which belongs to Mr Baillie of Glenelg we witnessed cases in which whole families had been living on the gleanings from diseased potato fields for weeks, and whose only hope seemed to be that the herrings which have appeared in Loch Eishort would soon appear also in Loch Kintail.' James Baillie (more accurately of Bristol) was one of the largest sheep-farmers in the west. His estate, worth £100,000 had trebled its value since 1800. When the famine began he was one of several proprietors who petitioned the Government, unsuccessfully, to advance money at low interest to provide employment for the people. Much of the land he now had under sheep had belonged to the Macdonells of Glengarry.

Elsewhere in Glengarry the *Courier's* man discovered that 'the cotters and crofters are in an equally destitute condition. In one instance eleven cotters had been kept from starvation by the kindness of a large sheep-farmer; and in another a farmer had thrown open his potato-field to some poor creatures who were digging for sound ones with all the earnestness that a dervish would search for gold.'

Distress and destitution increased as winter approached. It was no mild season this year, but the old cruel Highland winter of wind, snow and black ice. The population moved aimlessly before starvation and the cold. 'Fathers in rags carry the rude implements that are to be the bringers of bread,' reported a journalist, 'Mothers scantily clad bear children in arms, and children bare-headed and bare-footed are loaded with trifling articles of furniture that may assist in supplying the new hovel or, disposed of, avert hunger for an hour.'

It was to the credit of the proprietors (though perhaps no more than should have been expected of them) that they put their hands into their own pockets for once. The second Duke of Sutherland was said to have spent £78,000 in relief during the year of the famine and those following. James Matheson of Achany, who had bought the vast Lewis estate for £190,000 in 1844, spent £40,000 on meal for the people there. But the money from the landlords alone was not enough, and was too rarely distributed impartially. More was collected from public charity, in the Lowlands, England, Canada, Australia and South Africa.

The funds obtained in this way were administered by two Destitution Boards, one in Glasgow and another in Edinburgh, and until they provided themselves with paid staffs and an intelligent system of distributing relief they operated in the usual inefficient and wasteful manner of such bodies. Edward Coffin helped them by establishing food depots at Oban and Portree. The potato-crop failure of 1846 was followed by another in 1847 of a lesser degree, and the effects of both lasted for five years. Though the Destitution Boards prevented the Highlands from becoming another Ireland, they were able to do little more than anaesthetize the pain of those years, and when they had exhausted the £151,532 they collected in money or kind, the people may have passed through the worst they were called upon to suffer but they still endured poverty and hunger.

When the Glasgow Board wound itself up it admitted that it had been of no real assistance to the people. The Edinburgh Board's attempt to introduce new industries for the homeless and the starving – the knitting of hosiery, for example – had brought little improvement at the time and nothing of permanence. As late as 1849 in Wester Ross there were over three thousand people on relief, and in Skye there were five thousand.

When the Boards were established, in January 1847, the *Inverness Courier* said: 'There never was a time when there need be less fear of famine. In the shipping ports of the south the granaries are choked full.' Had the Government considered it part of its purpose to set fixed prices on this grain, and to direct its distribution to where there was the greatest need, the funds collected by the Destitution Boards might have been sufficient to meet the demand. As it was, charity became a honey-pot for the speculators.

Relief was given in return for work, a labour test upon one of the family. 'A whole day's hard labour,' said the *Courier*, 'is not exacted for a pound of meal. The rule practically acted upon is to give the maximum allowance of 1½ lb. of meal for eight hours fair labour; the relief officer having it in his power to give only one pound when the working-time is idled away.' The day's work also entitled a man to an extra half a pound of meal for every child under the age of employment. 'While the wife, by spinning, or in certain cases by mere attention to personal and household cleanliness, can earn her three-quarters of a pound or a pound per day, Sunday included.' Ministers of the parish determined the fitness or merit of those asking for relief, and in return for their meal the men worked on the roads, on drains, on the improvement of the landlord's property.

The Reverend Norman Macleod, now Chaplain in Ordinary to Queen Victoria, was active in stimulating the charity of the Lowlands and England. To obtain material for his many public addresses, he wrote to ministers and factors all over the Highlands asking one question: 'What is now doing for the poor?' He received some terrifying answers.

From Bracadale Manse in December 1846, Mr Norman Mackinnon wrote: 'My only fear is that relief will come too late. They are now in actual want of everything in the shape of food; some of them days past told me that they had not eaten anything for two days but a salt herring which they said "kept them in good heart". ... I have attended already death-beds that may be said to have died of starvation. This day a great number of them came to my house, who said they had not a bite and the meal store was run out; a Government store-ship having come into the loch on her way to Portree, they thought I could get them to land some of it, but this could not be done. Oh, send us someing immediately, whatever may be done again. If you can send but a few pounds at present, let it come, for many are dying, I may say, of starvation.'

John Lamont, minister of Swordale, said that he did not know what to do for people who came to him daily, asking for food. 'A woman with a suckling child at her breast had not tasted anything for some time, until going some distance she got some food in another house, and nearly fainted upon tasting it. Misery and want are plainly depicted in the very faces of the people, and unless something is done, and done *soon*, the consequences must be of the most deplorable kind you can imagine.' He admitted that the proprietors were helping to relieve the distress in his parish, 'but they cannot, *with any justice to their own interests**, do anything like what will be required.'

From Lochmaddy, Norman Macleod was told that deaths from starvation were inevitable. On Iona the Reverend Alexander MacGregor said that all his people were now dependent upon charity for whatever they could get to eat. William Robertson, who had a sheep-farm at Kinlochmoidart, discovered that there was more to his lease than wool and mutton. 'I believe that one-fourth of the population of my estate would have died of famine ere now, had I not supplied them with food. This I have hitherto done at vast expense, inconvenience and sacrifice. Were it not an imperative sense of duty, I would not remain in the Highlands and see so much that pains me.'

On the island of Mull a factor called David Ross had been doing his best to form relief committes, raise money, and purchase wool 'to employ the females'. Daily, men and women came to him for bread, and one woman told him that she and her husband had lived on three-halfpennyworth of barley for two days. In the bitter weather of January 1847, Ross was told by one cotter that he had sold his last blanket to buy meal for his eight children. 'Another family's case stood thus: The husband had just one morsel of bread in the morning and went out to trench at Dunnipie. The wife, a boy and a girl, had not a single morsel. The girl, toward evening, got a little broth in the School of Industry, and the mother and the boy had nothing but a little cold gruel from one of the neighbours in the dusk.'

Archibald Clerk, at his manse of Kilmallie, told Macleod that

*My italics. J.P.

more than half of his parish in Lochaber, three thousand people, were in need of 'urgent aid'. And from Barra, the Royal Chaplain heard that women, young and old, had died from hunger. 'Unless aid is immediately given there must be deaths. The prospects for the future are dismal in the extreme.'

Norman Macleod published all the letters he had received in reply to his question. The picture they gave was supported by the reports of a young journalist called James Bruce, whom the *Scotsman* sent to the Highlands in February. Bruce, however, was a proprietor's man, or at least the conclusions he drew from the things he saw were pleasing to a landlord's ear. He described the hunger and the poverty and the destitution, but decided that there were too many people in the Highlands anyway. 'I cannot help looking on the fact of a fruitful population living in a barren country as a proof of indolence and want of proper spirit. ... The rising population must, as soon as they are able to labour for themselves, be removed from the vicious influence of the idleness in which their fathers have been brought up and have lived and starved.' And when, on Mull, a cotter told Bruce how grateful he was to the proprietor for giving him work so that he might earn money for bread, the *Scotsman*'s special correspondent reported this with all the contempt which Lowlanders had long felt for the Highlandman :

It is encouraging to find that such opinions are making their way among poor men who recollect well that their fathers and grandfathers contrived somehow to live while their employment mainly consisted in walking about all day with their hands in their pockets, and at night sitting down and telling traditions about great lords and mighty chiefs, and stories about ghosts and fairies, while their mothers and grandmothers, though living on the poorest fare, would have looked upon themselves and their families as eternally disgraced if it were to get out to the public that they had sold a dozen eggs.

Bruce's reports, later published in book form, prepared Scotland for the great emigrations to come, and made it possible for Lowlanders to approve of the dispersal of the people whom they were later to romanticize and imitate. The Highlanders themselves, always conscious of *Mi-run mor nan Gall*, the Lowlander's great hatred, expected no more, perhaps. Yet their pride and their dignity, already injured by thirty years of betrayal and eviction were scarcely enough to support them during these years of famine. And Bruce may have been speaking with some truth when he wrote impatiently: 'They are positively getting proud of so much looking-after, and of so many enquiries being made into their condition.'

If the people in the Western Highlands were passive during the famine, in the East they were frequently violent. The only grain-ships seen on the west coast were those that occasionally unloaded cargoes for the depots at Oban and Portree, but from the Moray and Cromarty Firths in the east ships left weekly for the south with their holds full of wheat, barley and oats. Desperate attempts were made to prevent their departure, and were sometimes successful. In February 1874, three hundred men and women from Evanton in Ross stopped the shipment of five wagonloads of grain. They gathered on the beach at Foulis Point, kindled great fires and waited all night. In the morning they met the wagons near Waterloo and, despite protests and threats from the Sheriff, turned them back. Sixty men of the 7th Regiment were sent to Avoch in the Black Isle in answer to an urgent appeal from Mr George More, a farmer and corn dealer there. According to the *Inverness Courier* poverty and destitution in Avoch were as bad as anywhere in the Highlands, and the people were enraged by hunger. Helped by local fishermen they unmoored the ship on which More wanted to load his barley, and tried to pull it out into the firth, but the soldiers of the 7th drove them off, and the barley went south.

At Burghead, when the *Ceres* was loading meal for Leith, a crowd boarded her and took the cargo ashore again. Constables from Elgin, armed with ash-sticks, beat the crowd from the quay, arrested the ring-leaders and lodged them in the Grant Arms. But the mob broke down the doors of the inn and carried away the prisoners. A hundred men of the 76th Regiment came up from Edinburgh by steamer, and guarded the *Ceres* with their bayonets until she loaded and sailed.

In Macduff young men barricaded the quay and successfully prevented a schooner from taking aboard three cart-loads of meal. At Banff more men and boys laid booms across the harbour-mouth and stopped the sailing of the *Boyne* for Leith. When it was rumoured that the Duke of Richmond's agents were buying up grain and storing it for the use of the town of Huntly only, a great crowd came out of the hills with sticks and stones, mobbed the few constables there, burnt effigies of the Duke and his agents, turned off the gas supply and rioted in the darkness. Soldiers from Aberdeen drove them out. In Port Gordon a meeting of Justices, convened for the purpose of swearing in special constables against imminent riot, was broken up by the people who then laid siege to the house of the local corn-dealer. He was protected by the guns of a coast-guard detachment until the soldiers from Huntly arrived.

Then, for a few weeks, there was quiet. 'This has been accomplished,' said the *Courier*, 'by assurances being given to the people that meal will be placed in ample quantities within their reach at fair prices.' There was more optimism than truth in the assurance. The situation in Skye was typical of most districts. There Lord Macdonald, Macleod of Macleod, and other proprietors announced that 30,000 bolls of meal would be needed to support the islanders at subsistence level until October. Then there must be seed-potatoes and grain for next year's planting. Nobody knew where to find the £68,000 that all this would cost. It was hoped that Skye workmen, who had gone to the Lowlands to find employment on the railways, would send £5,000 home to their families, and a grant of £13,000 had been applied for under the Drainage Act, but this was scarcely enough.

In the last week of February, the food riots broke out again, the most savage and desperate of them in Caithness and Ross.

On the 20th of that month the Sheriff of Caithness asked for soldiers at once, saying that the mob was plotting to scuttle a grain-ship at Wick. Two companies of the 76th Regiment, under Captain Evans Gordon, came promptly by steamer, landing at Ackergill and marching into Wick with drums beating and bayonets fixed. They were in action immediately, for the streets were full of rioting men and women. Gordon put a lieutenant and twenty men on the wharf to guard the ship, and then marched the rest of his command to the meal-store where the carts were being loaded. From the moment the soldiers were placed on the wharf they were under bitter and sustained assault from the crowd, and several of them, including the lieutenant, were injured by stones. Fishermen tried to drag them into the sea by running at them with an extended rope, but the soldiers leaped over it and drove the sailors away with the bayonet.

When Gordon brought the carts down to the harbour he was halted by a barricade that kept him from the ship and the twenty men on the wharf. For an hour his men, most of them young recruits, stood in the open by the carts and under volleys of stones. Women hung from the windows on either side, urging on their men and shouting for bread. At last the Sheriff read the Riot Act and Gordon sent his men forward. They broke into sections and advanced with barking hurrahs, their bayonets down. The struggle was short and ugly. Women beat at the muskets with sticks, and one who attacked an officer was knocked to the cobbles by 'a pretty severe sword cut'. Many of the crowd were wounded on the arms and legs by the bayonets before they broke and left the harbour to the soldiers.

The ship was loaded and drawn out to the safety of the bay.

The 76th formed ranks and marched back towards their quarters with several prisoners they had taken, and now the mob swarmed down a hill upon them, hurling stones which, said the *Courier*, 'rattled on the soldiers' accoutrements like hail'. Gordon brought his men into line with their muskets at the present, and shouted a warning to the crowd. He was answered with more stones, and he gave the order to fire. The volley was aimed high, but two hundred yards from the redcoat line the falling shots broke a man's wrist and tore a hole in the breast of a young girl.

That night Wick was bloody and bruised, and the grain-ship it had hoped to scuttle lay off Pulteneytown waiting for a fair wind that would take it to the south.

A week later (when Captain Gordon and the 76th were marching northward still to quell another food-riot in Thurso) the officer commanding at Fort George received a hysterical call for help from John Jardine, the aged advocate who had succeeded Macleod of Geanies as Sheriff of Ross. He said that the people of Invergordon and the hills about were rioting against the export of grain. They had broken into stores and mixed the sacks to make them unmarketable and unfit for sale as seed, and they were now threatening to intercept and overturn all wagons sent to the harbour. His constables were unable to control the mob, and he wanted soldiers to escort farmers' shipments to the wharves at Invergordon. On Tuesday, 2 March, one hundred men of the 27th Enniskillen Foot, who had just arrived at Fort George in the *Birkenhead*, were sent to the Cromarty Firth in the same ship and under the command of their Colonel.

Mr Jardine, other sheriffs of the county, the Procurator-Fiscal, a retired lieutenant-general, a retired major, two baronets, and a dozen other gentry were waiting with relief on the quayside at Invergordon to welcome the Irish soldiers, in whose own home-land at this moment skeleton women were shrieking for food and maddened animals were gnawing at human corpses. The 27th formed up on the quay in scarlet and pipe-clay, tapped their muskets on the stones, and marched off with the gentry for Ross-keen two miles away. There a farmer called Baxter had several wagons of grain he wanted to ship to the south.

A mile from Rosskeen soldiers and gentlemen were halted by the mob. The people had already stopped Mr Baxter's convoy, driven off the few constables guarding it, unloaded the wagons and sent them back to the farm. The 27th formed in line across the road and the fields on either side, and Mr Jardine came for-ward to read the Riot Act. Not much of the Act was heard above the shouts of 'Starvation!' but when he had finished the Irish advanced and drove the people away with the bayonet. The carts were brought back, reloaded, and taken into Invergordon. A half dozen prisoners were locked in the inn.

The loading of Mr Baxter's grain began by torchlight that night, and was completed successfully under the protection of the soldiers. But the mob poured down on the empty carts as they were returning to Rosskeen, tore them to pieces and chased the drivers into the heather. The people then assaulted the inn where the retired lieutenant-general and the rest of the gentry were guarding the prisoners. They broke down the door with one of the gentlemen's own carriage-poles, rescued two of the prisoners, and were then driven out of the inn by clubbed pistols and riding-crops. The gentry made frequent sallies on the mob, shouting defiance, until a picquet of the 27th came up at the double and cleared the streets until dawn.

The little war continued the next day, when the Sheriff-Substitute and seventy-five soldiers went again to Rosskeen to escort some empty carts needed for carrying grain from the store to the harbour. But all they found was a great fire of burning wood. They faced about and marched to Ballintraid, where thirty loaded carts should have been waiting for them. Once more the people had forestalled them, and were already cutting open the sacks when the soldiers came running in with the bayonet. The carts were re-loaded, but all the way to Invergordon the 27th had to fight off a great crowd of men and women* who threw stones and cried, 'Starvation! Starvation!' Women who took the bridles of the horses in an attempt to turn them were beaten back with musket butts.

The convoy was a mile long, and the soldiers had difficulty in guarding all of it. The teamsters were often left alone, swinging their whips against the crowd. In Invergordon the difficulty increased. 'In the course of the march through the village to the harbour,' said the *Inverness Courier*, 'three successive bayonet charges were made, in the course of which several people received slight wounds.' Waiting on the quay was a company of the 76th, brought that morning by the *Birkenhead*, and at the sight of them the people lost heart. They went home in listless and hungry despair.

Picquets of the 27th and the 76th patrolled the empty streets of Invergordon for the rest of the day, and throughout the night while the ships were loaded with grain. On Friday the town was

---

* Many of them were the children and grandchildren of the Men of Ross who had been evicted from Strath Rusdale in The Year of the Sheep fifty-five years before.

still deserted, and Mr Jardine decided that the worst was over. But in the afternoon he heard that a band of men, in what appeared to be disciplined order, was coming down the road from Tain with a piper at its head. The General Assembly was beaten on the drums of the 27th, and the Irish formed up across the quay. The gentry came out of the inn with their pistols and crops, and Mr Jardine stood ready with the Riot Act once more in his hand. It was not needed. The threatened mob turned out to be 'sixty fine-looking young men from the Duke of Sutherland's estates, with knapsacks on their backs and sticks in their hands', who had left the land of Improvement to find work on the railways in the south. They knew nothing of the riot, and showed no desire to join it. The gentry were so relieved at this that they put their hands in' their pockets and gave the Sutherlanders money 'to buy beer and bread to refresh them'. Though where they might buy bread in the hungry streets of Invergordon was not explained to them.

Rioting increased with the second failure of the potato crop that year. Three-quarters or more of the population of most parishes were existing, or trying to exist, on the relief given them by the Destitution Boards. It was never sufficient. Sixty-nine 'poor inhabitants' of Evanton in Ross declared that for weeks they had lived on a few turnips, and now that these were gone they had nothing. Queen Victoria ordered her household to eat no more than one pound of bread per person daily, and seventeen 'distinguished persons', headed by the Dukes of Bedford, Norfolk, Rutland and Grafton, published an advertisement in the *Inverness Courier* pledging themselves 'to reduce in our families as far as practicable the consumption of bread and flour'. Lord John Russell decided that a banquet given by the Lord Mayor of London was a suitable occasion on which to advise other people to do the same. In Arisaig, seven hundred people were saved from death by starvation by the gift of 10½ bolls of meal which lasted them two days, and the Marquess of Abercorn rented a shooting-lodge on Loch Laggan for £2,000 a year.

The people were a burden – to themselves, to the proprietors, and to the Government. In the west a meeting of landlords put

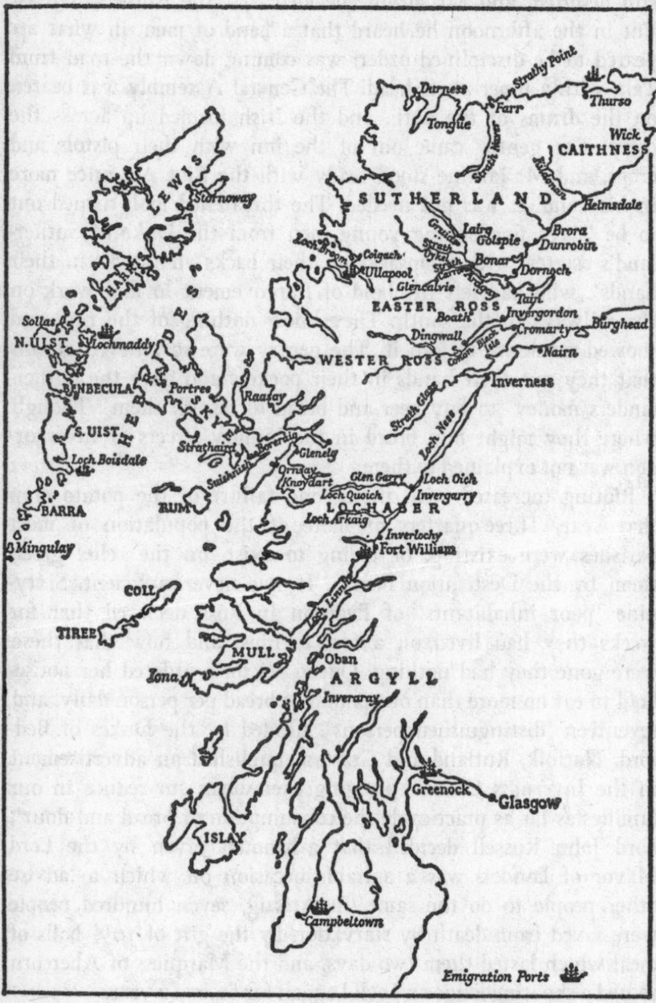
Strathy Point
Durness
Farr
Thurso
Tongue
Wick
Strath Naver
CAITHNESS
Kildonan
LEWIS
Stornoway
SUTHERLAND
Helmsdale
Lairg
Brora
Golspie
Dunrobin
Loch Broom
Coigach
Bonar
Ullapool
Dornoch
HARRIS
Glencalvie
Tain
EASTER ROSS
Invergordon
Sollas
Boath
Burghead
Cromarty
N. UIST
Lochmaddy
Dingwall
Black Isle
Nairn
HEBRIDES
WESTER ROSS
Inverness
BENBECULA
Portree
Raasay
Strath Glass
SKYE
S. UIST
Loch Ness
Strathaird
Boreraig
Glenelg
Loch Boisdale
Suishnish
Ornsay
Knoydart
Glen Garry
Loch Oich
Invergarry
Loch Quoich
BARRA
RUM
LOCHABER
Loch Arkaig
Inverlochy
Mingulay
Fort William
COLL
Loch Linnhe
TIREE
MULL
Oban
Iona
ARGYLL
Inveraray
Greenock
Glasgow
ISLAY
Campbeltown
Emigration Ports

into words and on to paper what men had been thinking for some time. The people should go. The meeting resolved to ask the Government to assist emigration from the Highland counties of Scotland. 'I see the hills, the valleys and the slopes,' cried the bard Kenneth Mackenzie,

> But they do not lighten my sorrow.
> I see the bands departing
> on the white-sailed ships.
> I see the Gael rising from his door.
> I see the people going,
> and there is no love for them in the north.

'Cha till mi tuille, *we shall return no more!*'

EMIGRATION had begun long before the coming of the Great Cheviot. According to John Knox, the London bookseller who toured the Highlands in the seventeen-eighties, twenty thousand people left for the Colonies between 1763 and 1775. In one year alone fifty-four emigrant ships sailed from the western sea-lochs. Though some of the emigrants were the families of soldiers who had fought in the Americas, and who had chosen to settle there on grants of land, most were led and organized by small tacksmen who wished to escape the rack-renting of their chiefs. In 1769 all tenants and sub-tenants left the Skye estates of Macdonald of Sleat, forcing him to import others from the mainland. A growing population, a decaying economy, recurrent famines and bitter poverty made exile inevitable for increasing numbers. Others left to be free from the religious intolerance of their lairds, of men like Colin Macdonald of Boisdale who beat his tenants into the Presbyterian Church with his cane, and thus earned for it the enduring name of *Creideamh a' bhata buidhe*, the Religion of the Yellow Stick.

From the beginning the emigrants were the victims of speculators and ship-masters, of typhus, cholera and dysentery. They were deceived in most of the promises made to them. In July

1773, two hundred people of Ross, thirty-three families and twenty-five single men, boarded the *Hector* at Ullapool on Loch Broom. The ship was so rotten that the emigrants were able to pick away its timbers with their finger-nails. It was owned by two Englishmen, Pagan and Witherspoon, who had bought unbroken land in Nova Scotia which they proposed to settle with Highlanders, rightly concluding that these were gullible or desperate enough to believe that they would receive a farm for every family and a year's free provisions for all. The people left in good spirits, and when their piper was ordered ashore because he had no money to pay for his passage 'they pleaded to have him allowed to accompany them, and offered to share their own rations with him in exchange for his music'.

The voyage was long and hard. Off the Newfoundland coast gales drove the *Hector* back into the Atlantic, adding two more weeks to its bitter passage. Eighteen children died of smallpox or dysentery. Water in the barrels was green and almost undrinkable, and in the end it was so scarce that the emigrants were unable to eat the little salt meat that was left. They searched the ship's hold for scraps of mouldy oatcake they had previously thrown away. In Nova Scotia they went ashore behind their piper, wearing the tartan that was still under proscription in Scotland, and some of the young men carried broadswords at their hips. But nothing they had been promised was awaiting them. Many were sent into the timberland without food or the tools to build houses. It was October, too late to break the land or plant it. That winter men and women walked eighty miles through the snow to exchange their clothing for potatoes. Some tried to live on the bark of trees or by hacking clams and oysters from the ice. Others bound themselves away as indentured servants to earlier settlers. Then they rose in protest, mobbed the owners' stores, bound the agent who had brought them from Ross and since deserted them, took what they needed in food and clothing, and left notes against their willingness to pay when they could. A company of militia ordered out against them refused to march. 'I know the Highlanders,' said its captain, 'and if they are fairly treated there will be no trouble with them.'

In the spring only seventy-eight of the original two hundred emigrants were left on the settlement.

The American Revolution checked the flow of emigration for seven years. In 1783 it began again, stimulated by a famine during which, said the Sheriff of Caithness and Sutherland, 'many people are dying in great numbers for want of food'. And now sheep had come to the Highlands. 'It need be no matter for surprise,' said Knox, 'if a gentleman should embrace the tempting offers from sheep-farmers. One man will occupy the land that starved fifty or more families; he gives a double or treble rent and is punctual to the day of payment.' The fifty or more starving families walked to Greenock, to Fort William or Ullapool, to Thurso or Wick, or any port at which emigration agents advertised their sailings. During the first three years of the nineteenth century ten thousand people left for Nova Scotia and Upper Canada, driven from the Highlands by poverty, by eviction and by sheep. In 1801, said Thomas Telford, eleven ships sailed from Fort William with 3,300 emigrants. In the verse of the people there was now a hopeless melancholy, an acceptance of despair. *A Dhomhnaill, a ghràidh mo chridhe . . .*

> Oh Donald, love of my heart,
> I am sorrowful, heavy and weary
> in solitude, as I think
> of all the misery that pursues me,
> and of all my kinsmen lost to me.
> It is not offended pride, not rage,
> not a fierce and savage gloom,
> not War even (that would be little),
> but that Islay now has so few
> of the youth that once were here.
> They have been driven away
> to America across the sea,
> and there is no one left
> with kindly feelings, or peace in him.

The *Inverness Journal* certainly had no kindly feelings when it reported the departure of one hundred and thirty emigrants who left Thurso in October 1807, aboard the brig *Rambler*. 'Most

criminal infatuation!' it declared, 'that can thus lead men to
emigrate from their native homes into a state of voluntary
banishment, peril and toil the most laborious, to a country where
they have not only to till but make the field, half of which exertion and labour would have made the country they thus abandon
pregnant with every blessing.' When it later announced the
wreck of the *Rambler*, with the loss of all but three of the emigrants, the *Journal* did not say that this was probably Divine
Judgement, but it did choose the occasion to lament the fact that
so many people were leaving Scotland 'when recruits for our
standing army and militia are hard to find'.

In its sustained disapproval of those who 'wantonly left the
Highlands and safely arrived in the western hemisphere', the
Journal had the support of all good men in the country, particularly those who took turns at governing it. So long as Highlanders were needed to fill the uniforms emptied by French
musketry or West Indian fevers, emigration was regarded as an
evil, though few men suggested that the economic causes of it
might be greater evils still. The Government's attitude was also
part of the paradox of Britain's imperial growth, that whilst the
country acquired large areas of the earth's surface it was dis-
inclined to people them with anything more than convicted
felons. In this it may have been mindful of the fact that thirteen
colonies of largely respectable emigrants had recently decided to
govern themselves. But until the Napoleonic Wars ended, and
until a sheep economy made destitution too great a problem to
be solved by anything other than emigration, the Government
did its best to keep the people at home (and in employment) by
encouraging the construction of the Crinan and Caledonian
Canals, the building of 875 miles of roads and bridges in the
Highlands. The cost of these works, to the State, county authorities and proprietors, was more than £1,500,000, of which nearly
half went in the eighteenpence or half a crown a day paid to the
labourers. Though hundreds of evicted men were able to find
work on the roads and the canals, the rate of removals and the
growth of the population outstripped the work available. Emigration increased in the second decade of the century.

There is probably a definable rule governing the exploitation of the many by the few in times of suffering, if it has not already been stated as The Law of Demand and Supply. Before the end of the eighteenth century there were men like Pagan and Witherspoon who saw an opportunity for quick profits in Highland emigration. Many were merchants who formed partnerships for the chartering of emigrant vessels. Others went further, again like Pagan and Witherspoon, and bought land in Canada which they never saw but to which they committed hundreds of Highland families. Some were retired or half-pay officers, buying shares in a single emigrant ship, or in a fleet. According to Sheriff-Substitute Brown of Western Inverness, writing in 1800, a Major Simon Fraser at Fort William 'has made a trade of the business since 1790'.

One of the most successful contractors was George Dunoon of Fort William who, with his partners, made a comfortable fortune shipping Glengarry and Strathglass people across the Atlantic to Pictou in Nova Scotia. On one of Dunoon's ships, said Sheriff Brown, fifty people died of cholera. 'I saw the ships when at Fort William. They were much crowded. When the passengers landed in America they were shut up in a point of land, and all communication betwixt them and the rest of the country people cut off, to prevent the contagion of disease.'

Emigrant sailings were advertised in an encouraging and deceptive prose:

NOTICE TO PASSENGERS

for

NOVA SCOTIA AND CANADA

A SUBSTANTIAL COPPERED Fast Sailing Ship will be ready to receive passengers at Fort William on the 10th of June and sail for Pictou and Canada on the 20th.

All those who wish to emigrate to these parts in Summer will find this an excellent opportunity, as every attention will be paid to the comfort of Passengers, and they may depend on the utmost punctuality as to the date of sailing.

For particulars application may be made to Mr John Grant, Merchant in Fort William.

In none of the advertisements was there any suggestion that death from fever, or from dysentery, was inevitable for some of the emigrants on every ship. Nor was there a warning that if the ship did not make the landfall it confidently promised, starvation would be added to the normal hell of the passage. The cost of the voyage was high, and many small tenants placed themselves and their families under indentures in Canada in order to meet it.

FOR PICTOU DIRECT
The Fine Brigantine
GOOD INTENT
220 Tons Burden
E. HIBBARD, Supercargo,

will be ready to sail from Aberdeen in March, and intends calling at Cromarty about the end of that month, if a sufficient number of passengers offer.

This Vessel has most excellent accommodation for Passengers, and Mr Hibbard, the Supercargo, will pay every attention.

The Fares are as follows, and payable at going on board:

Cabin passengers	10 guineas each
Steerage ditto	7 guineas each
Ditto, from 7 to 14 years old	5 guineas each
Ditto, from 2 to 7 years old	3 guineas each
Infants go free	

An early application from those who intend going by the Good Intent is requested, that the owners may determine whether the vessel shall call at Cromarty.

The sailing of an emigrant vessel was a deeply emotional experience, for those leaving and for those who remained. The Highlanders were like children, uninhibited in their feelings and wildly demonstrative in their grief. Men and women wept without restraint. They flung themselves on the earth they were leaving, clinging to it so fiercely that sailors had to prise them free and carry them bodily to the boats. A correspondent of the Inverness Courier watched the departure of some Kildonan people from Helmsdale: 'Hands were wrung and wrung again, bumpers of whisky tossed wildly off amidst cheers and shouts; the women were forced almost fainting into the boats; and the crowd upon the shore burst into a long, loud cheer. Again and again that cheer was raised and responded to from the boat, while bonnets were thrown into the air, handkerchiefs were waved, and last words of adieu shouted to the receding shore, while, high above all, the wild notes of the pipes were heard pouring forth that by far the finest of pibroch tunes, *Cha till mi tuille*, We shall Return No More !'

Conditions aboard the emigrant ships were seldom better than abominable, and for fifty years selfless humanitarian societies fought for Acts of Parliament that would bring a slight improvement in them. The ships that sailed from Dublin or Belfast were the worst of all, but because steerage passage on them cost thirty shillings only, a quarter of what it cost from Greenock, many Highlanders crossed the Irish Sea to sail from there. In the beginning, before Parliament attempted to control the contractors, emigrants were loaded into the ships like bales of merchandise. In 1773, for example, a ship of three hundred tons left for the Carolinas with four hundred and fifty passengers. All were crammed into a hold measuring sixty feet by eighteen by six, each emigrant having a little over two square feet of deck on which to spend ten or eleven weeks at sea. The pure water with which the shipmaster was supposed to supply his passengers was in fact sour, and was stored in casks that had previously contained indigo. Dysentery killed twenty-three of the emigrants before they reached America.

In the summer of 1801, George Dunoon advertised the sailing of the *Sarah* and the *Dove* from Fort William for Pictou. Had the laws then governing slave-ships applied to these emigrant vessels, they would not have been allowed to carry more than 489 passengers. Dunoon filled the tiny holds with 700, emigrants from Lord Reay's country, from the clan-lands of Seaforth, Fraser and Cameron. If they believed his promise that in Nova Scotia they would find a tree that supplied fuel, soap and sugar (he probably meant the maple) they may have found the nightmare voyage endurable, but it is unlikely. Forty-nine people died on the *Sarah* alone, and the suffering of all was so terrible that it was remembered in Nova Scotia for more than a century.

Two years after the departure of the *Sarah* and the *Dove* Thomas Telford, then surveying the coasts and Central Highlands for the Treasury, was asked to give his views on emigration. His report was placed before a select committee, and he urged that something be done to prevent over-crowding, to guarantee adequate provisions for all emigrants. The Passenger Act of 1803, which followed, produced some odd responses. Two ministers protested against it on behalf of 'one hundred illiterate crofters in Inverness and Ross', saying that the new regulations were making it impossible for their poor parishioners to escape hunger and destitution. Less disinterested was William Allen, a shipowner of Leith, who petitioned the Treasury and the Commissioners of Customs, ridiculing a clause in the Act which obliged him to ship the following provisions for every child he carried: 52 gallons of water, 84 lb. of beef, 84 lb. of biscuits, 24 lb. of flour, 36 lb. of oatmeal, and 6 lb. of butter.

Neither ministers nor ship-masters worried for long. The new regulations made little impression on the self-interest of contractors or the indifference of authority. Overcrowding continued and disease increased. When the little brig *James* reached Halifax in 1826 every person on board, crew or passenger, was ill with typhus. Reporting this to William Huskisson, the Colonial Secretary, a Governor-General of British North America added: 'I really do believe that there are not many instances of slave-traders from Africa to America exhibiting so disgusting a picture ... The most favourable account that reached me of one vessel admitted no sort of comparison between her and a French slaver brig captured by me four years ago when in command of a frigate on the Leeward Isles.'

Another Act, in 1828, tried to establish the amount of space which should be given to each emigrant, and the amount of provisions that should be supplied, but both were the pitiful minimum only, and both were largely ignored. Thirty thousand people were now leaving Britain for Canada every year, and the profits were too tempting for shipowners to limit them by obeying regulations which nobody seemed inclined to enforce.

From the moment they agreed to sail on a vessel the emigrants were bound to the contractor or his agents. They pledged themselves by depositing half the passage-money, and those who had no money sold their property to the agent at his valuation. Only when this was done, when a passenger-list was filled, was a ship chartered. Weeks, sometimes months would pass before she sailed down the Clyde, Loch Linnhe or Loch Broom (where the road to Ullapool was now known as 'Destitution Road'). During the long wait the emigrants were fleeced by the managers of boarding-houses owned by the contractors. Told by the agent that his company's 'fine coppered vessel' would be no more than six weeks at sea, the emigrant bought provisions for this period only, and usually exhausted them before Canada was reached. He was then obliged to buy more from the master, who would charge him two shillings for a stone of potatoes that had cost the owner threepence only.

For every emigrant who was fortunate enough to have the 30s. or £6 needed to buy himself three square feet on the lower deck of an emigrant brig, there were two or more with no money at all. They earned it by what work they could find in Glasgow, Greenock or Fort William. They were plucked by touts and brokers who sold them tickets for ships that could not sail for weeks, if indeed they existed at all. And where the ships did exist they were something that imagination could not have created. In 1836 the Colonial Office was told (and this after the passing of a third Emigration Act) that when the Ceres and the Kingston arrived at Nova Scotia the former was without water, and the latter had enough for half a day only. The Kingston, with 340 passengers, was carrying far more than the legal number, and aboard the Ceres* the rotten wood of temporary berths had collapsed, killing two children. Despite certain suffering, and possible death, many people without the passage money stowed away aboard the emigrant ships. This happened so frequently

*See p. 180.

that Customs officers took constables and coastguards aboard when they checked the sailing-lists, and they searched each ship before it sailed.

By the eighteen-thirties the Government, having no major war but too many people on its hands, was raising no objection to emigration from the Highlands. Where James Loch had once declared that the idle alone thought of leaving their country, sheep-farming proprietors were now saying that Canada and Australia needed those virtues which only the commonality of the Highlands possessed. These were the years of 'The Great Emigrations'. In 1831, 58,000 people left Britain for Canada, and in the following year the figure was above 66,000. Emigration to New South Wales was also growing, and in twenty years would be greater than that to Canada. Prompted and probably paid by the shipping-contractors, hack writers produced pamphlets of advice in which fact and fiction were engagingly mixed: 'The average length of a voyage to Quebec is from four to five weeks in spring, the proper time for an agricultural emigrant to go out. . . . Provisions must be taken for the longest period, as it would be very miserable to one blessed with a good stomach to have nothing to put into it during the latter weeks of a voyage lengthened by accidental circumstances.' The Highlander, who received special attention from these writers, was told that a man with his digestion and appetite would need four stones of oatmeal, four of cutlings for gruel, four stones of biscuits and a half of sugar, half a pound of tea, four stones of butter, twenty stones of potatoes, 'and a few dozen eggs which should be well-greased to exclude the air, and consequently preserve them fresh.'

Gentlemen who took cabin passage on the emigrant ships published accounts of their voyage for the entertainment of their friends and the education of their descendants. John Hood, of Stonebridge in Berwickshire, sailed for New South Wales on the *Lady Kennaway* in 1841. He paid £50 for his passage, and found the food ('Roast mutton, boiled mutton, mutton-pies, sheep's-head; pork roasted, fried, boiled and broiled') tolerable, and even enjoyable after a while. The claret was good too, and after tea every afternoon the cabin passengers sat on deck to await the coming of 'brilliant stars and splendid moonlight'. It was unfortunate that he found it difficult to sleep at nights for the noise which the steerage passengers made, and the lack of proper segregation for their women was deplorable. 'I am told that in some emigrant ships even partitions are dispensed with, that decency is entirely disregarded, and that a sentry and lights are the only protection.'

As late as 1854, after four Acts of Parliament to control and improve conditions aboard emigrant ships, *The Times* published this account of one:

The emigrant is shewn a berth, a shelf of coarse pinewood in a noisome dungeon, airless and lightless, in which several hundred persons of both sexes and all ages are stowed away, on shelves two feet one inch above each other, three feet wide and six feet long, still reeking from the ineradicable stench left by the emigrants on the last voyage ... Still he believes that the plank is his own, and only finds when the anchor is up that he must share his six feet three with a bedfellow. He finds that cleanliness is impossible, that no attempt is made to purify the reeking den into which he has been thrust, and that the thirty days voyage he has been promised will not, from the rottenness of the rigging and the unsoundness of the hull, be completed in less than sixty. He is lucky if the provisions correspond to a sample, if the water can be served out according to contract, or if he can prevail upon the cooks, selected from among the emigrants, to dress his meals in such shape that he can eat them without mortal loathing.... After a few days have been spent in the pestilential atmosphere created by the festering mass of squalid humanity imprisoned between the damp and steaming decks, the scourge bursts out, and to the miseries of filth, foul air and darkness is added the Cholera. Amid hundreds of men, women and children, dressing and undressing, washing, quarrelling, fighting, cooking and drinking, one hears the groans and screams of a patient in the last agonies of this plague.

Twenty-nine emigrant ships had left for America in November of the previous year. Of the 13,762 passengers who sailed in them, more than a third had been attacked by cholera, and over a thousand had died.

Yet all this was worth enduring if survival of the voyage meant relief from the hardships at home and an escape from the Great Mountain Sheep. 'Oh, young men of Ness,' wrote Donald Campbell from Upper Canada, 'I want you to come here and be not afraid. Leave the poor fishing of the Ness. Oh, my brothers and sisters, and all of you, be sure and come here, and don't live starving where you are!'

'That you should feel pain in leaving, is natural'

THERE was a reluctance to believe that conditions aboard the emigrant ships were as bad as reports indicated. The slight inconvenience of the voyage, it was thought, was a small price to pay for the good life at the end of it. 'Highlanders, it is well known,' said the *Inverness Courier*, 'can exist on very little when necessity requires them to do so. If each grown person, therefore, lays in one boll of oatmeal, and another of potatoes, there is no fear of him starving, and thus, for somewhat less than four pounds he will reach the promised land.' The *Courier* was reporting the plans of 'two respectable agents who, partly as a trading speculation and partly as an act of philanthropy' were offering to transport Skyemen to Cape Breton Island for two pounds a head. It left its readers to decide between this murderous optimism and a letter it published from a young Sutherlander who had left Cromarty in a small brig crowded with 220 emigrants: 'Nearly the whole of the passengers were attacked by a severe fever owing to bad water. The water had been put into palm-oil casks, or some other obnoxious stuff was in them formerly, and we could neither use it for tea, coffee, or anything else, and of which we got a very small allowance. We lost nine passengers in all.'

And of course there was the *Asia*. Three hundred Ross-shire emigrants sailed in her, but she got no further than Plymouth. There her rotten hold filled with water and she was declared unfit. Her passengers, who had been close to starvation since she left Cromarty, were put ashore and all record of what happened to them is lost.

The landlords' demands for 'an extensive system of emigration to relieve the destitute poor of the Highlands' reached Parliament in February 1841, when Henry Baillie, the Member for Inverness and a cousin of James Baillie the sheep-farmer, moved for a Committee of Inquiry. He said that there were forty thousand Highlanders in need of assistance, and since a passage to Canada cost £3 a grant of £120,000 should settle the whole business. No such grant was made by the Government, of course, and the landlords were later rebuked by the Assistant-Secretary to the Treasury, Sir Charles Trevelyan, who told them that it was their fault the land was over-populated and destitute, and that they would receive the real benefits of emigration by way of increased rents and a diminished liability to support paupers under the Poor Laws. Not that Trevelyan was moved by any great compassion for the destitute. During the Irish Famine later he was to say 'Dependence on charity is not to be made an agreeable mode of life.'

Baillie got his Committee, and when it issued its second and final report in June it said what everybody knew, that there were too many people in the Highlands. 'This excess of population,' said the *Inverness Courier*, 'who are for the most part, for a period every year, in a state of great destitution, is variously calculated at from 45,000 to 80,000 souls.' The Committee said that an efficient system of emigration was urgently needed, and on so vast a scale that it would be impossible without State assistance.

No assistance was offered. The Government, which had moved from one side of the House to the other that month, probably felt that its predecessor had adequately covered the problem the previous year by the establishment of a Colonial Land and Emigration Department, though this was never much more than a filing-cabinet for statistics and reports. The potato blight came, and with it a second great wave of evictions in Ross, Glengarry and the Isles. Toward the end of the decade destitution and over-population were worse than they had ever been. Landlords were now hysterical in their descriptions of the good life awaiting emigrants in Canada or Australia. Thomas MacLaughlan, in a series of letters he wrote for *The Witness*, accused them of hypocrisy and deceit, and that 'while the law is banishing its tens for terms of seven or fourteen years as the penalty for deep-dyed crimes, irresponsible and infatuated power is banishing thousands for life for no crime whatever'. And as for the 'promised land' which proprietors and Press said was awaiting the emigrants :

We would bring them to the emigrant sheds at Quebec or Montreal, and we could tell them that during the last great emigration hundreds, we might say thousands, died in these sheds of a fearful pestilence. We would bring them to Cape Breton or the district around Pictou in Nova Scotia, and we suspect we could point out an amount of destitution among old settlers not to be outdone by that of the Hebrides.... We could bring them to the Lewis Highlanders on the Salmon River who, after ten years of settlement, have hardly been able to pay the small sum due as the price of their lands; and lest they should suppose that this state of things merely existed among the *lazy* Highlanders, we could tell them of an English settlement in the same neighbourhood of several years standing where a friend of ours was told within the last year or two, on unquestionable authority, that there were forty families who had not twenty-four hours' food in their houses at a time, nor the means of purchasing it.

In 1851 something like planned emigration was evolved. It was by compromise, of course, with the Government acting like a parent, giving advice and some financial assistance to private emigration societies which were expected to find the bulk of their funds in the pockets of the public. The Board of Supervision, the central administrative control for the Poor Laws, had been in favour of emigration for some time, and was in a constant state of irritation over the people's reluctance to leave their homes. It was of the light-headed opinion that the best way to convince them of the necessity of emigration would be to put the burden of immediate poor relief on the shoulders of local authorities. This would soon starve the Highlanders into submission. At the beginning of the year the situation in the Highlands was as bad as, if not worse than it had ever been. The funds of the two Destitution Boards were exhausted, and the potato harvest of the previous year had been a failure. In Portree, the minister of Snizort wrote to the Home Secretary, 'Death from starvation must be the inevitable result if we are denied extraneous aid, as we have no local resources of any kind.' In February 1851, Sir John MacNeill, chairman of the Board of Supervision, went north for a gloomy tour of the Highlands. He went at the request of the Home Secretary.

The report made by this conscientious, fatherly old man was depressing. It strengthened the Board's argument that emigration was the only solution to destitution, and it accused the Highlanders of laziness, and of expecting relief as a right. 'The fact is unquestionable that a people who some years ago carefully concealed their poverty, have learned to parade, and of course exaggerate it.' Money expended by the proprietors, as well as that given by the local authorities for the relief of destitution had resulted in nothing that 'would justify the conclusion that any practicable amount of additional expenditure for the same purposes would place the present inhabitants in a condition to maintain themselves where they now reside'.

The people must emigrate. There should be no increase in poor relief.

The Highland and Islands Emigration Society was the direct result of MacNeill's report. It began, in September 1851, as the Skye Emigration Society under the chairmanship of Thomas Fraser, Sheriff-Substitute of the island, declaring that it had been formed to 'procure help for those who wish to emigrate but have not the means of doing so, to afford information, encouragement and assistance to all whom emigration would be a relief from want and misery.' It issued a public statement, telling the people that immigrants who were peaceable, orderly, moral and hardworking would be welcome in Australia and Canada, and it told them that the Highlands could no longer offer them either employment or subsistence.

That you should feel pain in leaving your own country is natural, and proceeds from a praiseworthy sentiment; but is the sacrifice of this feeling which emigration demands peculiar to you? Remember the families that were most respected in this country twenty years ago. How many of them have gone abroad? Is it harder for you to leave your native land than it was for them. They have subdued the feeling of pain, and so ought you, for you have stronger reasons for emigrating than they had.

We will do what we can to assist you, and we will endeavour to procure assistance for you from others ... and remember that you should convert into cash every article of property you possess to procure the means of carrying you to the Colonies.

The Society was to work with Government assistance supplied by the Colonial Land and Emigration Department, which after ten years of pigeon-holing was now called upon for action. Its Commissioners, said Fraser, would provide passages for suitable emigrants.

... but the emigrants require, first to make a deposit in money of £1 per head in certain cases, £5 in others, and £11 in others. Second, to provide a suitable outfit or clothes etc. Third, to find their way at their own expense from their homes to the port of embarkation.

Those emigrants who could find no money for the deposit, for clothes, or for transport to the ports, would be assisted from the funds collected by the Society. 'Let each consider well,' said Fraser chidingly, 'and answer the question for himself. Is it not his duty to endeavour to remove to a country where his services would be valued and would readily procure for him not only plenty of food and clothing, but the means of rising to a comfortable and respectable independence?'

This little Skye organization quickly grew into a national and imperial body – The Society for Assisting Emigration from the Highlands and Islands of Scotland. It had its headquarters in St Martin's Lane, London, and a committee of management that included the Lord Mayor, the Governor of the Bank of England, the Duke of Buccleuch, the Earl of Shaftesbury, Baron de Rothschild M.P., Macleod of Macleod, Macpherson of Cluny, and, of course, its humble founder the Sheriff-Substitute of Skye. Mr Fraser, surrounded now by his wealth and position, resigned his chair to the Assistant-Secretary to the Treasury, Sir Charles Trevelyan.

Queen Victoria's husband (his affection for Scotland made manifest by the wearing of the kilt and the designing of a tartan) graciously agreed to become Patron of the Society, and this was not without dramatic irony. 'Much as we rejoice in our beloved Sovereign's visits to our country,' Thomas MacLauchlan had grumbled two years earlier, 'we fear that they may hasten the consummation of making our Highlands a great deer-forest by inducing a larger number of our English aristocracy to flock to them for the purpose of sport.'

The Society became the machinery by which thousands of the Highland poor left for Australia and Canada. Each one of them was first examined by Commissioners from the Colonial Land and Emigration Department to determine 'condition, circumstances and character', and presumably to satisfy the Government that the applicant came within the Society's own definition of a deserving case: 'A burden to the British community in the Mother Country ... a support to it when transferred to the Colonies.'

Highland proprietors welcomed the Society with enthusiasm and relief (three of them sat on its committee). To judge from an interim report, they gladly paid for the opportunity to be rid of a people whom they wished to replace with sheep. 'The owners of the properties from which the emigrants depart will be expected, and, so far as they have been applied to they have not declined, to pay one-third of the sum disbursed by the Society towards the expenses of the emigration.' The remaining two-thirds were begged from the public which, as usual, responded with the generosity that should put Governments to shame, but never does. Quartermaster Sergeant Hoban of the 13th Light Infantry, for example, sent 4s. 2d., and there was 'A Widow's Mite of Twenty Shillings'. Highland soldiers abroad donated a day's pay, and Scots settlers already in Canada or Australia sent messages of encouragement with their collections. The Queen gave £300, and the Prince Consort £100. The Dukes of Sutherland, Argyll and Buccleuch each gave £100, and the Bishop of Argyll and the Isles sent ten shillings (but he did preach a sermon on the subject of emigration at St Matthew's, Spring Garden, and collected £36 1s. 11d. from his congregation).

In May 1853, five ships were placed at the disposal of the

Society by the Emigration Commissioners. The first to sail, two months later, was the *Georgiana* from Greenock for Melbourne. She carried 312 emigrants, most of them from Skye – 60 married men and women, 115 single men and women, 125 boys and girls, and 12 infants. Mr Chant, agent for the Commissioners, travelled with them to the Clyde from Skye (where, he said, 'it is not too much to say that many of the swine in England are better fed and better housed than are the poor of this island'). He assured the Commissioners that the *Georgiana* was

... one of the best emigrant ships I have seen. Her great height between decks, breadth of beam, and her excellent ventilation, render her the most desirable vessel of the service. Captain Temperly has put on board half a ton of oatmeal, in addition to the usual supply, to enable the people to have porridge for breakfast, for which they are very thankful. This is an arrangement of the greatest importance to Highland emigrants, and will, I have no doubt, prove very beneficial to the health of the passengers by this vessel.

Standish Haly, Secretary of the Society, went to Glasgow for the sailing of the ship. He told Trevelyan that the emigrants were 'exceedingly well-looking, even robust in appearance', and he was afraid that Chant, in selecting the people, had not realized that the Society wanted to relieve *destitution* by emigration. What Mr Haly did not realize was that Mr Chant, as an agent of the Government, was under obligation to send the able-bodied, not the sick, to the Colonies. Meeting the emigrants was a startling experience for Haly, and he was quite affected by their unrestrained emotions. He was also slightly shocked.

I should much have desired to have found a Gaelic clergyman who would have devoted himself to instruction on board, and also a more efficient matron for the girls. The person who is appointed to this post speaks not one word of Gaelic and wrung her hands at the girls' want of knowledge of the broadest Scots which she possesses in abundance. And as the young ladies, too, had generally never seen a plate, and have not as yet the refinements necessary to the more Lowland accomplishments of a knife, fork and spoon, her tribulations seem much increased at having such a charge.

I found, too, that there was a total want of books, and very few

Bibles on board; also a very general absence of hair-brushes and combs. These, to the best of my ability, I made provision for. I ordered Bethune and Macdonald to send down a plentiful supply of the latter articles immediately, and also a barber from this place to put the people's hair in order, and initiate them into the mysteries of combs and brushes.

Though the emigrants' ignorance of knives, forks, spoons and plates is hard to accept, the lack of Bibles was real enough. Before the *Georgiana* went down the Clyde, the Reverend Doctor Norman Macleod came aboard with a large supply of them, and also a hundred Psalm Books and three thousand religious tracts, all in the Gaelic. The emigrants sang Psalm 23 as they sailed. 'Cold indeed,' said the *Glasgow Constitutional*, 'must be the heart from which an earnest prayer ascends not to heaven, that God may be pleased to bring them in safety to the place of their destination, and prosper them in their undertakings.'

Australia was happy to welcome the emigrants, and those whom the Society sent later in the *Militiades*, the *John Gray*, the *Chance* and the *Flora*. They were offered immediate employment. On sheep-stations. These had been virtually deserted since the opening of the gold-diggings, and it was not only Australian flockmasters who were anxious for the Society to send more Highlanders. Yorkshire woollen manufacturers were alarmed by the thought of a failure in the supply of Australian wool. Few of them, however, thought it was their business to support the Society with money, even though Mr Bonamy Price, a member of the Committee and lately mathematics master at Rugby, wrote to them in a language they should have understood : 'I am making no appeal to your charity. I address you as a Yorkshire manufacturer deeply interested in procuring an adequate supply of wool from Australia. I venture to hope on [the Society's] behalf for the vigorous support of you and your brother capitalists, as an instrument pre-eminently adapted to accomplish your object.'

Since 1845, however, in Ross and in the Isles, the Great Cheviot Sheep had been making sure that its cousins in Australia would not want for drovers.

5

THE MASSACRE OF THE ROSSES

'I would have no place to take bread and cheese!'

THE MEN OF Strathcarron in Easter Ross had been out in the
Year of the Sheep, and their women had taken a stand across the
road at Culrain in 1820, when Sheriff Macleod came from Dingwall to serve writs of removal in Strath Oykel to the north.
Though the years since had emptied the glens of Ross-shire one
by one, and filled the ships for Pictou and Geelong, Strathcarron
in the parish of Kincardine had been left untouched by its laird.
It was a shallow green valley, an arm reaching westward from
the Kyle of Sutherland for nine miles and then clawing at the
escarpment of Bodach Mor with three fingers – the narrow
ravines of Strath Cuileannach, Strath Alladale and Glencalvie.
Down these ran three streams to make the black roll of the River
Carron. The land was divided into two estates, Greenyards which
formed most of the valley from its elbow to the Kyle, and Glencalvie where the waters of the ravines met on an *urlar*, a green
grass floor by the township of Amat.

Four to five hundred people lived in the strath, and their little
holdings were pinned to the shawl of the hills by brooches of
birch and oak. Most of them were Rosses or Munros by name,
though their *sennachie*, their bard and historian, was John Chisholm, a blind old man who lived at the mouth of the valley. Sitting at the door of his cottage in a blue coat with yellow buttons,
a Glengarry on his head, he told the people stories of their ancient
feuds with the Mackays. He said that there had been Rosses in
Strathcarron for five hundred years, and that they were the true
descendants of the Earls of Ross (though in any glen, anywhere
in Ross, an old man could be found to make the same claim).
Sixty men of Strathcarron, he said, soldiers with Lord Macleod's

Highlanders, had died in the great siege of Gibraltar when he was a boy. And he remembered those who had gone to Calabria and Egypt with Patrick Macleod of Geanies.

The people supported a poor teacher for the education of their children, and their minister was Gustavus Aird. His church was at Croick, a mile up Strath Cuileannach from the *urlar* of Glencalvie, and on a bend of the Black Water where an angle of hills breaks into the valley like the stem of a ship. It was, and is, little more than a grey stone cabin sheltered by wind-crippled trees, one of forty-two which Thomas Telford built in the Highlands for Parliament and eternity. A fierce and independent pride made the people of Strathcarron seem sullen to outsiders, and in Tain and Dingwall they were called 'The Philistines'. But they greeted each other in the old way, crying '*Failte duibh! Sith gun robh so!*' Welcome to you! Peace be here! Though they had as yet received no writs of removal, they had lived in dread of them for forty years. To the north, the south and the west, the Great Cheviot flocks were a sea surrounding them. Their rights by tradition had been taken from them. They were forbidden to graze their stock beyond their own pasturage. They could no longer take salmon from the Carron, hunt deer, shoot grouse or blackcock on the braes of Carn Mor. The right to slaughter these at their leisure had been purchased by a gentleman from Warwick and another from Lanark (who did not think they had a bargain, however, complaining to the laird's factor that the lodge was uninhabitable and that they were forced to stay at the inn of Ardgay). For centuries Highlanders had been free to take timber from the woods when it was needed to build a bridge or repair a house. In 1821 the people of Strathcarron lost that privilege too, when the laird imposed a fine of £20 upon them for stealing (as he called it) his trees. Since there was not that money in the strath, the minister paid the fine.

John Robertson, a southern journalist who reported the removals in Glencalvie for the *Glasgow National*, found the way of life in this little enclave both admirable and distasteful. 'Wonderful is the power of the affections which link human love to dark, dirty turf-huts with earthen floors and heather roofs, half kraals and half cow-sheds. All the cabins, with the exception of the stone cottages, filled me with disgust.' And he could not fit the people into a pattern of Victorian behaviour that might have given their savage virtues some value.

The Highlander's soul lives in the clan and family traditions of the past, the legends of the ingle, the songs of the bards. The master-idea of the English mind – the idea of Business – has not dawned on his soul, has not developed its peculiar virtues in his character. He is loyal but not punctual, honest but not systematic. The iron genius of economical improvements he knows not and heeds not.

The lairds of Strathcarron were the descendants of William Robertson, a seventeenth-century merchant from Inverness, a property dealer who bought himself the lands of Kindeace on Cromarty Firth. After Culloden the fifth laird acquired Strathcarron from a bankrupt Munro of Culrain. These Robertsons took commissions in the Sepoy regiments of the East India Company, in the Black Watch and the Ross-shire Buffs. They married into great Highland families, and were proud that their wives brought them the blood of Bruce, Plantagenet and Stuart. Their coat-of-arms was a red shield emblazoned with three silver wolves' heads, their crest was a right arm holding an imperial crown, and their motto claimed that glory was the reward of courage, in Latin of course. In 1842 another William Robertson, aged seventy-seven, was the sixth laird of Kindeace. A Justice of the Peace, he had ridden with the gentry in 1792, and in 1820 he had put his name to the bond by which all Ross-shire proprietors declared their loyalty to a mad old king and a profligate Regent. Not inappropriately, his wife had been a sister of The Chisholm who began the great clearing of Strathglass.

Old Kindeace came rarely to his land in Strathcarron, preferring a house in London to anything north of Highgate, but on one of the rare occasions when he did visit it he stopped at a cottage for food. The woman of the house spoke to him boldly as he sat at her door, and asked him if it were true that he intended to remove all the people in the glen. He said 'Far be it from me, you go on improving.' And he laughed. 'If I cleared Strathcarron I would have no place like this to take bread and cheese.' Toward the end of 1841 he instructed his factor to issue writs of removal on all the tenants of Glencalvie.

This factor was James Falconer Gillanders of Highfield, who had recently evicted twenty families from an estate he had bought for himself at Rosskeen. He was a hard and ambitious man, managing other property besides that of Kindeace (whose granddaughter he was later to marry). In Strathconon he drove out four hundred people, and when they took shelter in the Black Isle he drove them from there too. On 9 February 1842, obeying Robertson's instructions, he published an advertisement in the *Inverness Courier*:

FARMS TO BE LET ON

THE ESTATES

OF

GREENYARDS & GLENCALVIE

In the Parish of GLENCALVIE

The Sheep Walk of Greenyards presently possessed by Mr Alex. Munro.

The Sheep Walk of Glencalvie presently possessed by Mr Malcolm Mackay, etc.

The above farms will be let on Leases of such duration as may be agreed upon, with entry at the term of Whitsunday, 1842.

William Ross, Ground Officer at Bonar Bridge, will show the Farms in the Parish of Kincardine. Further particulars will be communicated by James F. Gillanders, Esq., Highfield by Beauly, to whom offers are to be addressed.

It was decided to proceed first against the sub-tenants at Glencalvie. If and when they went without trouble, then evictions at Greenyards would follow. Eighteen families, eighty-eight people, lived on the *urlar* in turf cabins indistinguishable from the brown hills, growing barley and oats, herding cattle and sheep on a total holding of no more than twenty acres. According to *The Times*, which sent a man there later: 'The most incredible rent of £55 10s. has been paid for the same land no farmer in England would give £15 for at the utmost.' Rents had been paid for generations without arrears, except for some weeks during the famine of 1836. The little community had no paupers on the poor roll, and the last relief given, said *The Times*, had been '5s. *a year* to a widow now dead, and 4s. 6d. a year to a sickly girl who was unable to do anything'.

I am told that not an inhabitant of this valley has been charged with any offence for years back. During the war it furnished many soldiers; and an old pensioner, 82 years of age, who has served in India, is now dying in one of the cottages where he was born.

Four tenants only were responsible for the rents of the property. The first was a Donald Macleod, an absentee who lived at Kingsburgh on the Isle of Skye. The others were of one family, David Ross and his son David, and Alexander Ross who may have been a brother or another son. Each was known (when the Law came to put their names to paper) as 'Ross alias *Greusaich*', meaning Shoemaker, and they had lived on the *urlar* for generations. The rest of the eighty-eight were relatives of these Rosses, cotters or squatters. The old pensioner, dying in his cottage, was Hugh Ross who claimed descent from Earl Farquhar, but most of the people, said John Robertson, 'do not know when their forefathers came there'.

Their cottages and holdings vary from huts in which the paupers of the community live without paying any rent, upward to the only stone cottage whose occupant pays a rental of about eight pounds a year. Of those who pay rent the highest pay eight pounds, the lowest two pound a year. Sixteen cottages pay rent, three cottages are occupied by old lone women who pay no rent, and who have a grace from the others for the grazing of a few goats or sheep by which they live. This self-working poor-law system is supported by the people themselves; the laird, I am informed, never gives anything to it. They are exceedingly attached to the glen. Their associations are all within it. Their affections – all the flower and beauty of their lives – are rooted, and grow like red buds of the coarse grass in the clefts of the rocks, out of their bare, bleak, wild mountain home. Their hearts are rooted to their hearths.

Since the Shoemakers were responsible to the laird for the

rent, collecting it from the others, they were also regarded as spokesmen and leaders of the community, and it was they who went to Gustavus Aird in February 1842, asking the minister what they should now do. Aird was a young man of twenty-eight, and new to the parish, but his influence over his congregation had been deep and strong since the first day of his arrival. He had come in a snowstorm thirteen months before, and before he entered his little manse by the Black Water he had led the people in the singing of a psalm of joy. Though he understood the bitterness of his parish, and shared it, he did not believe that Kindeace intended to turn the people out. Like Donald Sage, he had a weak admiration for the gentry, and would later prepare and publish a genealogy of the Robertson family.

On 14 March he wrote to James Gillanders, telling him that shortly after his induction he had been assured by Major Charles Robertson, the laird's heir, that 'so long as they paid the rent they were then paying, he would not think of turning out so many poor people, and I really think that if he were in the country that he would still be of the same feeling'. He reminded Gillanders that the tenants were ready to pay more rent, equal to any offer made by an outsider, if only they might remain.

If the offer of another is preferred, and theirs refused, these eighty-eight souls will then be set adrift, without knowing where to go or look for shelter. At home there is almost no prospect of their procuring any place; and to emigrate would prove to most of them but total misery, as, after reaching any of the colonies, they would not have the wherewithal to support themselves. . . . I sincerely hope that they will not be set adrift, but that the example of the Good Samaritan will be followed toward them.

Major Robertson was in Australia with his regiment. Old Kindeace was far south in London, and father and son were content to leave their affairs in Gillanders' hands. The factor sent Aird a brief reply on 21 March. He had, he said, given the people his 'tender consideration', and was prepared to leave them where they were, 'but only on the event of their giving a full rent for the farm, which I do not consider they pay at present.'

He invited them to compete in the bidding and, if they were successful, to give him security that the increased rents would be paid without arrears.

Aird read the letter to the Shoemakers, who told him that they were ready to pay the increase and asked him to arrange a meeting with Gillanders for the following Monday. But on the Friday before this, 25 March, before any answer had been received from the factor, Sheriff-Officers rode down the strath with writs of removal addressed to David Ross alias *Greusaich* Senior, David Ross alias *Greusaich* Junior, and Alexander Ross alias *Greusaich*, all tenants on the *urlar* of Glencalvie. By order of John Jardine, advocate and Sheriff of the shires of Ross and Cromarty, and by a statute of 1555 entitled *An Act Anent the Warning of Tenants*, the Shoemakers were ordered

To flit and Remove themselves, Bairns, Family, servants, subtenants, Cottars and dependants, Cattle, Goods, and gear forth and from possession of the said Subjects above described with the pertinents respectively occupied by them as aforesaid, and to leave the same void, redd and patent, at the respective terms of Removal above specified, that the Pursuer or others in his name may then enter thereto and peaceably possess, occupy and enjoy the same in time coming.

The Shoemakers were also warned that any attempt to oppose the officers in their duty would be punishable by a fine of £10, payable to Mr Robertson of Kindeace.

The Sheriff-Officers crossed the Black Water at the mouth of Strath Cuileannach and rode southward for a mile to where the land narrowed and the Carron and the Calvie came out of their glens to meet, and to hold between them the green and low ground that was the *urlar* of Glencalvie. To the south-west the hills rose abruptly to a brown peak known as the Cairn of the Sparrow-hawk. The only way to the *urlar* was by bridge across the Carron, and before this was gathered a crowd of women. Smoke, milk-white and sharply-scented, tumbled from a peat fire that had been lit by the bridge. The women smiled and called out to the officers, asking for the writs of removal, and when the papers were handed to them they threw them on the fire. The officers grinned, shrugged their shoulders and rode back to Tain.

Only Gustavus Aird realized that this was not the end of the affair, that the officers would come again, and with constables to enforce the writs. They would come as soon as fresh papers were prepared at Tain. He pleaded with the people. 'Receive the officers civilly,' he said, 'Say to them, Gentlemen by what hour must we be gone? Collect your cattle, your furniture, carry your sick, your children, and come in a body to the nearest town South. If you break the law you make it impossible for any like your minister to say a word for you. God bless you !'

On Monday there came Mr Cameron, Sheriff-Substitute, the Fiscal, Sheriff-Officers and a band of constables. They were met at the elbow of Strathcarron by Aird, who showed the Sheriff the letter he had received from Gillanders. Cameron was angry that the factor, after writing such a letter, 'should request me and these constables to serve the summonses'. But he had no power to reverse his instructions (nor, perhaps, did he think Gillanders' letter sincere), and he moved on, with Aird trudging unhappily by his side. Before they reached the Craigs, and crossed the Black Water on to the Amat property, they heard the shrill piping of whistles calling the people to the bridge over the Carron. It was cold, and it began to rain. Half a mile from the bridge a small group of men and women, armed with cudgels, watched the officers approach. 'We will use our sticks,' they said, but when they saw Gustavus Aird's familiar cloak they fell back. Both the Carron and the Calvie were in spate with the Spring thaw, meeting in a white and tumultuous embrace below the bridge. Before it stood a crowd of tenants from Glencalvie and Wester Greenyards, and the smoke of another fire was held to the ground by the heavy rain. The Sheriff-Substitute (exaggerating no doubt, in the manner of defeated generals) said that there were two hundred people gathered there to deforce his officers. He said that most of them were women, and in this he was probably right.

As the riders approached the bridge the tenants shouted to Aird, telling him to leave the officers. They were angry and disappointed. 'You have no business in such company!' they said. When officers and tenants joined there was a confused, sliding mêlée on the muddy road. A woman grasped Cameron's plaid to pull him from his horse, but released it when Aird shouted 'He's not a constable, he's the Sheriff. Don't lay hands on him!' The Sheriff-Substitute had the Gaelic too, and he pushed forward, shouting for silence. When he could be heard, he said, 'I greatly regret that so many people should be turned adrift, but by resisting the law you are only injuring yourselves. If you'll receive the summonses, after writing such a letter to Mr Aird, Mr Gillanders could not show his face if he turned you out.' The crowd laughed, and Cameron raised his voice. 'I don't believe you'll be turned out, and I'll do all I can to prevent it, if you'll take the summonses and not break the law!'

Despite their intention to hold the bridge by force if necessary, the tenants were in good humour, and the Sheriff-Substitute dismounted and walked among them. One took his arm and pointed to the river. 'What shall I do if I'm turned out,' he asked. 'Shall I lay my sick wife and children in that?' With the Fiscal, the Sheriff moved closer to the bridge, shouting 'Let me cross!' But the people held his arms and laughed again, pointing once more to the Carron. 'Shall we throw him in that? Let's see how well he can swim.'

But they let Gustavus Aird cross to the *urlar*, telling him to take shelter from the rain in a cottage. Angrily, the Sheriff-Substitute ordered up the constables with the summonses. John Robertson was told that the women mocked the officers, pretending they were lovers come to a tryst.

Some say the women took affectionately the hand of a constable, held the summonses in the hand clasped in rough dalliance, and applied the lighted peat to the end of the summons, and as the flames advanced up the paper the fingers of the constables themselves pushed forward the summonses to a state of tinder. According to other accounts the women simply burned the papers. But as there would be a struggle for the summonses it seems most probable they were destroyed whenever an edge of them appeared in the grasp of the constables. On coming forward, the Sheriff ordered the constables forward, the people blocked up the way, and the functionaries of the law retired, having, it is said, sustained no further injury than a wound on a hat.

Fiscal, Sheriff, constables and officers, retreated to a game-keeper's cottage on the Amat property near the mouth of Strath Cuileannach. The whole business had been more ludicrous than dangerous. His pride hurt by the refusal of his offer of help, Cameron decided to secure evidence against the ringleaders, if he could determine who the ringleaders were. He asked the game-keeper for the name of a man in a white hat whom he had seen with the tenants. The gamekeeper, having no wish to offend his neighbours or the law, said that he had seen no one in a white hat 'but Mr Andrew Ross the Justice of Peace Clerk'. And had he seen a woman with a stick in her hand? He had. For what purpose, did he think? 'I cannot say. It might have been a support for her corset.'

So the Law went back to Tain, and contented itself for the time being with a peremptory demand that the young people of Glencalvie should come down to the town to be examined before magistrates. They sent a cheerful reply. They would indeed come, if Mr Jardine would give them an assurance that they would not be put in 'the sharp-pointed house', the old Tolbooth with its spired cap.

And there, surprisingly, the matter rested. No more officers came to Glencalvie that year, or in the year following. Perhaps James Gillanders, acknowledging the tactical error of his letter to Aird (which was now public knowledge), decided that it would be foolish to insist upon evictions at this moment. Perhaps old Kindeace, on his death-bed in Hackney, wanted nothing immediate on his conscience when he was so close to Judgment. The Major, his heir, was too far away in Australia to make his wishes quickly known to the factor.

In 1843 the Disruption of the Church of Scotland emptied parish churches throughout the Highlands as men turned their backs on what was unashamedly the religion of Improvement, Clearances, Sheep and the Lairds. In many districts there was riot and the marching of soldiers to enforce the appointment of unwanted ministers. Landowners refused to grant sites for the building of Free Churches, and in Sutherland they were forbidden altogether. In Strathcarron Gustavus Aird took all but two families of his parish with him when he left the Establishment for the Free Church. Thomas Telford's greystone church at Croick was left empty, and without a minister. Aird preached to his people on the hillside, and later in a wool-shed offered him by a farmer of Rosemount.

And in 1844 William Robertson, fifth laird of Kindeace, died and was buried in Homerton Cemetery. Now Gillanders, acting with the authority and approval of the Australian absentee, ordered the three Shoemakers to meet him at Tain. They went in the belief that their offer to pay a new rent had been accepted, but once in Tain they were each handed a writ of removal, and this time there were no women present to burn them. Pleased with the little stratagem, Gillanders magnanimously told the Rosses that they might have until the following spring to flit and remove peacefully. Their stock would be taken at his valuation (he thought that £100 would be adequate) and they were free to take away the timber of their houses, 'which is really worthless,' said John Robertson, 'except for firewood'. The Rosses sadly accepted the writs, and their acceptance was noted and attested by the Witnesses appointed by Sheriff Jardine. They promised to lay down no crops that year, and the two tacksmen of Strathcarron, Munro and Mackay, became bound for their good behaviour until they were gone.

All over the county of Ross the people were again in wretched movement. It would have surprised James Gillanders to learn that the eviction of eighty-eight people from the *urlar* of Glencalvie would shortly be given wider publicity and cause greater concern than the four hundred sub-tenants he was at that moment driving from Strathconon to the Black Isle.

'James has shown his nature, a brutal chamberlain'

IN THE SPRING of 1845 John Delane, Editor of The Times, received a letter from Charles Spence, Solicitor before the Supreme Court of Scotland. On behalf of a committee of northern gentlemen who had appointed him their spokesman, Mr Spence wished the newspaper to publish the following advertisement:

CLEARING THE HIGHLANDS OF MEN

GLENCALVIE — NINETY ROSS-SHIRE COTTAGERS REMOVED WITHOUT HOUSES WHERE TO TAKE SHELTER. The following sums have already been received for the Relief of these Poor People. It is hoped that they may yet be saved from the necessity of encamping in the CHURCHYARD, as the aged could not be expected to survive the effects of exposure to damp and cold in such a situation, especially labouring as they are under heavy depression of spirits produced by expulsion from the land of their fathers, where for centuries they have been located. It is earnestly entrusted the Subscriptions will be liberal, and that the sympathy of the public will yet help to cheer the sufferers amidst their cloudy prospects.

The 'following sums' amounted to £37 2s., contributed by nineteen people including the Earl of Buchan, an East India Company general, Two Ladies, A Young Man, a Friend, and, of course, A Widow. Mr Spence was treasurer of the fund, and his committee of eight was headed by Gustavus Aird who may, perhaps, have been responsible for its formation.

Delane had no intention of publishing the notice without first satisfying himself that the facts were true and the cause genuine. He knew, also, that if ninety people were about to be abandoned in a churchyard this was too good a story to be buried among the advertisements on the front page of his paper. Highland destitution was at this time a running story, but The Times had not as yet given it its Olympian attention. Delane had perhaps been waiting for a dramatic opportunity to make a thorough examination of it through the dispatches of one of his 'Special Commissioners', those anonymous and often amateur feature-writers who were one of his greatest contributions to journalism. He wrote to Spence immediately, saying that he would 'send down a gentleman of experience and talent', and this Spence joyfully reported to his committee. The Commissioner whom Delane sent was a lawyer whose name has survived on no record.* He left for Scotland in the second week of May, and took his lodgings in the Inn of Ardgay at the mouth of Strathcarron. His reports, brave, compassionate and angry, brought the reality of eviction and improvement to the breakfast tables of the nation. The opening words of his first dispatch (written at the Inn and filling two columns of *The Times*) were pitched on a note of indignation that was sustained throughout.

Those who remember the misery and destitution into which large masses of the population were thrown by the systematic 'clearances' (as they are here called) carried on in Sutherlandshire some 25 years ago under the direction and on the estate of the late Marchioness of Stafford – those who have not forgotten to what an extent the ancient ties which bound clansmen to their chiefs were then torn asunder – will regret to learn that the heartless course, with all its sequences of misery, of destitution, and of crime, is again being resorted to in Ross-shire.

He had arrived in time to witness the departure of the Glencalvie people. At the end of April the Shoemakers had gone to Tain to see the Kindeace law agent, Donald Stewart, and to learn from him what compensation they might expect for their stock, and what arrangements, if any, had been made for their resettlement. They were told that each family would receive £18 'as their distributive of the £72 10s. agreed to be given to them to emigrate on going out peaceably.' It was the first they had heard that the laird wished them to emigrate, and they were

---

*Though admitting that there is no proof, the Librarian of *The Times* today suggests that this man may have been Thomas Campbell Foster, a legal writer who was called to the Bar in 1846. In that year, twelve months after Glencalvie, Delane sent him to Ireland as a Special Commissioner, with instructions to report the famine and destitution there.

given little reason to hope for resettlement elsewhere on the Kindeace estates.

When Gustavus Aird took *The Times* man down to the glen, all the cottages on the *urlar* were empty with the exception of one, and in this Hugh Ross, the pensioner, was dying. The rest of the people were seated on a green brae by the Carron, 'the women all neatly dressed in net caps and wearing scarlet or plaid shawls; the men wearing their blue bonnets and having their shepherds' plaids wrapped about them. This was their only covering, and this was the Free Church. There was a simplicity extremely touching in this group on the bare hillside, listening to the Psalms of David in their native tongue and assembled to worship God.' They sang Psalm 145: *The eyes of all things wait on Thee, The Giver of all good....* In the Parliamentary church at Croick *The Times* man was shown the two families who had not followed their neighbours into the Free Church, ten men, women and children holding a service in English and the Gaelic. 'And for what are all these people to be reduced from comfort to beggary?' he asked.

For what is this virtuous and contented community to be scattered and driven into destitution? I confess I can find no answer. It is said that the factors would rather have one tenant than many, as it saves them trouble. But so long as the rent is punctually paid, as this has been, it is contrary to all experience to suppose that one large tenant will pay more than many small ones, or that a sheep walk can pay more rent than cultivated land. Now, no doubt there is an object in driving off the people – namely fear of the New Scotch Poor Law compelling the heritors to pay toward the support of those who cannot support themselves.

He was wrong in assuming that sheep-walks could produce no more profit than cultivated land in the Highlands, but there was great truth in his charge that the proprietors were reluctant to pay their proposed share under the Poor Laws. The less people on their lands, the less their financial responsibility in the growing destitution. The laird of Kindeace, said the Commissioner, 'NEVER GAVE ONE FARTHING, the poor supported their own helpless poor, the wealthy let them do so unassisted'.

That weekend the only refuge for the people was the one that had been feared by Mr Spence and his committee, the churchyard at Croick, a little walled enclosure sheltered by a few bent trees. Although it was May, the weather was wet and cold.

Behind the church, a long kind of booth was erected, the roof formed of tarpaulin stretched over poles, the sides closed in with horsecloths, rugs, blankets and plaids ... Their furniture, excepting their bedding, they got distributed amongst the cottages of their neighbours; and with their bedding and their children they all removed on Saturday afternoon to this place. In my last letter I informed you that they had been round to every heritor and factor in the neighbourhood, and 12 of the 18 families had been unable to find places of shelter. With the new Scotch Poor Law in prospect, cottages were everywhere refused to them.

I am told it was a most wretched spectacle to see these poor people march out of the glen in a body, with two or three carts filled with children, many of them mere infants; and other carts containing their bedding and their requisites. The whole countryside was up on the hills watching them as they silently took possession of their tent.

A fire was kindled in the churchyard, round which the poor children clustered. Two cradles with infants in them, were placed close to the fire, and sheltered round by the dejected-looking mothers. Others busied themselves into dividing the tent into compartments, by means of blankets for the different families. Contrasted with the gloomy dejection of the grown-up and the aged was the, perhaps, not less melancholy picture of the poor children thoughtlessly playing round the fire, pleased with the novelty of all around them.

There were twenty-three children in the churchyard, all under the age of ten, and seven of them were ill. There were also some young and unmarried men and women, but most of the refugees were over forty. Aird called them to him, and told them that his companion was an Englishman who had come from a great newspaper in the south. They crowded about *The Times* man, shaking his hand. 'Their Gaelic I could not understand,' he told Delane, 'but their eyes beamed with gratitude. This unbought, spontaneous and grateful expression of feeling to you for being their friend is what their natural protector – their chieftain – never saw, and what his factor need never hope for.' He admired their dignity and their pride, but believing, like most of his Scott-fed generation, in the fierce spirit of the Highlander, he was puzzled by their docility. Yet this too was admirable. 'Were any such clearances attempted in England, I leave you to conceive the excitement which it would be certain to create, the mob procession, the effigy burning, the window-smashing . . .'

Within a week the churchyard was empty. Where the people went, to what southern town or what emigrant colony is not known. The six families, for whom Gillanders claimed he had found resettlement, were followed by *The Times* man. David Ross and his son, *Greusaich* Senior and Junior, 'got a piece of black moor near Tain, 25 miles off, without any house or shed on it, out of which they hope to obtain subsistence'. Another old man was given a small lot at Edderton, and these three alone received anything from which they might confidently expect to get the barest of livings. The other three families were given turf huts near Bonar Bridge. 'The rest are hopeless, helpless.'

The Commissioner moved on from Glencalvie to see and to report more of Highland destitution which, he said, was the result of 'a cold, calculating heartlessness which is almost as incredible as it is disgusting'.

One man, a respectable miller whose father, and grandfather before him, had rented a mill of one of the heritors in this neighbourhood (Fodderty parish in Ross), having taken the part of a poor woman who was ejected from her holding to make room for some improvements, and who on applying to her landlord to do something for her was beaten and driven from the door by him *with a stick*, walked 10 miles yesterday to tell me his own case. In the midst of a winter's night, with deep snow on the ground, he and his aged mother were suddenly turned out of his house under a decreet of removal, and his mother is now bed-ridden from the consequences.

In one of his dispatches he quoted a letter he had received from a Free Church minister of Ross:

Nothing short of a visit to this quarter and conversation with the poor creatures themselves could give an idea of the misery and wretchedness to which the people of this parish are reduced by the heartless and cruel tyranny of their oppressors. Here there is a kind of slavery ten times worse than that which for so long disgraced Britain. The poor are starving, and yet so much afraid are the people (who are tenants-at-will) of being removed, that lately I could get none to sign as witnesses to the petition of a pauper who required relief from the heritors and the Kirk Sessions. They said if their names were seen as witnesses, how clamant ever the case, they were sure of being thrown upon the wide world at next term. I have a list in my possession of from 50 to 60 who since the Disruption were turned away from houses and lands, and service and employment, by an heritor of this parish because they would not become residuaries and denounce the Free Church.

The immediate result of these *Times* dispatches was that Mr Spence's committee for the relief of Glencalvie people was encouraged to grow into 'The Society for the Protection of the Poor'. Its life was brief, and no more than *The Times* could it prevent the successive waves of evictions which continued for another ten years, and which threatened to make all the Highlands one great sheep-walk. The Society was formed at a public meeting held in the Waterloo Rooms, Edinburgh, at the beginning of June, under the chairmanship of Sir David Brewster, philosopher, physicist, a one-time licensed preacher and the inventor of the kaleidoscope. After the singing of Psalm 41 (*Blessed is he that wisely doth the poor man's case consider!*), Mr Spence told the meeting that there were now 200,000 paupers or destitute persons in Scotland, and that he thought (as in the case of Glencalvie) 'a collection might be raised throughout the country on their behalf, for the purpose of providing them with coals and candles and other necessaries in which they might stand need.' He was followed by other speakers, most of them ministers of the Free Church, and the Reverend Mr Begg was answered by prolonged applause when he asked if it were not true that the landlords 'proposed to extirpate the people because they would not be as quiet as sheep'.

The meeting concluded with a resolution that although they might not 'be able to secure for the people of Glencalvie the restoration of their farms, they might be able to prevent another Glencalvie affair from rising'. They were, of course, hopelessly optimistic. James Gillanders and other factors, the lairds they represented, were no more worried by The Society for the Protection of the Poor than they were disturbed by Parliament when it considered the Ross-shire evictions at the end of May. Answering a question, the Home Secretary, Sir James Graham, said that his attention had been directed to reports (in *The Times*) 'that four hundred tenants in the shires of Ross and Cromarty, including with their families probably four thousand persons, had been served with summonses of removal'. While he condemned such proceedings, he hoped that the reports were exaggerated. If anything, said the *Inverness Courier*, they were an understatement. In July, Graham was asked again for his comments, and this time he bored the House with a long communication from the Lord Advocate of Scotland in which his lordship, leaning heavily on the side of the proprietors, said that while he did not approve of wholesale removals either, the reports were indeed greatly exaggerated.

And by now the famine in Ireland was holding everybody's fascinated attention.

One silent voice during the evictions in Glencalvie had been that of the Chief of Clan Ross, Mr Ross of Pitcalnie, whose father or grandfather had acquired the title when Admiral Lockhart inherited the lands of Balnagowan. Pitcalnie held a house and land at Amat, between Strath Cuileannach and Strath Allandale. The tenants on the *urlar* were his most immediate neighbours, and while *The Times* Commissioner said that his wife 'is spoken of as doing much good to the poor', Mr Ross was an absentee laird and rarely came to the land of his forefathers, except when the shooting was good. He, however, has an enduring monument in Strathcarron today, an eroded obelisk against the railings of which sheep are inclined to scratch their backs. The bards of the Rosses made no complaint against this Pitcalnie, but of Gillanders they said

> James has shown his nature,
> that he is a brutal chamberlain
> like his grandfather before,
> wasting and stripping the poor.

He is a poor creature, without responsibility,
without honour, understanding or shame.
An unpleasant boor, he will be
doubly judged for driving
away the Rosses of Glencalvie.

When they took shelter in the graveyard at Croick, some of
the people scratched their names and brief messages on the
diamond-paned windows of the church. They wrote in English,
as if acknowledging that their own tongue would pass with them
and would not be understood in time. The words they wrote are
still there:

'Glencalvie people was in the church here May 24, 1845 ...
Glencalvie people the wicked generation.... John Ross shepherd
... Glencalvie people was here ... Amy Ross ... Glencalvie is a
wilderness blow ship them to the colony.... The Glencalvie
Rosses ...

'A singular, perverted feeling of insubordination'

WHEN James Gillanders decided that he could now complete
the clearance of Strathcarron by evicting the remainder of
its sub-tenants from his father-in-law's property at Greenyards,
no Times Commissioner came north to report the bloody result,
and nothing was heard from The Society for the Protection of the
Poor, if it still existed. The indignation of Press and Public, in
their concern for oppressed minorities, was directed against Tsar
Nicholas I, upon whom war was declared three days before thirty-
five constables from Dingwall and Fort William broke the skulls
and kicked the breasts of the women of Strathcarron. But for
one man, little would have been heard of this obscene affray before it was quickly disposed of by Lord Justice-Clerk Hope and
the Northern Circuit Court of Justiciary in September (when,
in any case, Scotland was more anxious to hear how many
Russians the Black Watch was killing in the Crimea, than to
know how many Highland women had been maimed by constables' truncheons in Ross-shire).

This man was Donald Ross, a Glasgow lawyer who left little record of himself but his writings on the evictions and a list of his addresses in the Glasgow Directory (the earliest being Brunswick Place in 1849). He was a Highlander by his name, and although it is a common enough one he may have been the Donald Ross of Dornoch who collected money for Mr Spence's Glencalvie fund in 1845. He had friends in Ross-shire, and it was in answer to their letters that he left Glasgow at the beginning of April and arrived in Strathcarron within ten days of its invasion by the Law. What he was told by the people there, what he saw, he put into long letters to the *Northern Ensign*, and when the editor baulked at printing all of them he published them himself, a pamphlet form with a trumpet-challenge for a title.

The Russians of Ross-shire
or
THE MASSACRE OF THE ROSSES
in
Strathcarron, Ross-shire
by
policemen when serving the
tenants in Strathcarron with
summons of Removal in March
Also a warning against
THE CLEARING OF THE GLENS

'Talk of secret diplomacy,' he said, 'and Russian intrigue and aggression forsooth! Are not whole straths and districts bargained for, and quietly let to some rich sheep-farmer and sportsman months before the unhappy occupants know about it!'

Some such secret agreement, he claimed, had been reached by Gillanders, Major Robertson of Kindeace, and Alexander Munro the tacksman of Greenyards soon after the Glencalvie removals. To prevent disquiet, or outside interest such as the troublesome curiosity of John Delane, they proposed to clear the property piecemeal, one tenant and his dependants at a time. Since there were four tenants only on the rent-book (though close to four hundred people in all) it was hoped that the evictions would be executed quietly and efficiently within four years. But, said Donald Ross, 'Munro who had up to this period remained a frigid bachelor, now married a young girl next door to him, and this interesting business occupied his attention so much that for the last three or four years he forgot to give the necessary instructions to his law agent.' Though he had the facts correct, Ross had got the wrong principal. The frigid bridegroom was James Gillanders who, in 1852 and at the age of forty-one, married Kindeace's daughter, Margaret.

The area to be cleared was a long, green stretch on both banks of the Carron, eastward from its second bend to the low ground at Gledfield by the mouth of the strath. Here the river flows more slowly than at the mountain angle of Glencalvie, turning in black coils about flat meadows. The hills above it are gentle and brown. The people, who lived in turf and stone townships at calling distance, had uneasy memories of Glencalvie. Some could remember Culrain thirty-four years before, and there were a few whose memories stretched as far back as The Year of the Sheep. In the early weeks of 1854, when rumours that they were to be evicted at the next term grew stronger, they talked of resistance, and in their determination to burn the papers and deforce the officers the women, as always, were stronger than the men. As the snow-line receded up Bodach Mor look-outs were placed on Ardgayhill, young boys and girls to watch the firthside run of the Tain road, and others to guard the drove-path that came down the Great Pass from Alness. Among these children were two or three men, armed with guns which they were to fire as soon as the officers were seen approaching.

Early in March Alexander Munro left his house at Braelangwell, on the north bank of the Carron opposite Wester Greenyards, for a secret (he thought) meeting in Tain with Gillanders and Kindeace's law-agent Stewart. Between them they decided on the day of delivery for the summonses. When Munro returned, the sub-tenants called on him and asked him for an assurance that he was not planning their removal. 'Calling his Maker to witness,' said Donald Ross, 'he declared that he had not authorized anyone to apply for warrants in his name.' And when they later pressed him to disprove the rumours they heard, he again invited Heaven to judge him if he lied.

Satisfied with this solemn oath, and believing that the tacksman would support them, the women ran from their houses on Tuesday, 7 March, answering the warning of hilltop whistles. Two hundred yards from Braelangwell, they halted Sheriff-Officer William Macpherson and his Witness, Peter Mackenzie, a constable. According to the evidence both men gave in September before the Court of Justiciary, they were attacked by 'a mob or a number of disorderly persons', who threw them on the ground, burnt their papers, stripped them of their clothes and drove them four miles down the strath to Bonar Bridge. Donald Ross, closer to the event, was told a different story :

The females laid hold of Macpherson, searched his pockets and took the summons from him, and burnt them. They made no attack whatever but treated him very gently; and one or two of the men who came up after the summonses were burnt went with him and with his assistant 'Peter' to the Inn at Ardgay and treated them to refreshments and some spirits.

It probably was a gentle, even humorous affair, but if it happened as Ross said it was not something that a Sheriff-Officer would care to admit to before a court. Two weeks later another attempt to deliver the summonses was made by a heavily-whiskered Preventive Officer called Dugald MacCaig, and his two assistants. Ross said that they were merely drunk, and that they sallied out of the Ardgay Inn and down the strath shouting that they were 'sheriff officers on their way to warn out the tenants of Greenyards', just for the joy of it. But in court later they were acknowledged as officers authorized to carry the writs. Whatever they were they, too, were met by women gathered by the whistles. They lost some of their courage then.

'One of them,' said Ross, 'a long, ugly-looking fellow with huge moustacheos, confessed that they were only practising a small bit of imposition on the excited people and begged to be let away as they were excisemen.' But the women, who were enjoying the encounter as much as the drunkards had hoped to, solemnly protested that this could not be so, for no excisemen would practise such a cruel trick. MacCaig offered them money which they gave back to him. Then he was fool enough to pull out a pistol, and a boy 'seeing the gauger's pistol levelled at his mother's head, took out an old, rusty pistol he had for frightening away crows, and told the gauger that if he dare meddle with his mother he must stand the consequences'. The excisemen ran from Strathcarron, and when they reached Tain they told a story of riot and deforcement and retreat before heavy odds. In this account, and a later one which MacCaig gave to the *Glasgow Herald*, they appeared to be very noble fellows indeed. 'Accordingly,' said Ross ... 'private meetings were held in Tain, the great heads of the evicting firms and the great sheep lords consulted together, and it was resolved upon to go to the district with a strong police force in order, as they said, to uphold the majesty of the Law, and to strike terror if not into the hearts at any rate into the skulls of the opposing females.'

These meetings, if they took place, were probably organized by the Kindeace law-agent. Certainly he insisted that when the writs of removal were again sent to Strathcarron they should be accompanied by a large body of officers and constables. And so it was. Early in the morning of Friday, 31 March, while it was still dark, twenty Ross-shire constables and fifteen from Inverness marched from Dingwall under the command of Superintendent Cumming of that town, and of Superintendent Mackay of Fort William. They came over the hills from Alness and down the Great Pass to Midfearn where they waited two hours for the arrival of Sheriff-Substitute Taylor of Tain, the Procurator Fiscal, and Donald Stewart the law-agent.

After several bottles of ale, porter and whisky had been drunk, and the roll called, the police stood in a row and the sheriff administered the oath to them. Between Sheriff, Fiscal, Law Agent, Jehus and policemen, there were more than 40 men convened in this place on that dark and dismal morning, binding themselves under a great curse like the wicked Jews of old, that they would *eat* nothing until they had maltreated the women of Greenyard. It is presumed, however, that they excluded from the oath all reference to *drink*, for they brought with them large baskets full of alcoholic liquors, of which they drank copiously.

By seven o'clock, in a water-colour dawn of blue and milky grey, the 'baton brigade', as Ross called them, entered Strathcarron by Gledfield. They heard firing from the hill above them, and whistles blowing, but Sheriff Taylor put his head out of his carriage and told them to be of easy mind, this was the Rosses' usual method of warning. Four miles down the glen, as they came through a wood by the march of Greenyard, their road was blocked by sixty or seventy women, with a dozen or less men standing behind them. The women had drawn their red shawls over their heads, and were waiting silently.

Taylor, the Fiscal and Stewart got down from the carriage and walked to the head of the police. Taylor shouted to the women in Gaelic and told them that they must clear the way for the Law, and when they did not move he took out the Riot Act and began to read it.* Now the women shouted that Alexander Munro the tacksman had denied all knowledge of warrants issued in his name, and they pressed forward on the constables. Taylor thrust the Riot Act into his pocket, struck the ground angrily with his stick and looked over his shoulder to the police superintendents. 'Clear the way!' he ordered. Several of the women later said that he added: 'Knock them down!'

The constables went forward with their truncheons lifted, and, according to the *Inverness Courier* (which got the information from Taylor), the Strathcarron men immediately ran for the hills, leaving their women alone. Although some men must have remained, for two were injured and one was later charged, the absence of all the others is hard to condone, as it was at Culrain, Gruids and elsewhere. The assault of the police was short, brutal and bloody. The *Courier*, again reporting Taylor perhaps, said that there were three hundred women there, and that they were armed with sticks and stones. If they were, they were remarkably inefficient in the use of them, for no policeman suffered more

---

* Ross claimed that the Riot Act was neither produced nor read.

than a bruise or a dented hat. 'The police struck with all their force,' said Ross, '... not only when knocking down, but after the females were on the ground. They beat and kicked them while lying weltering in their blood. Such was the brutality with which this tragedy was carried through, that more than twenty females were carried off the field in blankets and litters, and the appearance they presented, with their heads cut and bruised, their limbs mangled and their clothes clotted with blood, was such as would horrify any savage.'

Twenty women and girls were seriously wounded in the baton charge, and Ross interviewed all or most of them, putting their names and their injuries, the words that they said and the oaths that answered them into his letters. Christy Ross, aged fifty and the wife of John Ross at Greenyard, one of the four tenants to be warned out, stood in front of the women when the police came. 'She was for showing the Sheriff a letter, signed by Munro and addressed to Major Robertson, denying that he had ever authorized these removals.' She was immediately struck by three constables, knocked down by their sticks, kicked on the back of the head and, as she rolled over in pain, kicked again by nailed boots on the face, the breasts and the shoulders. 'Reason had been thrown completely off her seat,' wrote Ross sadly, 'and the victim is now insane, in short a maniac.'

When Ann Ross, a woman of forty, was knocked down she cried out 'Murder!' and another constable, coming up, said, 'I'll put you from crying!' and he beat her as she lay on the ground. Margaret Ross, the youngest daughter of Thomas Ross, tenant at Amat-na-tuath at the far end of the glen, defended herself with her fists. She was struck three violent blows on the breast with truncheons, and she staggered from the road to the field by the Carron, pursued by constables. She hid in a thorn-bush but the police kicked at her head until she crawled out.

The police now proceeded to put handcuffs on her, one of them actually kneeled on her breasts while adjusting and holding up her hands, while another put them in irons. Margaret had no corset on at the time, and nothing intervened between her flesh and the hard ash batons of the police but her shift and thin cotton morning gown.

Another Margaret Ross had her head split by two great wounds, and she was struck again when she fell. Losing a great deal of blood, she was taken in irons to Tain Gaol. 'Alienation of the mental faculties very perceptible,' reported Ross with clinical detail, 'headaches, vomitings, cold and sudden perspiration.' Elizabeth, her sister, was also knocked down and kicked on the breasts. The batons left a deep cut, 3¾ inches long on her head, tore away part of her scalp and shattered the frontal and parietal bones. The marks of hobnails, said Ross, remained on her breasts and shoulders for days. She was, or had been, a tall and pretty woman, but now 'her long hair, clotted with blood, could be seen in quantities all over the ploughed land.' Ross said she died later.* Another sister, Janet, running forward to protect Elizabeth, was struck on the shins and 'then the policemen rolled her over into the ploughed land and there she was with her face in the earth and the blood gushing from the wounds in her head and shoulders.'

Broken by the baton charge, the women ran up the brae, pursued by the stumbling, swearing constables, who caught at hair, arms and legs, throwing the women down and beating them. Margaret Macgregor Ross, a woman of forty-seven and the mother of seven children, was hit on the shoulder and then on the left ear. Her skull was broken, said Donald Ross, and she died later, 'as cruelly murdered as if a policeman had shot her on the links at Tain'. Ann Ross of Hilton by Langwell, a spinster of fifty-six, 'had no more thought of resisting the police than she has at this moment of going to join the insurgents in Greece. Her linen cap was riddled with blows, her blue derry gown torn to ribbons. Her elbow was broken. Had she been attacked in a den of tigers she could not have been in a worse state.'

The wife of William Ross *Greusaich* (a cousin of the Glencalvie Shoemakers) was on the other side of the river when she 'heard the awful moaning and groaning of the bleeding and wounded

---

*Donald Ross of Letchworth, her grand-nephew, tells me that in fact she survived these incredible injuries. He remembers her in her extreme old age.

females'. She waded through the Carron where it was knee-deep, tearing her apron into strips for bandages. Two constables charged her, and she ran from them, stumbling across ditches and drains. The policemen struck her on the shoulders, the head and the back, but she continued to run until she fell into the river. The water carried her down toward Gledfield, where her husband (one wonders where he had been all this time) pulled her out.

Catherine Ross also came over the ford to help the wounded. She was the young wife of a tenant at Langwell. Two policemen seized her as she came out of the water, and she fought with them. They knocked her down with a stone, and one constable put a knee on her breast as he tugged a pair of handcuffs from his pocket. 'Leave her alone,' said the other. 'She's dead.' But she was not, and when they were gone she crawled into the bushes. Grace Ross, the daughter of a cotter at Ca-dearg, was well-known for 'her clean and tidy appearance as well as for her good conduct and amiable disposition'. A policeman 'struck her a savage blow with his baton on the forehead, which felled her as if a cannon-ball had gone through her heart'. When she recovered, she was attacked again, and she ran into the river and stood there, blood running from her forehead to the water. Naomi Ross, another young girl, 'was most violently kicked on the breasts and also in the most delicate part of her person. Had poor Naomi been wandering on the banks of the Danube and been ill-used there, I could understand it; but in Christian Scotland to be butchered alive, who can think of it without a blush of shame?'

And so it went on. Ann Munro, 'a stout and active woman of Cornhill by Langwell', twisted a baton from one constable's hand and pitched it into the Carron. Pursued by three others, she swam across the river. Helen Ross, of Wester Greenyards 'was brought home on a litter, and for the space of eight days thereafter she could not move her hands or feet'.

Two men and two boys seem to have been all the male population to stand with the women. Donald Ross, sixty-eight and a Waterloo veteran, was beaten down by batons and kicked as he lay on the ground. 'The old man declares that although he was at nine battles on the Continent he never saw such treatment of wounded soldiers or prisoners of war as he saw of the helpless and inoffensive women of Greenyards.' There were two 'poor lads', George and Donald Ross, who went to help the women and were quickly knocked down. A policeman from Inverness, a Maclean or a MacLaren, stood over the boy yelling obscenities, '*Marbh as am b – r righinn dubh!*'. David Munro, a man from Culrain, gave the police the only serious resistance they had to meet. He was attacked by three constables. Struck on the head by the first 'he seized the policeman by the waist and pitched him five yards', and then the other two beat him into insensibility.

Then it was over. Sheriff, Fiscal, law-agent and police marched over the bloody earth and executed their summonses. They refreshed themselves with whisky in the house of Alexander Munro, and went back to Tain, dragging with them four women who, to give the dirty little affair some dignity, were referred to as 'ring-leaders in the riot and mobbing'. They were: Margaret Ross, twenty-five, daughter of Alexander Ross, Amat-natuath; Margaret Ross, eighteen, daughter of Thomas Ross, Amat-natuath; Christy Ross, fifty, wife of John Ross, Greenyard; and Ann Ross, forty, Greenyard. Two days later, upon the intercession of Gustavus Aird and others, including Dr Gordon, who came from Tain to care for the injured, the women were released on bail.

The *Northern Ensign*, though it was an opponent of evictions, shared its readers' refusal to believe all that Donald Ross wrote in his reports. 'We think it right to state,' said the editor in a postscript, 'that we have considerably modified some of the statements in the foregoing, as they represent the conduct of the Sheriff and its results in such a light as to be almost incredible, and require the strongest testimony before our readers could be induced to read them.' No more than any journalist then or since, Donald Ross could do little against sub-editorial caution and scepticism, but he took with him from Strathcarron ghoulish relics of the battle, 'patches or scalps of skin with the long hair adhering to them',* which to his mind were testimony enough. 'Dirty work,' he said, 'must be done by dirty hands, and a cruel business is most generally entrusted to cruel hearts and to ferocious dispositions.'

When he arrived in Strathcarron, Ross went to see Alexander Munro at Braelangwell. He found the tacksman (in whose name, as tenant, the warrants were issued, and who played an equivocal role in the whole business) still maintaining his innocence. 'He summarily declared in the presence of witnesses, and he also stated, that he always told the tenants that he did not authorize the application for warrants against them.' But his name was on the warrants.

The *Inverness Courier*, upon which Ross had wasted no paper, ink or postage, refused to believe the stories which its rival, the *Ensign*, was publishing. It said that unnecessary violence would not have been permitted by Superintendent Cumming, 'whose services as an officer on many occasions have proved invaluable; he acted with great tact and caution and succeeded in suppressing the formidable attempt at deforcement'. It fairly reported the story that many women had been badly injured (it could scarcely do otherwise, since two doctors had been called to the glen), but it also quoted unidentified witnesses as saying that the police were only doing their duty, 'less firmness might have proved fatal to themselves'. It then lectured the sub-tenants of Greenyards, and through them all Highlanders who were reluctant to make way for sheep, improvement and the Law: 'The people of Strathcarron are evidently not guided by the best advice, but are deluded into the belief that the law is tyrannical and ought to be disregarded – a dangerous doctrine of which the clergy and influential persons in the district should seek to disabuse them.'

---

*These words were written by Donald Macleod of Strathnaver, who met Ross in Glasgow. 'Sutherland and Ross-shire,' he wrote, 'may boast of having had the Nana Sahib and his chiefs some years before India, and that in the persons of some whose education, training, and parental example, should prepare their minds to perform and act differently.'

On Wednesday, 12 April, the Messenger-at-arms in Tain went to Strathcarron with two policemen. Of the four women arrested, only one was to be charged, Ann Ross, *alias* Taylor. The Messenger had come to look for a 'ringleader', a man. They arrested Peter Ross, *alias* Bain, and took him to the gaol at Tain. Donald Ross made no mention of his part in the battle, but he was involved in the deforcement of Sheriff-Officer Macpherson, and in what was now known, with amusement or indignation, as 'The Gauger Affair'.

Home again in St Enoch Square, Glasgow, Donald Ross wrote to the Lord Advocate on 19 April, urging him to call 'an immediate inquiry into the conduct of the police force and of the Sheriff'. He sent a copy of the letter to the *Northern Ensign* which printed it in full under the headline 'SLAUGHTER IN STRATHCARRON'. Ross said that an inquiry was necessary for the sake of good government, 'for independent of the rash and reckless conduct of the Sheriff, and the brutal and savage conduct of the police, people are labouring under the impression that Her Majesty sanctions, nay, encourages and authorizes, these evictions, specially as the batons broken and left on the battle-field have the letters V.R. painted in large characters on them'. He did not defend the women for obstructing the police, and he said that had he been there at the time he would certainly have advised them 'to allow the Law to take its course'. In this he was being more than tactful. All of those who wrote against the inhumanity of the evictions (with the exception of Donald Macleod of Strathnaver) believed that cruel though they were, resistance to the Law which supported them was unpardonable. Though it was three-quarters of a century since the American colonists had fought in defence of the principle that men should make the laws that govern them (and two hundred years since the English Levellers had done the same), even the friends of the Highlanders demanded that they should obey a Government which neither consulted nor represented them.

Despite his respect for the Law, however, Ross did not believe that its instruments were ennobled by it, and he told the Lord Advocate that 'the local authorities are in a league with the proprietors for the expatriation of the people'. What other explanation could there be for the behaviour of the police?

Such indeed was the sad havoc made on these females on the banks of the Carron on the memorable 31st of March last, that pools of blood were on the ground, that the grass and earth were dyed red with it, that the dogs of the district came and licked up the blood; and, at last, such was the state of feelings of parties who went from a distance to see the field that a party (it is said by order or instructions from headquarters) actually harrowed the ground during the night to hide the blood !

My lord, I have every reason to believe this statement ... for there was shown to me in Strathcarron two table-cloths filled with clothing which the unfortunate victims had on them at the time, and these were completely dyed red with their blood. There were caps with holes on them where the batons tore and carried the thin cotton with them into the skulls of the women; and there were pieces of the cotton of the caps afterwards abstracted by the doctor out of the heads of these unhappy sufferers. There were several strong ash batons left on the field, broken with the blows which the police gave with them. There are pieces, or patches of the skin, which the police with their batons stript off the heads and shoulders of the women when they were beating them.

Presumably his lordship replied to Ross's letter, though he said nothing which either the lawyer or the *Northern Ensign* thought necessary to put into print. And in September Her Majesty, through her Lord Justice-Clerk, made it plain that her police, with their monogrammed batons, had been in Strathcarron with her authority. Before the Northern Circuit Court of Justiciary, Ann Ross, *alias* Taylor, and Peter Ross, *alias* Bain, were accused of 'mobbing and rioting, breach of the peace, and assault on officers of the law in execution of their duty'. The charges referred to the deforcement of William Macpherson and Peter Mackenzie on 7 March, the comic repulse of Dugald Mac-Caig and his preventive men on 22 March, and the resistance given to Sheriff Taylor, Superintendent Cumming and thirty-five policemen on 31 March. On the advice of their counsel (who hoped that the court would 'deal leniently with the prisoners'),

Ann Ross and Peter Ross pled guilty to a breach of the peace, and this modified charge was accepted by the Advocate-Depute. No doubt there were many who were happy that he did so, for as a result there was no discussion, no argument, no examination of witnesses. Indeed, the Court seemed unaware of the fact that, by Donald Ross's account, Margaret Macgregor Ross of Greenyard was dead from a broken skull.

Lord Justice-Clerk Hope (who had come to Court in Inverness after a pleasant holiday shooting on his son's estate in Sutherland) spoke at some length, addressing the prisoners in a legal English which they must have had some difficulty in following, if they understood it at all:

The course of the Law must have its effect with all, in order to protect all persons high and low; and all must submit whatever their feelings, or rank, or perverted notions of right and wrong, to the authority of the Law.... It is fortunate for the deluded parties that no life was lost on this occasion, for there was no degree of vigour, no exercise of authority that the Sheriff-Substitute might not have been fully authorised and justified in resorting to in order to accomplish his purpose. It is quite essential therefore, that such a spirit as that which these pannels exhibited should be repressed. Neither they nor their neighbours can be allowed to suppose that they can live in this kind of wicked and rebellious spirit against the Law. They must be taught submission in the very first instance...

He sent Ann Ross to prison for twelve months, and he sentenced Peter Ross to eighteen months with hard labour. He thanked the jurymen for their attendance, and he hoped that none had been put to serious inconvenience by it. They had performed a most important duty in ensuring the conviction of Ann Ross and Peter Ross. 'You are aware,' he said, 'that there exists a singular and perverted feeling of insubordination in some districts of the Highlands against the execution of civil processes in the removal of tenants. This feeling is most prejudicial to the interest of all, and it is absolutely necessary to suppress it.'

6

WHERE ARE THE HIGHLANDERS?

'My business lies with the poor and oppressed!'

THOMAS MULOCK was an eccentric, and thus not all that could be hoped for in a champion of the evicted. He had little of Donald Macleod's obstinate courage, and less of the objective integrity shown by *The Times* Commissioner. But he had passion, and anger, and if he treated the Highlands as a skittle alley, rolling woods at the proprietors for the pleasure of seeing them fall, he was sincere enough while the game lasted. With a cry of 'Justice to Scotland!', and with the little *Inverness Advertiser* under his control for eighteen months, he attacked the clearances with sustained violence and occasional brilliance. He then retired to France, where he became a hired hack for Louis Napoleon.

He was sixty when he arrived in the Highlands in 1849, a tall, white-haired Irishman, handsome, witty, and a darling at conversation provided nobody interrupted him. The great pride of his life was his daughter, 'a very celebrated writer, kind and obedient to me, and worthy of every respect and honour'. Celebrated though she was in her time, her father's polemics now make better reading than *John Halifax, Gentleman*. That she had written so splendid a novel was always a consolation to him, and sustained him in his old age when he was summonsed for non-payment of his rent, or sent to prison for contempt of court, or committed to Stafford Asylum 'through the influence of some magistrate whose displeasure I had incurred'.

He was born in Dublin, first son of the third son of Thomas Mulock of Kilnagarna, Comptroller of the Stamp Office, and one of the many oddities of the man is that although he was Irish (at least Anglo-Irish and small gentry), he never wrote in defence of the Irish peasantry. But, to be fair, he did take up causes more as a result of geographical accident than selection, and had he received a newspaper appointment in Wexford rather than Inverness he might have attacked Irish oppression as boldly as he did that in the Highlands. When young, after a promising career at Oxford and a short term as Private Secretary to George Canning, he decided to read for the Bar. With a man called Blood, he opened a law firm in Liverpool. The people he met there did not know what to make of him, except that their acquaintance was likely to be brief, and they remembered him, guardedly, as 'perhaps the ablest man, as well as the most original genius who has temporarily resided in Liverpool'.

He turned from law to literature for greater excitement, lectured to the Pitt Club, and attacked the Whigs in the Press over the signature 'Six Stars'. But he was too vain for anonymity, and when he boasted his identity the Whigs laughed at him and nicknamed his firm 'Bloody Moloch'. He lampooned Byron in a pamphlet called *An Answer Given by the Gospels to the Atheism of all Ages.* 'This gentleman seems to be my great admirer,' said Byron, 'so I take what he says in good part.' Instinctively, Byron recognized that this furious iconoclast was in fact a tragic figure, a man of considerable ability, greater ambition, and no discipline. 'I thought there was something of wild talent in him, mixed with a due leaven of absurdity, as there must be in all talent let loose upon the world without a martingale.'

He married the daughter of a tanner, an anticlimax almost, and a marriage that crippled any social pretensions he may have had. He left Liverpool and the law, appeared in Geneva as a *savant*, and again in Paris, lecturing on English literature. Thomas Moore, who attended some of these lectures, found them irritating and absurd. 'He talked of persons going to the wellspring of English poetry in order to communicate what they have quaffed to others.... Dryden was no poet. Butler had no originality, and Locke was of the school of the devil!' When Moore heard that Mulock intended to speak on his poetry, he stayed away from the lecture in protest, and was ashamed afterwards, because the Irishman had in fact praised his work.

The lectures were a dismal failure. Mulock turned to divinity, entered the Baptist Ministry and founded a chapel at Stoke-on-Trent. This he conducted on highly original lines, of course. Resenting privilege by birth or wealth, and power by inheritance, he created his own 'elect', selecting the Godly and the righteous from among his congregation and giving them a special corner of his chapel, railed off from lesser men. Most of those so chosen were his friends and his creditors. He was always in debt, borrowing heavily to pay for the numerous law-suits in which his writing involved him, and which he rarely won. He armed himself with the Almighty's approval when he asked his friends for a loan: 'I must ask you to send me two pounds and no more. I do not wish to be constrained to ask of anyone but yourself, to whom the Lord hath given a largeness of heart not to be found but in specially gifted gospel creatures.' When this friend later ran out of patience, or money, Mulock denounced him from the pulpit as 'a blasphemer and the greatest heretic that has arisen since the days of the Apostles'.

Mulock left Stoke and the ministry in 1831 and became a wanderer again. He reappeared in Liverpool, writing articles for the *Chronicle* on 'The Duke of Newcastle, England's Scribbling Liberator'. He had a sniper's skill with a well-aimed phrase. The Lord Lieutenant of Ireland, he said, was 'paid £5,000 every quarter for opening letters'. Thomas Carlyle was 'an amateur statesman and an uninspired prophet', and Disraeli was 'that Jew-Gentile romance-writer'. His dark suspicion of the Prince Consort was like a grumbling appendix, always demanding relief. When Albert promoted the Great Exhibition, and thereby won some belated popularity with Press and public, Mulock stood firm in his distrust of the humourless man. 'Prince Albert is a mere nose of wax in this business; and a sort of fashionable joint stock company (very like some of the railway concoctions) is at the bottom of the whole affair.' He had no approval for Albert's habit of lecturing industry and the arts at public dinners, the only form of intellectual exercise available to the consorts of queens. He called it 'the Prince's post-prandial eloquence'. He never thought a phrase could be spoiled by too much alliteration.

In 1849 he was in Scotland. Donald Macleod of Strathnaver,

who should have had more compassion for him, first liked Mulock and then despised him (for apologizing to the second Duke of Sutherland). 'He came to Scotland a fanatic speculator in literature in search of money,' said Macleod, 'or a lucrative situation, vainly thinking that he would be a dictator to every editor in Scotland.'

He first attacked the immortal Hugh Miller of the *Witness*, Edinburgh, but in him he met more than his match. He then went to the north, got hold of my first pamphlet, and by setting it up in a literary style, and in better English than I, he made a splendid and promising appearance in the northern papers for some time; but he found out that the money expected was not coming in, and that the hotels, head inns and taverns would not keep him up any longer without the prospect of being paid for the past or for the future. I found out that he was hard up, and a few of the Highlanders in Edinburgh and myself sent him from twenty to thirty pounds sterling. When he saw that was all he was to get, he at once turned tail upon us, and instead of expressing his gratitude, he abused us unsparingly, and regretted that he ever wrote in behalf of such a hungry, moneyless class. He smelled (like others we suspect) where the gold was hoarded up for hypocrites and flatterers, and that one apologising letter to his Grace would be worth ten times as much as he could expect from the Highlanders all his lifetime.

It was a bitterly unfair attack. Sutherland may or may not have bought off the Irishman, but if he did one suspects that Mulock would have made the apology a great deal more abject than it was. Probably Sutherland threatened him with a suit which Mulock, debt-ridden and emotionally exhausted, could not face. Macleod, seeing men as friends or enemies, was not able to understand the tormented Irishman who had nothing to live by but his pen, and little to gain by imprisonment.

He began his journalistic career in the north as an editorial writer for the *Inverness Advertiser*, a small paper recently started by a young man called James MacCosh. When MacCosh died of a heart attack, the paper's new owner put Mulock in the editor's chair *pro tempore*. Most Highland newspapers walked carefully through the squalor of the evictions, taking care not to soil their reputations or the proprietors'. Mulock took the *Advertiser* into battle on the side of the people with wild disregard for circulation and advertising revenue. He undertook what he called a 'close and impartial inquiry into the state of the Highlands', and when he went to the west and the Isles to report the results of the evictions there the *Inverness Courier* felt compelled to send its own man too, just to balance the picture.

Mulock went to Glenelg, a wild and beautiful estate on Loch Hourn. Once it had been Macleod country, belonging to the Dunvegan chiefs. It was sold for £30,000 in 1798, again in 1811 for £100,000, and in 1824 it was bought for £82,000 by Charles Grant, President of the Board of Trade. In 1831 he took his title from it when he was given a barony, and six years later he parted with it for £77,000 to the sheep-farmer, James Baillie of Dochfour (he who was once of Bristol, and was now to be 'of Glenelg'). With each successive sale of the property more of the small tenants were removed, and now, in 1849, five hundred of them were to be helped on their way to Canada by a grant of £2,000 from Baillie (he had been asked for £3,000) and £500 from the Destitution Board. The *Courier* made much of Baillie's liberality and of the strong desire of the people to leave their homes. Mulock thought this was humbug.

To suppose that numerous families would as a matter of choice sever themselves from their loved soil, abolish all the associations of local and patriotic sentiment, fling to the winds every endearing recollection connected with the sojourneying spot of vanished generations, and blot themselves, as it were, out of the book of 'home-born happiness', is an hypothesis too unnatural to be encouraged by any sober, well-regulated mind.

Forty or fifty families had been unable to find room on the *Liscard*, which took the Glenelg people to Quebec. They had sold most of what they possessed, and were now living close to starvation on the edge of Loch Hourn. Mulock called the heads of these families together, and asked them if they were indeed willing emigrants. 'With one voice they assured me that nothing short of the impossibility of obtaining land or employment at home could drive them to seek the doubtful benefits of a foreign shore. So far from the emigrations being a spontaneous movement springing out of the wishes of the tenantry, I aver it to be the product of desperation, the calamitous light of hopeless oppression visiting their sad hearts.'

His most inviting windmill was Sutherland. He read Loch's book and declared: 'It has no more weight with me than the history of Sinbad the Sailor. It is a laboured attempt to blacken a people whom it was resolved to oppress, and in order to vindicate tyranny he seeks to vilify those who were fore-doomed to slavery.' With his usual recklessness, he sailed close to the wind of criminal libel. When Sutherland claimed that he was making no profit out of his estates, Mulock suggested that he ask Loch and the agents where the rents were going. He criticized a grant made to the Duke by the committee of the Destitution Board, saying that a rich man should be able to put his hand into his own pocket to help his people, and not ask for the charity of others.

Mr Loch, the Duke's Premier, put the committee in mind that the Duke of Sutherland had formerly subscribed £1,000 to the Highland Destitution Fund, and conjoined with this reminiscence a supplication to the committee to grant his noble employer the sum of £3,500 to help towards the relief of the poor people of Sutherland! Subsequently the Duke's petition was acceded to, on condition the money was to be expended building a road bisecting His Grace's territory in the most favourable direction.

The second Duke of Sutherland had none of his father's serene indifference to public criticism. He wrote an open letter to Mulock, which was published in the *Courier*, and which said that if the wild man took the trouble 'to visit this country, and make yourself personally acquainted with local circumstances, I should not apprehend the sharp scrutiny you mention'. Mulock accepted the challenge with enthusiasm. He left for the north in October 1849. Those who suggested that he might think more kindly of the gentry if he cultivated their acquaintance were sharply reminded of his duty: 'I never obtrude myself on the hospitable walls of proprietors or their local managers. My business lies with the poor and the oppressed, and if I overcharge my statements of their case, I confess myself open to the censure of aggrieved proprietors or their officials who, it is to be hoped, will be more successful in their recriminatory scribbling than the Duke of Sutherland and his factor, Mr Gunn.'

He went with a copy of Macleod's book in his pocket, and his letters, as they were published in the *Advertiser*, made good use of it. He retold the story of Kildonan and Strathnaver and he accused the middle classes of Scotland and the Highlands of being accessory to the extirpation of a people.

At Inverness the Sutherland clearances received a sort of solemn sanction, proprietorship was re-enforced with supreme sway, and from henceforth the prosperity of the rich was to be secured by the ruin of the poor. The population, it was now decided, should quit for ever their former abodes on cultivatable land, be penally fixed on coasts where the reclamation of rocky land was to constitute their chief hope of subsistence.

He described the ruins in empty glens, a debased tenantry living on sterile coasts. He accused the Sutherland agents of continued extortion and exploitation. He said that they were determined to recover from the tenants, by increased rents, every penny given in 'charity' by the Duke. The majority of the people, at great sacrifice, managed to pay these increases.

I found the wretched inmates possessed one proof of probity, the last of a continued series of receipts for rents. Nay more, I saw clouds of printed notices threatening these same needy rent-payers with legal prosecution if they did not *repay* the Duke certain 'arrears of grain' delivered from Dunrobin during the appalling scarcity consequent on the failure of the potato: and the tendered payment of rent was refused until these said 'arrears' should be previously discharged !

He saw so much poverty, so much hardship and squalid destitution in the county that he wondered what had happened to the money which was said to have been spent for the relief of hardship there.

Perhaps the enormous outlay at Dunrobin, without and within that superb pile, may help to explain this mysterious expenditure; to which might be subjoined the lavishness that palpably prevails in providing costly buildings for opulent sheep-farmers, whereas the small holders of land have to house themselves at their own expense . . .

A thoughtless, selfish proprietor deprives his people of all incentives to industry, and all scope for profitable exertion. He denies them land, he renders the sea unprofitable, he places over them stony-hearted and iron-handed Commissioners and factors. . . . One of the functions of such factors is to obstruct marriage.

He [Sutherland] has a palatial residence at Dunrobin, and he has half a dozen sheep-feeding satraps lording it over his once-peopled but now deserted inheritance, and positively this is all that can be said of the princely possessions of Sutherland.

Mulock returned to Inverness thoroughly pleased with himself, and with every right to be; his letters had been masterpieces of polemic, but they had also been a hammer-blow at the Victorian gloss that was spreading over Highland landlordism. For their wider circulation and the payment of his debts, he published them in book form, and warned his readers that the gathering of the material had not been the work of a day. 'The discovery of truth is a painful and difficult process where oppression frowns on a crushed community. . . . At length, however, the real state of things becomes apparent to a patient investigator.' The only fault in this noble declaration was that it did not pay due credit to Donald Macleod of Strathnaver, whom Mulock had plagiarized with vigour and abandon.

When it was announced that the Queen was considering a visit to Sutherland, Mulock was delighted. Sardonically, he considered the *Inverness Courier's* glowing account of the pleasures awaiting her: 'The splendid palace . . . well-sheltered gardens . . . sweet-wooded and sequestered dells . . . wide heaths well-peopled with antlered monarchs . . . a loyal and peaceable, high-spirited race of peasantry of whom almost every woman is comely, and every man handsome.' Was some Scots Potemkin, Mulock asked, going to prepare all this? 'As the Queen has a decided taste for the picturesque, and sketches as well as she etches we recommend Her Majesty to try her hand at transferring to her album Kildonan and Strathnaver landscapes, interspersed with the blackened ruins of burnt-down cottages, where dwelt in former days the "loyal and peaceable and high-spirited race of peasantry".'

And, naturally, he could not ignore the Consort. 'If, instead of devoting his royal zeal to the feeding of porkers, Prince Albert were to dedicate his whole mind to the management of sheep, we admit that Sutherland's noble straths would afford His Royal Highness ample scope for contemplating the grandeur of a lonely shepherd's life on the large scale organized by the late Marquess of Stafford.'

In the same month that the Queen's visit to Sutherland was proposed, a great celebration was held at Dunrobin Castle upon the majority of Sutherland's heir, Lord Stafford, who had been recently married to Anna Hay-Mackenzie. Mulock was able to get no closer to this brilliant affair than the Inn at Golspie ('which, by the way, is an excellent hostelry'). He was cordoned there with other journalists, factors, ground-officers, and unimportant ministers of the Established Church. One of these last was a Reverend Mr Rose of Tain, who made the journey worth while for Mulock.

Mr Rose was on his road to Golspie for the purpose of mastication, deglutition and declamatory achievement when he was lucky as to see (without second-sight) two rainbows, one lovingly enclosing another and brighter one! The rev. gentleman treasured up these optical wonders in his mind's eye until a tenth toast enabled him to turn his rainbows to admirable account, by insisting that the larger and (he somewhat ungallantly added) the *faded* one meant Mrs Hay-Mackenzie, while the lesser and brighter rainbow radiantly imagined the youthful Marchioness of Stafford.

This bodes well for the congratulatory addresses to the Queen when received right royally at Dunrobin. If Mr Gunn fires off another loyal harangue, and the Rev. Mr Rose has the good fortune to pop upon another pair of rainbows (to suit the Queen and Prince Albert), the next Sutherland rejoicings will constitute a memorable affair.

He could not be allowed to keep this up for ever, of course. To duel in public with a hack journalist was not within the dignity of the Duke of Sutherland, beyond that one letter in the *Inverness Courier*. But something stopped Mulock's mouth, and we have only Macleod's word for the fact that it was gold. One suspects that it was exhaustion and old age. In 1853 he was gone from the Highlands, leaving behind that letter of 'apology'. It was a qualified one; he was too Irish not to go down fighting: 'My mind has undergone no change respecting the impolicy of Highland Clearances. But I feel conscientiously convinced that even unquestionable truths may be advocated with an angry pertinacity which impedes usefulness instead of promoting it.'

Macleod said that Mulock then went to Paris, where he started an English newspaper. 'For the service he rendered Napoleon in crushing republicanism during the besieging of Rome, etc., the Emperor presented him with a *gold pin*, and a few days afterwards sent a *gendarme* to him with a brief notice that his service was not any longer required, and a warning to quit France in a few days.'

Before Mulock left the Highlands, however, he had spoken his mind about the evictions then taking place in the Isles.

'Oh, dear man, the tears come on my eyes!'

THE GREAT CHEVIOT came to the Hebrides last of all, but it came to them all in time, to the Long Island and to Mull, to Raasay, Skye and Barra, to Mingulay and Tiree. Though the land that made this shield of islands offered less to the animal than Sutherland or Argyll, and although many of the sheep-walks were later abandoned, they were still a profitable alternative – the only alternative to men. By 1830 there were too many men in the Hebrides. At the end of the eighteenth century, when mainland proprietors had begun to remove their people, the lairds of the Isles were importing labour to work their property, and in Lewis and the Uists there were no songs sung about a land taken from the people, or of white-sailed ships taking away the best of the youth.

The reason was kelp, the rich vegetation which a restless ocean vomited on to the shores of the islands. For sixty years seaweed brought a twilight prosperity to districts where, shortly after Culloden, an Englishman had seen 'the poor prowling like other animals along the shore to pick up limpets and other shell-fish, the casual repast of hundreds during parts of the year in these unhappy islands.' Kelp could be made into a rich fertilizer, urgently needed as Britain's agricultural economy expanded. It required no planting, no cultivation, only a vast army of men, women and children to tear it from the rocks with hooks and sickles, to carry it to great kilns and there burn it over peat until it became hard, brittle and multi-coloured. Island lairds and tacksmen, clinging to their warrior patronymics, were in fact seaweed farmers, shipping thousands of tons every year to middle-men in Liverpool, Glasgow, Hull or Newcastle. Prices rose to £12 a ton, on which the landlord (paying a family £4 or £5 a season to work his shores) could expect to make a profit of £7. The supply, brought by willing tides, never faltered.

Hebridean proprietors had used all their influence to secure the passing of the Passenger Act of 1803, hoping that it would restrict emigration and therefore guarantee them a reservoir of labour. Because of kelp, the population of the Isles increased by 63 per cent overall, and in South Uist the figure was 118 per cent. The lairds grew rich. At the beginning of the nineteenth century, the second Lord Macdonald of the Isles had an annual income of £20,000 from kelp alone. Macdonald of Clanranald, whose people were spread across a dozen islands, large and small, as well as much of the mainland, received £18,000, most of which he spent as a Regency buck in London. Lord Macdonald, Clan-ranald, Lord Seaforth and the Duke of Argyll between them enjoyed the profits of nearly half of the industry. The rents of sub-tenants were increased beyond what their holdings could be expected to produce in cattle, and thus were the people forced to work on the beaches or at the kilns. An island rent-roll, once counted in swordsmen, now depended on the manuring of English fields.

But it ended. The price of kelp began to fall in 1811, having reached £20 a ton for some grades. With the close of the

Napoleonic Wars import duties on competitive products were reduced or lifted, and when the salt excise duty was abolished in 1825 kelp was no longer the green treasure-chest of the Isles. The industry continued in decline for another quarter of a century but long before then the people who had been drawn to the islands to work it were being driven out, and the great Seaweed Chiefs sank into a bankruptcy from which only the Great Cheviot could rescue them.

The wide Clanranald estates, stretching from Moidart and Arisaig on the mainland to South Uist in the Isles, were the first to crumble. Ranald George Macdonald of Clanranald, eighteenth captain of the clan, was more at home in London or Brighton than he was in Arisaig, and he had little feeling for his people, being inclined to remove them if he thought their cabins spoiled the view from his windows. Even one of his more merciful tacksmen, John Macdonald of Borrodale, did not question his right to do this (they 'being so close to your house and policies', he said), but he wished that *Mac-'ic-Ailein* had given the people earlier warning of the fact that they were not wanted. Clanranald began to dispose of his lands in 1813 by selling some to his tacksmen and kinsmen, continued by selling Arisaig and Bornish to the trustees of Lady Ashburton, and concluded in 1838 by parting with the whole of South Uist and Benbecula to John Gordon of Cluny, one of the most ruthless removers in the Isles. For all of his property, which his ancestors had held by sword or charter through seventeen generations, Clanranald received £214,211 11s. 7d. He was left with the island and castle of Tirrim, which supported his threadbare claim to be a landed chief for another thirty-five years.

'The clearances came upon us,' said Peggy MacCormack, who had been born a Macdonald in Clanranald's country. 'There was neither sin nor sorrow in the world for us, but the clearances came upon us, destroying all, turning our gladness into bitterness, our blessings into blasphemy, and our Christianity into mockery. Oh, dear man, the tears come on my eyes when I think of all we suffered, and of the sorrows, hardships and oppressions we came through.'

The land and the islands were sold and bought and sold again in the exchanges of Inverness, Edinburgh and London by speculators who rarely saw what they bought. Raasay, the green island strip that lies between Skye and the mainland, changed hands four times in sixteen years, and each time it lost some of its people. Barra, where MacNeils had lived for forty generations since Niall of the Nine Hostages sired the line, was sold twice in one year. General Roderick MacNeil (who claimed the hereditary right to sit down to his dinner before any prince on earth) accepted £42,050 for the island in 1839 from a speculator called Menzies. In 1840 Menzies put it up for auction again at Paxton's Coffee House in Inverness, but chose the wrong moment for it fetched £38,050 only, the buyer being Colonel Gordon of Cluny. In 1825 the whole estate of Lewis was brought to judicial sale before Lord Medwyn at a reserve price of £136,000. After some brisk opposition bidding from the Joint Stock Property Company of Edinburgh, Mackenzie of Seaforth bought it for £160,000. Twenty years later it was bought for £190,000 by the young millionaire, James Matheson. He was a benevolent proprietor, and was to spend nearly half a million pounds on the island in an attempt to improve it and to relieve the destitution of its people, but in the end the people went in hundreds to Canada and Australia.

The Isle of Skye became the property of several proprietors, who, in the four decades following 1840, would serve 1,740 writs of removal, involving nearly forty thousand people, all of whom, whether they were removed or not, had to pay 10s. for the cost of the summonses against them. On Harris the 78th Highlanders were called in to remove the proprietor's sub-tenants. He had been paying them £2 12s. 6d. for the collection of a ton of kelp that was selling for £2 10s. only in Liverpool, and not unnaturally he decided that he would do better with sheep (due to footrot in parts of England and Scotland that year, the price of Cheviot wedders had risen handsomely). On the Isle of Mull, from Mornish to Glen Moire, evictions were particularly severe, and the bard Angus MacMhuirich lamented the bitterness which followed.

> The jaws of sheep have made the land rich,
> but we were told by the prophecy
> that sheep would scatter the warriors
> and turn their homes into a wilderness.
> The land of our love lies under bracken and heather,
> every plain and every field is untilled,
> and soon there will be none in Mull of the Trees
> but Lowlanders and their white sheep.

In 1849 Lord Macdonald decided to evict a hundred and ten families, more than six hundred people, from Sollas on the island of North Uist. He was Godfrey William Wentworth Macdonald, fourth Baron of the Isles, descendant of the Macdonald chiefs of Sleat. His uncle, the second Lord (who had done so well out of fertilizer), had built a fairy-tale castle at Armadale on Skye to the design of James Gillespie Graham, the architect who introduced the horror of Gothic to the Highlands. Macdonald hoped that this absurdity would persuade his descendants to live on their property, and he also introduced the cultivation of hemp, drained marshes, built bridges, churches and mills. But it all depended on seaweed and an overblown population. The fourth baron had a wide property on Skye and North Uist, debts of £200,000, and impatient creditors who soon formed themselves into a body of trustees to intercept some of his rents against the money owing them. Macdonald was a humane man, concerned for the well-being of his people (which is more than could be said for some of his ancestors), and during the Potato Famine of 1846 he spent all of his resources on the relief of destitution among them. It was therefore an irony that one of the most bitter and best-remembered evictions in the Isles should take place on his property. But the pressures on him were as inexorable as those on less charitable lairds, the Great Cheviot could save him as much as them, and in the end he too was petitioning for 'an armed force to enable the constituted authorities to compel the people to give obedience to the Law'.

A central stud of the great Hebridean buckler, North Uist had once been one of the most profitable of the seaweed islands, but in 1849 it was impoverished and wretched. 'It is necessary,' said

Mr Finlay Macrae, minister of the parish, 'to find some proper outlet for the excess of population by emigration, and thus to increase the amount of land possessed by each family. At present it is notorious that there are no less than 390 families paying no rent, but living chiefly on the produce of small spots of potato ground given them by some of their neighbours and relatives.' Since the decay of the kelp industry, the five thousand inhabitants of North Uist had been living close to starvation, but their attachment to the island was fierce and strong. In 1847, Shaw, the Sheriff-Substitute, had told the Commissary-General that they stubbornly refused to go to the Lowlands for work. 'Emigration seems to me to be the only means of permanently improving the conditions of the people in these crowded districts, and I think that the cost of maintaining them in idleness or unprofitable employment for a single season would suffice to effect the removal of the superfluous number.'

It was therefore with the best of motives, and for their own good as it seemed to him, that Macdonald decided to eject the people. He offered to remit the arrears of their rent, to take their crop and stock at valuation, and to supplement the Destitution Board's offer of £1 per head (on condition of emigration) by whatever money was necessary to get them to Canada – if only they would go.

The district of Sollas was a square mile of flat ground in the north of the island. On the west it bordered a sandy, tidal bay. It lay in a trough between a three-mile drift of dunes and the slopes of the inland hills, over which climbed a wandering road from Lochmaddy. It was the best land on an island that consisted almost entirely of water. The six hundred people there lived in the townships of Dunskellar, Mallaglate (Malaclete), Middlequarter and Sollas itself. It was a brown, treeless country that took the first anger of the Atlantic weather, and where spring came late and winter early. Yet every corrie, rock and hill had been give a name and a legend, and even in their poverty the people loved the land. Those who belonged to Clan Donald had an independent pride, and an Englishman said that even the 'poorest and most despicable creature' among them was vainer than men of property because he carried the name. They called themselves the Children of Colla, the Irish prince who had once ruled the Isles, and they called themselves the Sons of Conn of the Hundred Battles, the High King of Ireland. A seventeenth-century bard had spoken of them as 'the race of Colla, of vast armies and many tributes, with their full-laden, white-sailed fleet they sail upon the oceans'. All of which was the stuff of dreams only by 1849.

Highland newspapers, with one exception, were sympathetic to Lord Macdonald's proposal to remove the race of Colla to Canada, and they praised his desire to make the island productive once more. The one exception, of course, was the *Inverness Advertiser*. When it was all over, Thomas Mulock hammered away at Macdonald, accusing him of replacing the people by sheep, of sheltering behind his agents, and of being a liar (or at best misinformed). 'Sollas was foredoomed,' he said, 'in order that the district should be partitioned among two or three prospective tacksmen who had found favour with your Lordship's functionaries. The old disposition of Naboth's vinyard is renewed on a larger scale by the Celtic Ahabs.' Far from the rents being in arrears for years, they had in fact been paid with regularity until 1848, and Mulock quoted a Macdonald factor in evidence of this.

'I respect your Lordship's rank,' said Mulock, 'I unfeignedly pity your painful position, but I cannot suffer your Lordship to be screened by the interposition of an underling. No privilege of your order can avail you here. . . . That the heathery hills of Scotland are suitable for sheep is a truth open to a traveller's observation, but the mighty man of sheep must have every valley as well as every hill. . . . Aye, but the rent, but the rent? cries some commissioner of Lord Macdonald, or of the Duke of Sutherland, or Mr Baillie of Glenelg.'

More probably murmuring, Aye, but my debts, my debts! Macdonald moved against the people of Sollas. From Whitsuntide to summer they evaded a direct answer to his offer to ship them to Canada, and to send one of his agents with them in guarantee of his good faith and concern for them. Mr Macrae, the minister, was also unable to persuade them. They said that the season was now too late, or too early, that the midsummer markets would offer better prices for the stock they must abandon, but their real fear was unspoken. They did not wish to leave the brown island and the grey sea, their boats and their cabins, the hills where their kin were buried. In July Patrick Cooper, Macdonald's Commissioner, went to Sollas with Sheriff-Substitute Shaw, and warned the people that they would be forcibly ejected if they did not move. They told Shaw that they would not harm him, for they had good memories of his father, 'but they threatened instant death to any officer who should attempt to evict them'. Cooper went back to the mainland complaining, through Macdonald, that the people were dishonouring earlier promises they had made, and the petition they had signed asking for aid in emigration.

'Your Lordship has been made the victim of some unworthy trick,' said Mulock later, 'for on two occasions the whole of the heads of families at Sollas emphatically assured me that they had never signed, never seen, never heard of any petition on the subject of emigration. I cannot yield to the supposition that fifty or sixty decent persons palmed a rank falsehood on me.'

On Saturday, 14 July, the first attempt to execute the writs was made by a Sheriff-Officer of Langlash in North Uist, Roderick Macdonald, with two assistants also surnamed Macdonald. They were driven from Mallaglate by stones. They tried again on the 16th, this time accompanied by Patrick Cooper, and by Shaw, the Sheriff-Substitute of the Long Island, with twenty officers. Once more volleys of stones repulsed them. A third try was made the next day, this time without Cooper. He said that he had heard the people threaten 'to murder certain parties whom I could name' (meaning himself, Shaw suspected). 'As you apprehend danger to yourself,' Shaw told him, 'you'd better not come forward. If the people yield, it will be easy for you to take possession. If not you are clearly better out of the way.'

At the approach to Mallaglate, Roderick Macdonald said afterwards, Shaw's party was stopped by a crowd of three hundred men and women, and there were warning signals flying: 'Namely, a pole with some black thing on it, but I couldn't say whether it was a flag or a bonnet. The first flag was about fifty yards from the house, and three flags were on top of a hill about a mile distant. The crowd said they would not allow us to go on with the removals. They did not strike, but were speaking, and said that if we attempted the removals we should see the consequences.' Rain came on, lowering Shaw's spirits still further, and he ordered another retreat to Lochmaddy.

At Armadale Castle on 19 July, Lord Macdonald wrote to the Home Secretary, asking for an 'armed force' to compel the people to obedience. He thought that forty men and officers would be enough, and he also told the authorities in Oban that he was appealing for soldiers. They were less anxious than he to have redcoats and bayonets doing the work for which their police were paid, and they told him that before the military were dispatched they would 'give efficacy to the Law by employing the county forces only'. There was great indignation over the resistance shown to Shaw. Highlanders were supposed to be bold and valorous in battle only. 'Their conduct,' said the *Inverness Courier*, 'was very unlike what Highlanders might be expected to exhibit, and some mischievous demagogue must have been among them. One man said that before they were turned out they would do as the Hungarians did with the Austrians !'

On Monday, 30 July, the steamer *Cygnet* arrived at Oban from Glasgow. It had been chartered for a week by Mr Mackay, the Procurator-Fiscal of Inverness-shire, and at seven o'clock that evening he boarded it with William Colquhoun, Sheriff-Substitute of the county, Superintendent MacBean, and thirty-three constables armed with ash truncheons. The Reverend Mr Macrae who had been on his way south for a visit, was persuaded to abandon the trip and return to the island in the hope that the Word of God might make the use of truncheons unnecessary. Also aboard was 'OUR OWN REPORTER' from the *Inverness Courier*, who later made a brave try for literary immortality :

The vessel proceeded to sea, reaching Tobermory before midnight. By three o'clock the vessel was again under steam, and her course was directed for the Sound of Sleat – the Sheriff and Mr MacBean having agreed on the propriety of communicating with Lord Macdonald before proceeding further. Rounding the point of Ardnamurchan (which, freely interpreted, is the point of the high-sounding waves), a heavy, tumbling sea convinced us that the name was no misnomer, but the bold, craggy shores of Eigg afforded shelter, and as the sun broke through the early clouds, pouring light on the bold hills of Arisaig, the wild scenery of Loch-Nevis, and the gloomier mountains around Loch-Ourn, we saw, in its most beautiful aspect, one of the grandest panoramas in the West Highlands ...

At Armadale, the wretched Lord of the Isles told the Sheriff and Superintendent that, by his latest news, the Sollas people were determined to resist. Joined now by Patrick Cooper, the seasick police sailed on through the 'short, crabbed, punching sea that rolls continually through the Minch', and arrived in Lochmaddy on the evening of 31 July. They could have been in no mood for sweet reasonableness.

The constables marched for Sollas in the rain the next morning, arriving on the hills above it at mid-day. There they waited for Fiscal, Sheriffs and Commissioner, those gentlemen having taken their time over breakfast at the inn. Three black flags were flying over the townships, and a great crowd was gathering. 'All were evidently in such a state of excitement,' said the *Courier*'s reporter, 'that it appeared more than questionable, should an ejectment be proceeded with, whether a promise made to Mr Macrae in the morning that no resistance would be made to the officers, would be fulfilled.' Much of the day was spent in argument, the police standing in wet, ill-tempered ranks while Cooper shouted against the wind, repeating Macdonald's promises and appealing to the people to accept the writs and emigrate. 'Mr Macrae and Mr MacBean added their arguments and advices in Gaelic, but the people resolutely persisted in refusing to leave the island, principally for the reason that it was now too late in the season.' Four or five families promised to leave immediately, but the rest sullenly refused. 'Although the demeanour of the men had been quiet and peaceable, almost all the women of the district, young and old, were assembled around a signal, raised at the top of an eminence, and seemed very much excited.'

At dusk MacBean and Colquhoun decided to withdraw, but a tactical victory had to be scored over the people. A squad of police moved suddenly on the men. There was a short, bitter struggle and Roderick Macphail and Archibald Maclean were dragged out in handcuffs. According to Shaw, they had been ringleaders of the earlier deforcements. When the constables and the gentlemen retired to Lochmaddy, the *Courier* reporter, who was a better newspaperman than his writing suggests, remained behind to get a statement from the people. It was a long and sad account of their hardships, but it confirmed Mulock's claim that 'no petition was sent to Lord Macdonald by the crofters praying for assistance to emigrate'. It also demonstrated that the people had positive ideas of how their happiness and prosperity might be secured without emigration. 'If Lord Macdonald,' they said, 'would increase the crofts to double the present size, for which there is sufficient improvable land, and would give leases and encouragement to improvements, we would be content to pay rents, and we would have seaware and stock sufficient.'

The black flags of defiance were flying again the next morning when the police once more marched down the Lochmaddy road to Mallaglate. Now there was no discussion, no arguments, no appeals. The police formed two lines down the street of the township. Sheriff-Officers asked one question only at the doors of the cottages, whether those within were prepared to emigrate on the terms offered. If the answer was no, and it invariably was, then bedding, bed-frames, spinning-wheels, barrels, benches, tables and clothing were all dragged out and left at the door. Divots were torn from the roof, and the house-timbers were pulled down ready for burning. Patrick Cooper, with a guard of constables, supervised each eviction. 'That a rash young man,' Mulock told Lord Macdonald in the *Advertiser*, 'flushed with sudden authority, and inflated with professional pedantry, should have been let loose upon the ancient retainers of the house of Macdonald, is not creditable to your Lordship's judgment.'

In the beginning the people made a moving protest of silence, but it could not last. When the wife of John Mackaskill rushed from her cottage with a child in her arms, crying '*Tha mo chlann air a bhi air am murt!*' (My children are being murdered!), there was a great shout of anger. The people of Dunskellar, Middle-quarter and Sollas, who had been watching from the hill about the black flag, ran down with stones in their hands. The police drew their truncheons and faced about.

Mr MacBean went up to the crowd, and explained what the men were actually doing in the house. He was listened to quietly; but as he returned a stone was thrown at him, and he had scarcely joined his men when a heavy volley of stones drove the assistants from the roof of the house, and a band of from fifty to one hundred women, with a few boys and men, came running up from the shore, shouting and armed with large stones, with which they compelled the assistants to fall back behind the police for shelter. Fresh supplies of large, sharp-pointed stones were obtained from the bed of a small stream, and several heavy volleys were discharged, most of them, however, falling short of the officers.

MacBean put his men into two divisions and sent them forward against the crowd with their batons. One took the women in the rear, the other on the flank, and drove them over barley-rigs and dykes, along the deep-pooled shore. Some of the women fought with the police, calling out to their men, 'Be manly, and stand up!' Thus constables and women, Highlanders both, fought on the wet heather and the white sand for the possession of Lord Macdonald's land, until MacBean's whistle recalled the officers and the women crawled away to bathe their bloody heads.

The threat of mobbing remained all afternoon to worry Patrick Cooper. Now and then young girls and boys sallied down the hill to throw stones and cry insults. He could not retire, he could not continue without the risk of killing somebody. On the hill maddened women were soon shouting 'such wishes as that the men might come down and wash their hands in their enemies' heart's-blood, and that the devil and his angels might come and sweep them out of the land'. Cooper was learning that however much he might belong to the Age of Steam and the Gas Lamp, the women of Uist were closer to Conn of the Hundred Battles when roused. Sheriff Colquhoun made his distaste plain by refusing to execute some of the writs, claiming that there were

faults in the wording of them, and Cooper now decided that if
he made ten token ejectments, and took some prisoners, the Law
could return to Lochmaddy without the loss of too much dignity.

Archibald Boyd and Roderick MacCuish, tenants of Mallaglate, were taken after a wild scuffle along the shore and placed,
securely handcuffed, in the middle of the police. Cooper then
ordered two last ejectments.

The ninth ejectment was that of a family in Middle-quarter, named
Monk, who had taken an active part in all the previous opposition to
the authorities. It was found necessary to remove the women by
force. One of them threw herself on the ground, and either fell or
pretended to fall into hysterics – (fortunately, I have not had experience enough to know the difference) – uttering the most doleful
sounds, and barking and yelling like a dog for five or ten minutes.
Another, with many tears, sobs and groans, put up a petition to the
Sheriffs that they would leave the roof over part of her house where
she had a loom with cloth in it which she was weaving; and a third
woman, the eldest, made an attack with a stick on an officer, and
missing her blow, sprung upon him and knocked off his hat. Two
stout policemen had difficulty in carrying her to the door.

And now the mood of the people changed. Suddenly, like an
island squall, their resistance was over. Macrae had been busy
among the men, most of whom were sullen spectators only, telling them that if they gave a promise to emigrate the following
year they would be allowed to remain in their houses for the
winter. They did not trust Cooper, they would not promise, but
they asked Macrae for guidance. Meanwhile, to show that he
meant business, Cooper ordered the eviction of the tenth family,
that of Peter Morrison, 'formerly Lord Macdonald's ground-
officer, but who was believed by the managers to have taken an
active part in fomenting discontent'. Whether or not he was
the 'mischievous demagogue' suspected by the *Courier*, he was
prudently absent today at the peat-moss. When his wife and
children had been turned out, his house unroofed, the heads of
the families were gathered at the school-house for their answer.

Still they were undecided. After a passionate appeal, Macrae
secured from Cooper an assurance that they could have until

the morning to accept the writs and sign a pledge to emigrate. Police and officers, Commissioner and Fiscal, then marched away in a wet, tarpaulin tail to the house of a gentleman of the neighbourhood, 'where Mr Cooper put in writing the terms he had before explained to the people, and a copy was sent to each of the four towns. This done, the authorities with their force retired to Lochmaddy, having appointed a meeting with the heads of families at the schoolhouse the next morning at nine o'clock.'

One by one in the morning, under pressure and persuasion from Macrae and Shaw, the tenants put their names to a bond, promising to emigrate to Canada whenever and however Lord Macdonald decided. All their stock they surrendered to Cooper at his valuation, with the exception of a cow and a pony to each family, the one for milk and the other for carrying peat. The four prisoners were released on Macrae's bail and his word that they would surrender themselves for trial when called. There was one last flash of spirit when some of the tenants boldly asked Cooper to put his name to a bond, promising to honour his part of the bargain. This was ignored.

At ten o'clock on Saturday evening, the *Cygnet* left Lochmaddy for Armadale and Oban. The rain had stopped. It was a gentle August night, and the isles were like surfaced whales on the still sea astern. The gentleman from the *Inverness Courier* finished his dispatch on deck. 'The bare, barren hills of North Uist are fading behind me, nor will I regret should they never rise before me again but in memory.'

The people of Sollas were members of the Free Church, and the absence of their minister, Mr Macdonald, throughout the whole unhappy affairs was never explained. The influence of Macrae had been personal, not spiritual. He was a minister of the Establishment.

By the middle of August Thomas Mulock was in North Uist, writing alliterative protests to Lord Macdonald, the Lord Advocate and the *Inverness Advertiser*. 'Is there no hope for landlords,' he asked Macdonald, 'but the expatriation of their humble and attached tenants? Is it a crime that the poor Highland peasantry should still cherish that instinctive patriotism which binds them to their native mountain nooks?' He said that Colquhoun had compelled the people to sign the bond of emigration under threat of pulling their houses down. He accused Macdonald, and other proprietors, of 'sueing *in forma pauperis* for savoury slices from a public charity, the pernicious, perverted Destitution Fund'. And he had no patience with talk of overpopulation, which he called 'the babble of Malthusian deprecators of progeny'.

In traversing large districts I have indeed found the peasantry crowded into some narrow, swampy spots, for which they have been forced to exchange their former patches of cultivated land, now added to the huge farms of some tacksmen up held by cash credits from an accommodating Bank. . . . I maintain that the people are not too many, but that their holdings are too small, their rents too high, their oppressions innumerable, their encouragements nil!

On 13 September the arrested men – Maclean, Macphail, Boyd and MacCuish – appeared before the great Lord Cockburn at Inverness, accused of mobbing, rioting, obstructing and deforcing officers of the law in the execution of their duty. There was strong sympathy for them, and for Lord Macdonald, who was regarded as the victim of events rather than a creator of them. Lord Cockburn found it necessary to clear his mind, and the jury's, of any question but 'Was the Law broken?' The Court could not concern itself with the rights or wrongs of evictions.

There are moral and political considerations involved in such questions with which you and I have no concern. Had I been appointed to settle the question of the propriety of those proceedings I would have declined the task; and I shall endeavour to cleanse my mind from such considerations. Your duty and mine is simply to uphold the majesty of the law; and it would be a grievous consideration for this country if the administration of justice in its Supreme Court could be so tainted. I have no facts before me from which to applaud Lord Macdonald or the people. I do not wish to give an opinion, and so help me God I have no opinion on the subject!

The jurymen had, however. They found the accused guilty, but recommended them 'to the utmost leniency and mercy of the Court in consideration of the cruel, though it may be legal, proceedings adopted in ejecting the whole people of Sollas'. When Cockburn finally silenced the applause which followed this recommendation, he demonstrated that he might have an opinion after all. There was, he said, no reason for a severe sentence; four months in prison would be enough. Justice is as wayward as public opinion. Five years later, in the same court, there was no recommendation to mercy, no public sympathy for Ann Ross and Peter Ross, and Lord Hope passed savage sentences upon them for resisting a bloody assault of police in Strathcarron.

Though he had secured the people's pledge to emigrate, Lord Macdonald was reluctant to send them away from Sollas, and it is not clear whether this was from compassion, doubt, or inefficiency. Whatever the reason, the people suffered from the delay and indecision. In January 1850, Cooper warned them to make 'every preparation within your power to go to America, or elsewhere as you may determine, in conformity with the written bargain existing between you and Lord Macdonald'. In July, when they should have been gone, they were still there. In September they were all removed to Loch Efort, in the south of the island, where each family was given twenty acres of land. These allotments, known as the Perth Settlement, had been made possible by a grant of £1,700 from the Perth Destitution Committee. Though the land was not as good as that at Sollas, had the move been made two years before (and at Macdonald's expense) the people might have been content. But their morale was broken, their energy wasted, and after one bitter season of failure they petitioned Macdonald to send them to Australia. Not unnaturally, the Perth Committee was angry, and accused the people of indolence. It denied that the holdings were poor and too far from the sea, but others, apart from the people, said that this was true, and that no man could hope to make anything of such land. Macdonald argued for months, and at last gave in. Those who were young, or healthy, could go to Australia. He could do nothing for the aged and the sick.

This was not his decision, but one made by the Government's

Emigration Commissioners, who handled the affair in the usual bloodless manner of civil servants. Since Australia had too many bachelors, and too few spinsters, all the young men of Sollas over the age of eighteen were told that they would be given no passage without a wife. Those who hoped to marry girls from their own townships discovered that these had been ordered to remain unwed. For weeks a hundred young men of Sollas wandered through Benbecula and South Uist, looking for wives. 'In such trying circumstances,' said the *Glasgow Herald*, reporting the matter with some astonishment, 'it was hard work to find suitable brides, but the task was accomplished to the great mortification of the young damsels who saw their sweethearts debarred from binding the matrimonial ties with their first loves. But we hope that the young girls will be happily mated at the diggings.'

Just before Christmas 1852, after three years of demoralizing delay, the people of Sollas sailed for Campbeltown in the steamer *Celt*. The old, the sick and the unwanted were left on the island, listening to a piper's lament until the ship could no longer be seen. At Campbeltown the people joined other emigrants from Harris and Skye aboard the frigate *Hercules*. She sailed on 26 December. When she stopped at Queenstown for water and mails, there was already smallpox below decks.

'Prompted by motives of piety and humanity'

HELPED by the Highland Emigration Society and by the Commissioners for Emigration – the one finding the money and the other supplying ships – the lairds of the Isles were now clearing their estates with sickening haste. In one season Colonel Gordon of Cluny removed two thousand people from Mingulay and Barra, Benbecula and South Uist. 'Hear the sobbing, sighing and throbbing,' wrote Donald Macleod of Strathnaver; 'see the confusion, hear the noise, the bitter weeping and bustle. Hear mothers and children asking fathers and husbands, where are we going? hear the reply *Chan eil fios againn* – we know not.' In August 1851, for greater dispatch and the saving of time, Gordon asked the Commissioners to send the transport *Admiral* to Loch Boisdale on South Uist. With maniacal fury his factor, Fleming, drove the people to the shore for a public meeting, and fined each absentee forty shillings. 'At this meeting,' Macleod was told by one of the people, 'some of the natives were seized, and in spite of their entreaties sent on board the transport. One stout Highlander, Angus Johnstone, resisted with such pith that they had to handcuff him before he could be mastered. One morning during the transporting season we were suddenly awakened by the screams of a young female who had been recaptured in an adjoining house, she having escaped after her first capture. We all rushed to the door, and saw the broken-hearted creature, with dishevelled hair and swollen face, dragged away by two constables and a ground-officer.'

The *Admiral* lay close to land, and some of those put aboard her swam ashore again. Fleming led the police and officers in pursuit of them, combing the curling hills to the north of the loch, beating the fugitives down with truncheons and bringing them in irons to the quay. Carts loaded with bound men came over the sand from Benbecula at low tide. Cottages were raided in the early mist of day, but even then some of the people managed to escape. 'Were you to see the racing and chasing of policemen,' Macleod was told, 'pursuing the outlawed natives, you would think that you had been transported to the banks of the Gambia on the slave coast of Africa.'

'Many a thing have I seen in my own day and generation,' remembered Catherine Macphee of Iochdar in the north of the island. 'Many a thing, O Mary Mother of the black sorrow! I have seen the townships swept, and the big holdings made of them, the people being driven out of the island to the streets of Glasgow and the wilds of Canada, such of them as did not die of hunger and plague and smallpox while going across the sea. I have seen the women putting their children in the carts which were sent from Benbecula and the Iochdar to Loch Boisdale while their husbands lay bound in the pen, and were weeping, without power to give them a helping hand, though the women themselves were crying aloud, and the little children wailing like to break their hearts. I have seen the big strong men, the champions of the country, the stalwarts of the world, being bound on Loch Boisdale quay and cast into the ship as would be done to horses and cattle. The God of Life, and He only, knows all the loathsome work of men on that day.'

On Catholic Barra, and on the little isle of Mingulay to the south of it, the evictions were organized by a Protestant minister called Beatson. 'He made himself very officious as he always does,' Macleod was told, 'when he has an opportunity of oppressing the poor Barra men. He is the most vigilant and assiduous officer Colonel Gordon has. He may be seen in Castle Bay, the principal anchorage in Barra, whenever a sail is hoisted, directing his men like a gamekeeper with his hounds, in case any of the doomed Barra men should escape.' One man took shelter on an Arran boat which Beatson boarded in a fury, demanding his surrender. The master lifted a hand-spike and threatened to split the minister's skull, man of God or no, if he did not get ashore with his dogs.

'I have lost my memory since I lost my means,' said Roderick MacNeil, long after he was evicted from the three hills of Mingulay, 'and since my people were scattered, some of them in Australia, some in Canada, and some mouldering in the dust. Oh, the turns of the hard world! Many a trick does it play, and so it was with me. My new house was burned over my head, and I burned my hands in rescuing my dear little children. Oh, the suffering of the poor folk, the terrible time that was! The land was taken from us though we were not a penny in debt, and all the lands of the township were given to a Lowland farmer. He had always wished to have them, and he was not content until he got them.'

Fifteen hundred people from Gordon's estates went to Canada. Six hundred were accepted as paupers and were supported by the colony. Many more begged for bread. They buried their dead in Quebec. 'They were in rags,' said a newspaper, 'their mourning weeds were the shapeless fragments of what had once been clothes.' They went to Upper Canada, where the *Dundas Warder* reported their arrival with indignation. 'We have been pained beyond measure for some time past to witness in our streets so many unfortunate Highland emigrants, many of them sick from want and other attendant causes. . . . There will be many to sound the fulsome noise of flattery in the ear of a generous land-lord who had spent so much to assist the emigration of his poor tenants. They will give him the misnomer of *benefactor*, and for what? Because he has rid his estates of the encumbrance of a pauper population.' Donald Macleod said that when Gordon bought the Isle of Barra his first intention had been to sell it quickly to the Government, for use as a penal colony.

All over the Hebrides the Cheviot tide rose. On Rum, one family only remained of the hundred who had once paid their portion of Clanranald's debts with black cattle and sea-weed. 'All was solitary there,' wrote Hugh Miller. 'We could see among the deserted fields the grass-grown foundations of cottages razed to the ground. It seemed as if man had done with it for ever.' Ulva was turned into a single sheep-walk. The blue isles of Tiree and Coll lost half of their people. St Columba's Iona, 'broad, fertile and fruitful of corn', became the deserted necropolis of fifty Scottish kings and countless forgotten chiefs.* On a dozen islands from Berneray to the Sound of Sleat there was no echo of voices in the hills, and the milkwort flowers grew unpicked by children on the *machair* by the sea.

In the summer of 1851 Alexander Macalister, who styled himself of Torrisdale Castle in Argyll, decided to put sheep on the Strathaird district of Skye which he had lately bought. He was generally regarded as an amiable and inoffensive fellow. That is, said Thomas Mulock darkly, he was 'a man who does all his harsh deeds by deputy'. His new land was a green opening on the west of Loch Slapin, below the black frown of Blaven and the Cuillins. He said that the people's rent had been in arrears

---

*Until the eighth Duke of Argyll, to whom it belonged, guaranteed its tourist prosperity by giving it to the Church of Scotland. He also had himself buried there, with his wife, in a fine marble tomb.

for twenty years ('Pretty factorship this!' thought Mulock), although they said that all they owed was one half-year which they would endeavour to pay, if Macalister would allow them to remain. The debt, he said, was £450, but he would waive it and advance them £1,200 on condition that they went to Canada or New South Wales, whichever took their fancy. Mulock, whose political ideas could occasionally leap-frog into the next century, said that if tenants were given this kind of money to improve their land it would profit both them and their landlord, and there would be no need to replace them with sheep. 'Ah, Mr Macalister of some Argyll ilk, how would you like to be transported against your Scottish will from Torrisdale to Toronto?' The thought of this intrigued the old Irishman. 'Stars and Garters! Just imagine the Duke of Sutherland under orders for some backwoods location!' It is still an interesting thought.

To evict the five hundred people of Strathaird Macalister's factor, a banker in Portree, needed the cooperation of Sheriff Colquhoun, two officers of the Destitution Board and, said Mulock, the threat of using two companies of the 13th, Prince Albert's Own. Donald MacInnes, a native of the isle and one of the Board's officers, first brought the writs to Strathaird, though it was scarcely his business. The people were less inclined to accept his authority than they were to acknowledge the decreets. They drove MacInnes out. He hurried back to Portree, interrupted the Sheriff and the banker at their dinner, and reported that 'The people will do all in their power to resist any number or force that may be brought against them, and they say that they will abide by the consequences'. This, said Mulock, was a lie. But Colquhoun, with unpleasant memories of the screaming women on North Uist, wrote to the mainland and asked for police and soldiers. All this, jeered Mulock, because of 'rebellion in Skye, an armed peasantry, and policemen deforced by two old women and a lame boy!'

Captain Smith of the Destitution Board then went to Strathaird. He read the people a lecture, which they did not understand, and pinned a notice in Gaelic on their church door which left them in no doubt. It told them that they would receive no more relief from the Board, for by Law they should not be there after next term. Since the relief promised them in February had not been paid, this may not have surprised them, but the threat of police and soldiers soon broke any will they may have had to resist. Mulock said that if the Strathaird affair were not an example of what was happening all over the isles, it would be comic.

MacInnes concocts a wicked fable for Captain Smith, and the latter (though fully apprised of its falsity, as we are informed) transmits it to the Highland Destitution Board. The Sheriff on his side is not supine. He sends it to the Lord-Advocate, who straightway orders the Sheriff of Inverness, his Procurator-Fiscal, and a body of police (to be paid for extra by the county) to be ready for immediate action in Skye! Sheriff Colquhoun diligently prepares some extempore harangues on the patriotic duty of emigrating to prevent the pulling down of houses; and the Procurator-Fiscal is quite on the *qui vive* to dictate precognitions of what witnesses never uttered, but for which fiscals must be honestly paid. To crown the whole, the Home Office must get an alarm ... two companies of the 13th, Prince Albert's Own, absolutely required if Strathaird is expected to form part of the British empire.

While the eight townships of Macalister's estate were being cleared, two miles to the east across the mouth of the loch the Trustees of Lord Macdonald were evicting the people of Suishnish and Boreraig. The first was high on a point of land where the sea-lochs of Slapin and Eishort are joined, the second was two miles to the east by an idling path. The people, most of them surnamed Macrae and MacInnes, were the descendants of men who had once formed part of the armed rent-roll of the Macdonalds of Sleat. They raised barley and potatoes, had boats for inshore fishing, and grazed some stock on the braes of Beinn Bhuidhe. Their life had been hard since the Great Famine. The Trustees of Lord Macdonald argued that he had been overindulgent to this community, that he had allowed the people to waste good land, and that it would be better for them and it if they were removed. Patrick Cooper, who was skilled at special pleading, let it be known that in evicting the people his Lordship had been 'prompted by motives of benevolence, piety and humanity, because they were too far from the church'.

Most of the people were removed without trouble in 1852 and sent to Campbeltown, where Emigration Commissioners put them aboard the *Hercules* with the demoralized tenants of Sollas. And for some of them, too, there was death from small-pox in Queenstown harbour. Thirty-two families were left in Boreraig and Suishnish, and when they heard what had hap-pened to their kin on the transport they asked Macdonald to let them remain in Skye, for no one could now claim that the town-ships were overpopulated. On 4 April 1853, they were warned that writs of removal would be executed against them in the autumn.

Macdonald, the factor of this district, was also a Sheriff-Officer and the local Inspector of the Poor, and he used the authority of two of these offices to rid himself of the responsibilities of the third. On a golden day in September, with the Sheriff-Substitute and a body of police, he came down the Portree road, crossed Loch Slapin from Strathaird, and began the removals. Most of the men of the townships were away, working in Glasgow or on the railways that were crawling like vines across the Low-lands, but some were in the hills with their cattle. They heard the crying of women, the barking of dogs, and a hammering as the officers nailed up the doors of the cottages. They came down in haste, and there was a short, brutal struggle on the shore by Boreraig. When it was over, Alexander MacInnes, John and Duncan Macrae were in irons. They were dragged thirty miles to Portree and their families followed them, weeping.

The evictions continued. 'The scene was truly heartrending,' Donald Ross, the lawyer, wrote to the *Northern Ensign*. 'The women and the children went about tearing their hair, and rend-ing the heaven with their cries. Mothers with tender infants at the breast looked helplessly on, while their effects and their aged and infirm relatives were cast out, and the doors of their houses locked in their faces. No mercy was shown to age or sex, all were indiscriminately thrust out and left to perish.' There was no word spoken of emigration, or of other land on Skye which, in an unguarded moment, Lord Macdonald had said might be theirs. The doors were nailed up and the people were told to go. When the officers left at dusk the women and children crawled into byres and sheep-cots. And waited.

At Portree, the two Macraes and MacInnes gave their word to appear before the Court of Justiciary in Inverness. Without food and without money, they walked a hundred miles, and arrived two days before their trial, surrendering themselves with dignity at the Tolbooth. Factor and Sheriff-Officers, who were to appear against them, had already arrived 'in their conveyances,' said Donald Ross, 'at the public expense, and lived right loyally, never dreaming but that they would obtain a victory and get the three men sent to the Penitentiary to wear hoddy, break stones, or pick oakum for at least twelve months.'

At their trial the men were defended by a persuasive and passionate advocate called Rennie. 'It really becomes a matter for serious reflection,' he said, 'how far the pound of flesh allowed by the law is to be permitted to be extracted from the bodies of Highlanders. Here are thirty-two families driven out, and for what? For a tenant, who, I believe, has not yet been found. But it is the will of Lord Macdonald and Messrs Brown and Ballingall that they should be ejected; and the civil law having failed them, the criminal law with all its terrors is called in to overwhelm these unhappy people. But, thank God, it has come before a jury !' And the jury, with great enthusiasm, returned a verdict of Not Guilty.

The Macraes and MacInnes went back to Loch Eishort, where their families and others' were living in the shelter of walls and huts. The men opened the houses, put back the roof timbers and lit peat on the hearths again. The little victory was brief. Notwithstanding the verdict at Inverness, the writs of removal were still valid in law. Five days after Christmas, in a bitter wind and drifting snow, the factor Macdonald came again with his men. In Suishnish they turned out all the MacInnes family, the old man Neil who was its head, and his sons Alexander and Donald. Bedding, furniture and crockery were thrown through the doors. Donald MacInnes was away looking for sheep in the snow when he heard the cries and shouts from Suishnish, and he came back at the run. His sick wife was cowering against a wall in a bedgown and with a child at her breast. He tore down the bars from his cottage and carried her inside again, and when the factor threatened him with prosecution he 'armed himself with a formidable oak cudgel which he promised to bring with all his strength over the head of the first who would meddle with his wife or with himself'.

In Boreraig the factor's men were floundering in the snow, dragging out the belongings of the Macraes. The mother of John and Duncan was eighty-one, and Macdonald yelled at her to take up her bed and walk. When she said nothing, but stared at him with dark eyes, he ordered her to be pulled out on her blanket. A Macrae child of seven stood before the factor crying, 'O nam bitheadh m'athair an so an diugh, co aig an robh a' chridhe so dheanamh oirnn!' (If my father was here today, who would dare to do this to us!) But it was done, and once more the houses were nailed up, and the snow fell on the little heaps of clothing, on the women and the children huddled against the walls.

Many of them were still there in February, living like animals in the open, when Donald Ross came from Glasgow with food and clothing. He found Flora Robertson, a widow of ninety-six, existing on half a crown a month from the Parochial Board. She had been living in a sheep-cot since the September eviction, and was starving. 'Anything more wretched than the appearance of this old woman I never yet witnessed. Her bed, a pallet of straw and some pieces of old blanket was on the bare floor. Her face and arms were the colour of lead. I asked her what was it she complained of most. She tried to raise herself up, and she replied, "I complain of nothing, but weakness and the want of food." '

He saw seven children, all under the age of eleven, lying in a shed on 'a collection of rubbish, fern, meadow-hay, straw, pieces of old blanket and rags of clothing'. Rain and snow fell upon them. They were so thin, and so light he said, that he could have carried them all in his arms for a quarter of a mile without feeling their weight. 'It would be insulting the feelings and commonsense of right-thinking persons to ask them if this is a fair and legal treatment of the poor. The injustice is so palpable, the inhumanity so great, that one can scarcely find language sufficiently strong to condemn it!' The Parish Relief for the families was rarely more than two shillings a month.

Eighteen people were still living on the shore at Boreraig when spring came, or on the muir about Suishnish. The others had gone, to Portree or Glasgow, or had died in the open like Flora Robertson. By the first warm days of summer the townships were at last empty, and in time Lord Macdonald's Trustees found a tenant for the land. The market for wool and mutton was uneasy that year, owing to the war in the Crimea. Fleeces that would have fetched 21s. 6d. a stone in 1853 were being sold for less than 15s. but the newly published *Wool Market Circular* in Inverness said that prices for ewes and wedders were still high, and this promised an early return of stability.

One of the last to leave Boreraig had been an old man of eighty-six. 'I have paid sixty-six rents to the Macdonalds,' he told Donald Ross, 'and I am not one farthing in arrears. To be cast out of my house and my home to make room for his sheep is what I never expected. It is breaking my heart.'

'Oh do not, I beseech you, lose sight of the poor'

WHEN Alistair Ranaldson Macdonell, 15th Chief of Glengarry, made that over-confident leap from a sinking steamer in Loch Linnhe he left his title, his example, and his debts to his son, Aeneas. The young man accepted the rank with pride, the example with caution, and the debts with horror. He did his best to be a romantic like his father, but he had neither the conviction nor the health to support the strain. The debts were more easily honoured, and when he reached his majority he evicted his people and sold some of his lands to pay them. Lord Abinger, the jurist (and father to General Scarlett of Balaclava) bought the mortgage on Inverlochy for £75,150. Edward Ellice, son of a founder of the Reform Club, became the laird of Glenquoich and, fortunately for the Highlands, a fierce critic of Poor Relief administration. When the estate of Glengarry itself was auctioned at the Old Signet Hall, Edinburgh, it was bought for £91,000 by William Ward, an Englishman and 11th Baron of the name. Ward resurrected the spirit of Alistair Ranaldson by wearing kilt and plaid, and by holding Highland gatherings for his friends. He also introduced the flavour of English squirearchy, organizing ploughing matches among those few tenants who remained between his sheep-walks.

All that was left to the 16th Chief was the far land of Knoydart, a knuckle of mountains on the west coast between Loch Nevis and Loch Hourn. When sales of his property were completed he emigrated to New South Wales. He left in October 1840, in comfort and in style. He took with him his wife Josephine and family, his servants, his piper, clothing, bedding, bolts of tartan, furniture, a comprehensive selection of agricultural tools, and a number of prefabricated timber houses. His departure, said the *Inverness Courier*, could not be considered without emotion and regret, and it was a comfort to know that the piper was going too. 'These Celtic strains will sound strange in the new world of the wanderers, so far removed from their native Loch Oich, the Rock of the Raven, and other magnificent scenery of the Glengarry mountains.' Word was heard of the Chief now and then, that he had arrived in New South Wales with all his gear and goods, that he had been guest of honour at a St Andrew's Day fete in Port Phillip, that he had 'announced his intention to proceed alone, with his family, to the great South Land.' Two years later a Scots traveller met him in an out-back inn. The chief was so well strapped with pistols that 'his countryman mistook him for a bushranger. An explanation followed and they spent the night together, discussing *Lochaber no more!* Glengarry had just bought 100 cows for £10 each.'

And then he was back in Scotland, prematurely aged and dying. The great South Land had not been all that he had hoped. In 1852 his widow buried him beside Alistair Ranaldson at Kilfinnan, and prepared to pay the debts which his heir (a minor, as seemed to be the way with these Glengarrys) had inherited.

With her son's trustees and his factor she planned the clearing and the sale of Knoydart.

Knoydart had been the most westerly of Macdonell lands. Its conical hills rise abruptly from the sea and from lakes of black glass. Columns of summer sunlight support the clouds above it, and its beauty is an eternity of melancholy. Marshal Wade broke no way into Knoydart, and Cumberland's burning infantry touched its shores only. In 1852 the road that reached it from the east was frequently impassable, abandoning incautious travellers in a blue wilderness. This road ran through Edward Ellice's estate for thirty miles, and here there were no townships, nothing but Cheviot wool. 'Had I been walking through the wild territories of the Hudson's Bay Company,' said Donald Ross, who went that way to Loch Hourn, 'I could scarcely see greater signs of desolation.'

Most of the people of Knoydart had gone to Canada during the long century of Macdonell emigration. Those who remained lived in townships on the coast. In 1847 there had been over six hundred of them, but the poverty which followed the Great Famine had scattered most of these. The land which the remainder worked was good, and had they received encouragement and help, thought Donald Ross, they could have grazed more sheep and cattle, raised vegetables and corn, and thus paid their rents with money to spare, though such modest husbandry would not have settled the debts of the 17th Chief. They were Catholics for the most part, and were cared for by a selfless priest, Coll Macdonald, known to them as *Maighstir Colla*. In an open boat, winter and summer, he took the Sacrament from township to township along the coast. By 1853 there were only seventy families in his parish, but all the people, Protestant or Roman, loved him. Half a century later the children of Glengarry in Australia and Canada were still calling their sons Coll in his memory.

Since they lived on the coastal fringe of Knoydart, and worked none of the inland valleys needed for a sheep-walk, the people were no real obstacle to the Great Cheviot. But no incoming tenant in the Highlands now wanted the financial responsibility of a near-pauper population. If the thought of their eviction troubled the conscience of Josephine Macdonell, her factor, an old man called Alexander Grant, eased it for her. The people were in arrears, the people were making ill-use of the land, the people wished to emigrate.... And, of course, Mr James Baird wished to buy the estate. He was a Lowlander, a great admirer of Robert Burns, who had bought the estate of Cambusdoon in Ayr because that was the poet's shire. When he had built himself a fine house there, on the banks of the Doon, he invited Miss Isabella Begg, a niece of Burns, to break a launching bottle of whisky over its door. Mr Baird's money came from iron and coal, and he was a generous benefactor of the Church of Scotland.

The arrears of rent in Knoydart were £2,300, or so Alexander Grant claimed, and Mrs Macdonell had apparently forgotten that this was due to the fact that after the Famine her husband had written to Grant from Australia, directing that no rent should be taken until better times, for he looked upon the people 'less as tenantry than as children and followers'. When a reader of the *Inverness Courier* questioned the ethics of ignoring the wishes of a dead man, Alexander Grant replied that Mrs Macdonell 'acting for her son, considered it a duty to remove a non-paying body of tenants.' The people of Knoydart, with uneasy memories of what Glengarry widows had done to their clan in the past, petitioned Grant at Martinmas in 1852, soon after the death of Aeneas, offering to pay what rent and arrears they could in return for a promise that they would remain on their holdings. They tried again in 1853, but by then Mrs Macdonell was making arrangements with the Highland Emigration Society and the Board of Supervision for their speedy dispatch to Australia. Having received Sir John MacNeill's approval, and a promise from the Society that a transport would be sent, she instructed Grant to prepare and execute the writs of removal. 'Just as if,' said Donald Ross bitterly, 'they had been a parcel of broken-down useless slaves she was desirous of getting rid of.'

At the end of August 1853, the Government transport *Sillery* came to Isleornsay on Skye, and waited there for the people to be ferried across the Sound of Sleat from Knoydart. The evictions began soon after her arrival, and Mrs Macdonnell came up from Edinburgh to Invergarry, to be near should there be papers to sign or orders to give. Under the direction of Grant, parties of men with axes, crow-bars, and hammers, visited each township, and daily the *Sillery's* boats rocked across the bronze sea to Inverie, Sandaig, Doune and Airor. Four hundred people were cleared from their homes, and those who refused to go in the boats ran to the hills and hid in caves. Grant ordered the destruction of each house immediately it was evacuated. 'Not only the houses of those who had left,' said Ross, 'but also of those who had refused to go. The inmates were ordered out, the thatch was pulled off, picks were stuck into the walls, the levers removed the foundations, axes cut the couple trees, and then roof, rafters and walls fell with a crash. Clouds of dust rose to the skies, while men, women and children stood at a distance completely dismayed. From house to house, hut to hut, and from barn to barn the factor and his menials proceeded.' The few huts left standing belonged to paupers on the poor roll of Glenelg parish. Grant warned them that if they gave shelter to the evicted, 'for one moment by day or night', they too would have their homes levelled.

One of those evicted from the township of Airor was Allan Macdonell, a widower with four children. Thirty years before he had gone to Edinburgh with Alistair Ranaldson, to support the chief's dignity before George IV at Holyrood. 'Commercially speaking,' said Donald Ross, 'Allan Macdonell now has no value at all. Had he been a roe, a deer, a sheep, or a bullock, a Highland laird in speculating could estimate his "real worth" to within a few shillings, but Allan is only a man. Then his children – they are of no value, nor taken into account in the calculation of the sportsmen. They cannot be shot at like hares, blackcocks, or grouse, nor yet can they be sent to the south as game to feed the London markets.' Macdonell said that he did not wish to emigrate, and would not go aboard the *Sillery*.

A widow called Elizabeth Gillies sat by her fire and refused to move. One of Grant's assistants threw water on the peat, two more pulled at the old woman's arms. She fought with them, screaming, and they struck at her fingers with sticks when she caught at her door-posts. She crawled on her knees to a dyke-wall, and watched as the agents threw out her furniture, 'broke down the partitions, took down the crook from over the fireplace, destroyed the hen-roosts, and then beat the hens out through the broad vent in the roof of the house.'

Charles Mackinnon, who was seventy and lived alone, was waiting at his door for the factor. Grant asked him when he was going. 'As soon as I can,' said Mackinnon. He put on his bonnet and plaid and walked away from the boats, up into the hills. Alexander Macdonell carried his pregnant wife to the shelter of a bush, refusing to put her aboard the *Sillery* when she was so close to labour. Catherine Mackinnon, sick in bed, asked that she be given God's time to recover, and then she would go to the boats, or anywhere the factor ordered. She was taken out and put in a ditch. These things were repeated again and again until all the cottages in all the townships were emptied and destroyed. 'No hand was lifted, no stone cast, no angry word spoken,' said Ross. 'Able bodied men who, if the matter would rest with mere trial of physical force would have bound the factor and his party and sent them out of the district, stood aside as dumb witnesses ... As far as the eye could see the face of the strath had its black spots, where the houses of the crofters were either levelled or burnt, the blackened rafters lying scattered on the grass, the couple-trees cut through the middle and thrown far away, the walls broken down, the thatch and cabers mixed together, but the voice of man was gone.'

The *Sillery* sailed. The russet Highland autumn was over. There were white frosts on the hills when sixteen families came down from the rocks and the caves and began to put their houses together. They stretched blankets over the walls, and built shelters from the timbers. Grant sent men to destroy these and to burn them, and to tell the people that they were tres-passers. Three families were living in the store-house, and this too was burned. 'The couples and rafters were of old mountain-pine, full of resin, the cabers dry as tinder. The thatch of old moss divot. The straw and heather covering, all dry, all combustible, blazed away magnificently, illuminating the whole district.' Father Coll visited the families regularly, tacking up the coast in his little boat. He collected money from other districts, bought a tent or two, and took seven old people back to his house at Sandaig on Loch Nevis, building them a shelter in the garden. He must also have been the 'much-respected clergyman' who wrote to Donald Ross soon after the *Sillery* sailed, telling the lawyer what had happened and of his fears for the winter. 'One of the young women lay for some time beside a bush; she was afterwards brought within the wall of her former house, where she lay for three days so ill that her recovery was very doubtful. The other woman, Mackinnon, is very unwell as yet, it is not unlikely that this cold weather will put an end to her suffering and her life together.'

Ross wrote to Grant, asking him for permission to send tents and blankets to Knoydart. The factor, who was busy explaining to the *Inverness Courier* why the widow Glengarry had been forced to clear her tenants, referred Ross to her law-agent in Edinburgh. He received no reply from this man at all, 'although there are four mails every day from Edinburgh to Glasgow'. Meanwhile he received another letter from Coll MacDonald. 'To-day, the 22nd October, is the stormiest day we have seen this year, and yet the servants from Inverie are after making their round, destroying the shelters of the outcasts! All those poor creatures are out there exposed to the raging elements. The officers and servants have broken their huts now six times with the first warrant. If this is legal, you know best. Oh do not, I beseech you, lose sight of the poor who are living without shelter in this dreadful weather!'

Collecting what clothing and tents he could, Ross left for Knoydart. He travelled by road to Loch Hournhead, and there hired a small boat to take him to the township of Airor, thirty-four miles away, where most of the people had collected. The voyage was rough for the first half of the journey. 'A strong current like a powerful tide rushed up the loch, boiling and raging, and had our bark the power of an ordinary steamer it would have baffled her to make head against such an element. We had to change our course, ply our oars, and soon got into smooth water again, and a gentle breeze soon starting, filling our unreefed sail, we steered along under the shadow of the high hills of Knoydart, rounded several rocky points, and reached the pier at Arar by seven o'clock at night, after a voyage of four hours and a half.'

He found and spoke to all sixteen families, took the names and ages of the parents, the names and ages of the children, and published them all before Christmas in a pamphlet called *Scenes at Knoydart*. Each wretched individual was given his careful, compassionate attention. 'Allan is still a fine specimen of a highlander, well-made, good-looking and muscular. He has fallen off very much of late, however, in consequence of exposure to cold and damp.' There was Angus Kennedy, a boatman, whose 'wife's complaint is caused by some mismanagement, and by want of proper nourishment and appliances after a premature birth.' Ross called at each hovel, each hole in the ground, greeting the people with respect and in the Highland manner: *'Failte na maduin duibh!'* (Hail, good morning to you). Children crawled from holes in the ground to stare at him with large, dark eyes. 'The boy was complaining very much of colic. He looked pale and very ill, and said he had sore arms. The father pointed to the hole where he and the boy had to lie all night. It was damp and rain from the level roof kept dripping on them.' One man had built a crude shelter for his family four times, and four times it had been destroyed by Grant's men. 'On one occasion they surprised the inmates boiling a pot of potatoes, they took the roof off the hut at one sweep, then put out the fire and ordered the wretched lodgers out at the door.' Ross told each story in detail, each family's agony, until they all became one pain that numbs.

'Had this Emigration Committee not been so very accommodating,' said Ross with restrained anger, 'had Sir John MacNeill not been so very ready with his promises of large ships, need I say that Mrs Macdonell would not have been so ready to warn out and evict the peasantry on the Glengarry property? Such conduct deserves exposure.' He did his best to expose it. He went back to Glasgow, wrote to the *Northern Ensign* and published his pamphlet. He appealed for food, clothing, meal, and justice. 'It is most unfair to bargain with "Committees", and to arrange about large ships fit to carry away the whole population of a Highland district without first consulting the population that is sought to be packed off.'

Throughout the winter he gathered and sent what supplies he could to Father Coll, and in February he made another bitter, snow-driven visit to Knoydart. He became a better newspaper-man with every letter he wrote to the *Northern Ensign*, and this time he told the story of the cold and starving people through the case of one of them only – Catherine Mackinnon, who had asked the factor for God's time to recover before he put her out. Ross headed his letter 'AUNTY KATE'S CABIN', taking theme and title from a novel then exciting the country. He presumed that few people had not read 'Mrs B. Stowe's' work, and he said that fiction was not 'so strange as the *simple* narrative of *facts* I am about to give'.

On 18th Feb. last I found poor 'Aunty Kate' under the bush and blankets covering her 'cabin' at Inverie ... After reaching the spot where I was told it stood I was surprised I could not see it. I went on a little further and then I observed a little mound, like some huge molehill, with some smoke issuing from the end of it. Approaching nearer I was satisfied it was the abode of a human being, for I heard through the openings a hard coughing inside. My friend now came up and we both went to the door of the cabin, and Mr Macdonald (*Father Coll: J.P.*) asked how Aunty Kate was. At first he got no answer, for the door, which consisted of empty sacks thrown double across a rope, was fast closed down, and two branches were thrown across from the outside, signifying that one of the two inmates was out. Mr Macdonald then went to the other side and having cleared away the snow with his staff, he lifted an old divot and cried 'A' cheat, coid an coir a tha airbh an duibh?' ('Catherine, how are you feeling this day?') Immediately the poor creature turned round in her bed and putting a little, withered hand out through the hole in the roof, she grasped her friend's hand firmly, telling him at the same time that she felt no better, but worse. I put my eyes to the little opening in the roof ... Aunty Kate has a very miserable look, her face is pale, her eyes black, and as she speaks from underneath the blankets at me the place puts me in mind of where I kept my pet rabbits as a boy. The cabin was in two divisions, one for sleeping, the other for cooking. The sleeping division I already noticed, the other is a small place about four and one half feet long, by four feet broad. The height is two feet nine inches. A small partition of staves and pieces of cloth divides the apartments, and the entrance to the sleeping apartment is just about the size of a door in an ordinary dog kennel.

In this Catherine Mackinnon, aged about fifty, lived with a niece. Most of the other families were no better housed. Allan Macdonald ('his head is swelled, his hearing defective now') lived with his four children in the space between a collapsed roof and a wall. Donald MacEachan at Airor, his wife, baby, and two small children, were huddled under an old sail. 'The mother's breasts were dry as corks, and although the poor infant continued pulling at them for nourishment, it could procure none.' Alan Mackinnon's wife was dying of consumption. Alexander Cameron's wife was advanced in pregnancy, and he was sick with asthma and rheumatism, and both were crouched in the roofless corner of a cottage. And so on. So on. And over all of them was the white, silent snow of a Highland winter.

In addition to the public disgust which Ross aroused by his letters, he also secured the powerful support of Edward Ellice who sent blankets and food to the people. As a member of Parliament and a substantial land-owner, Ellice was listened to with more attention than was the angry Glasgow advocate. He wrote to Sir John MacNeill, Chairman of the Board of Supervision, and freely gave a copy of his letter to Ross for publication. He said that parochial relief had been poorly given, if at all to some of the people. There was no medical man in the parish, or nearer than Skye across the Sound. Although Catherine Mackinnon was on the Poors' Roll as an infirm person, she had received no portion of meal sent to the Highlands for such persons, and had in fact been struck from the Roll for no given reason. He accused the local Inspector of the Poor of being party to the destruction of the hovels which the people had built, so that they might not become a demand on Parish Relief. 'I am not aware of the exact powers of the Board,' he told MacNeill, 'but if they can institute an official inquiry there seems to me to be, in this instance, a *prima facie* case for one. No inquiry, however, can be satisfactory in its results unless conducted by a neutral party, and ample opportunity given to the people of the district to state their alleged grievances.' He said that, to his mind, Knoydart was 'only *part of a system* of trying to starve people who, from age or infirmity, are unfit objects for emigration, into submission to being sent out of the country, or, at all events, out of the parish they properly belong to. Opposed to the common principles of humanity and good government, it appears to me to reflect discredit upon the country where it is permitted to exist.'

In the flutter this aroused, few heard the voice of Alexander Grant who was still pleading that it was neither his fault nor his employer's that people who had been offered a passage on the *Sillery* were now freezing, starving, and destitute. The Lord Advocate ordered George Young, Sheriff of Inverness-shire, to make a full inquiry, and to discover whether Ewen Campbell in Morar, the Local Inspector of the Poor, should be arrested on charges of neglecting his duty. The right of a proprietor to issue writs of removal against his tenants was not questioned, and nobody suggested an inquiry into the conduct of Alexander Grant, Josephine Macdonell, or the Trustees of the 17th Chief of Glengarry.

On Wednesday, 1 February 1854, Andrew Fraser the Sheriff-Substitute at Fort William left for Knoydart with his Clerk, the Fiscal, and Dr Crichton the senior medical practitioner of the town. The weather was bitter and angry, even for those parts, and it delayed them at Father Coll's house in Sandaig, where Ewen Campbell complained that his papers were in Glenelg. He was sent to fetch them. 'A distance by sea of upwards 25 miles,' Fraser reported to the Lord Advocate, 'The weather broke up the day after (he) crossed over to Glenelg by sea, the 3d, and it may give you some idea of the state of the weather when I mention that his boat did not get back till the 10th; he reached us, however, with the books, crossing the hills of Glenelg and Knoydart, two days sooner.'

Meanwhile Fraser, the Fiscal and the doctor had begun their inquiries, visiting the paupers whom Campbell was accused of neglecting, taking down statements from each, and making careful medical examinations. They travelled ten or fifteen miles every day in the company of Father Coll, who acted as witness, guide and interpreter. Their report, when they made it to the Lord Advocate, was precise and comprehensive. They said that in Knoydart and Glenelg the proprietors' contribution to Poor Relief was 1s. 2d. for every pound of rental they received, and that this amounted to £396 8s. None of the proprietors – the Glengarry Trustees, James Baillie, Lord Lovat, nor even the conscientious Mr Ellice – had ever attended a meeting of the Parochial Board to discover how this one and twopence in the pound was being spent. From the offhand manner in which Mr Fraser announced this, it does not seem to have been an uncommon thing.

The paupers examined were almost all women. 'Their houses are of the worst description ... the wretched inmates scantily and miserably clad. Their clothes, such as they are, being limited to one suit; they have no change of raiment, and are dirty and uncomfortable-looking in their persons, many are without shoes and stockings.... Their food is scarcely limited to potatoes, they cannot provide themselves with meal or other articles of diet sufficient to keep them alive during half the period.... One miserable family (Alexander MacIsaacs, Doune), consisting of a man cripple and blind of an eye, with a wife suckling an infant a month old, and six other children, whose allowance was 19s. 6d. per quarter, we found preparing their daily meal, consisting of potatoes and *dulse* gathered off the rocks, boiled and mashed together.'

When called upon for a sworn statement, Ewen Campbell admitted that he had known of the wants of the Knoydart paupers,* that their allowances were inadequate, that their ac-

---

* Only a handful of the evicted people of Knoydart were considered to be paupers within the Act, and entitled to Parish Relief.

commodation was deplorable, that he had given them 'no nutritious diet', that he had found them no medical attention. But, he said, 'he was acting under the orders of the Parochial Board who gave him no discretionary powers, limiting his duties to the simple payment of the quarterly money allowances fixed by the Board'. Sheriff Fraser thought it relevant to add that the minute-books of the Board did not show that Ewen Campbell had ever informed it of the conditions in Knoydart, or recommended an increase in the allowances. Two police constables from Fort William, however, had made a report to the Board of Supervision, but the members of the Parochial Board, when examined by Fraser, said that they did not know whether the policemen were telling the truth or not. 'I know nothing personally,' said James Stavert, factor to Baillie of Glenelg, 'regarding the state, past or present, of the Knoydart paupers. I never was at Knoydart but once in my life, and I never visited the paupers there.' Another member of the Parochial Board was the Reverend John Macrae, Protestant minister of the parish. He said 'I did not visit them, these people are of a different communion from me, and have their own priest to attend them.'

The Lord Advocate sent Andrew Fraser's report to the Solicitor-General who, in July 1854, laid it before Parliament. He said that the condition of the paupers disclosed by the precognitions was very distressing. There must have been some defective administration of the Poor Law, yet there was quite obviously a difficulty in proving a case of neglect against the Inspector. 'A conviction to some extent might perhaps be obtained, but it is more likely that the inspector would be acquitted while the Parochial Board might be blamed.' Rather than risk this injustice, he decided that criminal proceedings were not necessary.

Probably no one was more astonished than Ewen Campbell.

That summer the *Inverness Courier* reported briefly: 'Proceedings have been taken to remove those crofters who were allowed to remain in Knoydart at the time of the evictions last year.' Soon after they were gone, Mr Baird the ironmaster put his sheep on their hills.

'As to those ridiculous stories about the Duchess ...'

AT the beginning of 1853 more than half a million women
in Britain put their names to what *The Times*, grumbling on
behalf of their husbands no doubt, regarded as impertinent interference in another nation's affairs: *An Affectionate and Christian
Address of Many Thousands of Women in Great Britain and
Ireland to Their Sisters, the Women of the United States.* The
signatures filled twenty-six large folio volumes, and the address
was emotional. 'We appeal to you, then, as sisters, wives, and as
mothers to raise your voices to your fellow-citizens, and your
prayers to God, for the removal of this affliction and disgrace
from the Christian world.'

The affliction was slavery. The whole western world (with
the exception of Papal Rome where the book was of course
banned) was reading *Uncle Tom's Cabin*, a sentimental, melo-
dramatic and tendentious account of slavery written by a
woman whose personal knowledge of the subject had been gathered during a weekend in Kentucky.* It was no more a true picture of the slave-owning South than slabs of wood were ice in
numberless dramatizations of Eliza's flight across the Ohio. But
the book may be ranked with the Bible, the Koran, and *Das
Kapital* in its profound effect on human emotions and actions.
It made dumpy little Harriet Beecher Stowe one of the most
famous women in the world, and in Britain she was for a while
a greater literary lion than Dickens or Thackeray (neither of
whom thought much of *Uncle Tom*). When forty ladies of
Society gathered at Stafford House in March 1853, under the
leadership of the second Duchess of Sutherland, to decide what
should be done with those twenty-six folio volumes, they

---

*Goodbye to Uncle Tom, by J. C. Furnas (Secker & Warbourg, 1957)
contains a full account of her surprising ignorance. A far more
reliable account of American slavery was published in 1863 by the
actress Fanny Kemble in her *Journal of a Residence on a Georgian
Plantation in 1838–1839.*

resolved to send the *Address* to Mrs Stowe. Not only had she
inspired the feelings that had prompted it, but she was obviously
the one person to present it to her compatriots. At least, that
was the opinion of the Duchess, though many Americans were
inclined to agree with *The Times.*

Harriet Elizabeth Georgina Sutherland was a Howard, her
ancestry weighted by the coronets of Carlisle, Devonshire,
Marlborough, Sunderland and Bedford. Her marriage had been
one of the most brilliant achievements of the Countess Elizabeth.
She was beautiful, witty, charming and romantic. She was the
confidante of and Mistress of the Robes to Victoria for twenty
years, and at Court she had the good sense to behave 'like a head
housemaid', veiling her beauty and muting that wit. But when
the Queen was her guest – at Dunrobin where a new wing was
built for the occasion, or at Stafford House – she was the sun in
a galactic setting. 'I come from my house to your palace,' said
Victoria, peering at the wealth which the first Duke had hung
on the walls. The Duchess Harriet was an amateur architect and
landscape gardener, filling notebooks with details of the houses
she saw abroad, and when her husband built Cliveden in Buck-
inghamshire it was modelled on the Villa Albano near Rome.
She liked comfort and luxury (as the Duke had hastily reminded
himself after his father's funeral), but she could also weep for
the suffering and poverty of others. She entertained foreign
liberals like Garibaldi, and patronized the harmless oppressed at
home. When impoverished silk workers of Spitalfields brought
her a roll of cloth, in a colour they had called Magenta in honour
of Napoleon III's victory over those tyrannical Austrians, she
had it made into a gown, wore it to Court, and imposed the
fashion upon the country. At her invitation Shaftesbury held
many reform meetings in Stafford House. 'She was always ready,'
he said after her death, 'to give her palaces, her presence, and her
ardent efforts for the promotion of anything that was generous,
compassionate and good.'

And what could be more compassionate and good than the
abolition of slavery in the United States. With the Duchesses of
Bedford and Argyll, with Ladies Shaftesbury and Palmerston,

she organized that mammoth address to the women of America, and when the author of *Uncle Tom* visited England shortly afterwards she suffocated what real sensibility the woman had under extravagant attention and affection. At Stafford House, on her first visit, Mrs Stowe was received by two great Sutherlanders in kilt and plaid. They led her through treasure-chambers. Liveried servants called her name at every door of every empty room. Her memory, and later her pen, recorded the furniture of white and gold, the walls of green damask, the crystal, the paintings, the newness of costly things, the age of the invaluable. There was nothing like this in Cincinnati, Ohio. In the final room of all there was waiting this still-beautiful, middle-aged creature with creamy shoulders, dark hair and splendid eyes, one of the few women whom Winterhalter could paint without flattery. There too, by his wife's chair, was the Duke, old, white, exceedingly deaf and exquisitely polite.

The one Harriet instructed the other in the subtleties of British Society, introduced her to the Palmerstons, Russells, Gladstones, the right-thinking and the well-born. She was an American thrush among ospreys, and when she came again to Britain in 1856 she was welcomed by the Duchess less as a guest than as an old friend. It was no secret that on this visit Mrs Stowe was gathering material for a book, a journal of her European tour, and it was with the suggestion that she might find much to employ her pen in the Highlands that the Sutherlands invited her to spend a few days at Dunrobin. The Duchess of Argyll, who competed with her mother the Duchess Harriet in most things social or philanthropic, sent an invitation from Inveraray. Mrs Stowe was thus given an opportunity of seeing more of Scotland than she had ever seen of Kentucky.

Elsewhere than in the ducal drawing-rooms where she spent most of her time, men took an interest in her visit to the Highlands. Donald Ross wrote to her at Inverary, saying that he had read in the newspapers that she had come 'to make notes on the clearances and to report the result in your future "Memoirs of a Sojourn to the Highlands of Scotland"'. If indeed she had made such an announcement it would suggest that the Duchess Harriet's invitation had not been without a hook in the bait. Remembering Aunty Kate's Cabin in Knoydart, Ross sent her some of Donald Macleod's pamphlets on Sutherland, in the hope that they would help her to understand that not all Uncle Toms had black skins. He received no reply, no acknowledgement. He wrote to her again at Dunrobin Castle. From what he had heard of her visit, he said, he thought that she was – '... ill-prepared to write anything worthy of being read regarding the clearances and the cruelties to which the Highland people are subjected. At Dunrobin Castle you are in a manner tied to the Duchess of Sutherland's apron strings. You are shown all the glory and grandeur of the Ducal residence. You are brought to see extensive gardens, aviaries, pleasure-groves, waterfalls and all that is beautiful and attractive, and you are occasionally treated to a drive along the coast road for some miles, through rich farms and beautiful corn-fields, and to finish all you are asked to be present at an exhibition of stockings, plaids, winceys, and tartans made up by poor females from a distant part of the country. But you have not visited Strathnaver, you have not penetrated into Kildonan, you have not been up Strathbrora, you have not seen the ruins of hundreds and hundreds of houses of the burnt-out tenants.'

Indeed she had not, but the Duke had given her son Henry a magnificent plaid of the Sutherland tartan. The Duchess gave her a copy of Mr Loch's book, so that she might understand the nature and extent of the Great Improvements. The author she could not meet. He had died a year before at his house in Albemarle Street, and on the day of his death there had been evictions on the Sutherland estates of Tongue and Farr. At Achtoly near Tongue, John Mackay stood outside his cottage with his wife, his children and his furniture while officers of the estate cut the couples, tore down the back wall and felled the roof-tree. The next day the same officers went to the house of Christy Mackay, described by the *Northern Ensign* as 'a harmless, inoffensive but sensible girl'. The factor accused her of giving shelter to an evicted family, and of having in her cottage at this moment an aged pauper. The officers dug a hole in the ground and put the old woman in it, and then nailed up the house, leaving Christy Mackay weeping against a dry-stone wall. At Armadale, while his house was destroyed, Angus Sutherland led his family in the singing of the 43rd Psalm. . . .

On the day of James Loch's funeral his son wrote in his journal 'What eminent and great qualities he had! What a long and useful life! His whole existence is one long lesson. How simple, direct in his aim, sagacious, wise and fine!' Thirty gentlemen followed the hearse to Brompton Cemetery, led by the Duke of Sutherland 'very much affected'. While Mrs Stowe was at Dunrobin plans were already in hand to give James Loch a monument in the county. At the top of the steps leading to it was to be placed a commemorative tablet:

> To the honoured memory of
> JAMES LOCH
> who loved in the serene
> evening of his life
> to look around him here
> May his children's children gather here
> and think of him
> whose life was spent in virtuous labour
> for the land he loved
> for the friends he served
> who have raised these stones

In time Mrs Stowe published her account of her visit to Europe, calling it with some aptness *Sunny Memories*. That section which dealt with Sutherland was a loyal defence of Improvements, and leant heavily upon Mr Loch's book, and on letters from Loch which Lord Shaftesbury had allowed her to copy. It referred, obliquely, to Donald Ross and to Donald Macleod's pamphlets which the Glasgow lawyer had sent her. 'What led me more particularly to inquire into these facts was that I received an account containing some of these stories which had been industriously circulated in America. There were dreadful accounts of cruelties practised in the process of inducing the tenants to change their place of residence.' She was happy to say that such stories were mostly slanders put about by Sheriff

MacKid, and that Mr Sellar, against whom they had been directed, had been exonerated before the Court. She did not say that forty sheep-farmers occupied land that had once supported ten thousand people, and she did not think it necessary to repeat what Donald Ross had written to her: 'Upon the top of the hill, *Crockan-a-choillich*, you can set a compass, with 25 miles of a radius upon it, and go round with it fully-stretched, but, mark what I say, within this broad circumference you will not find a single human habitation, or one acre of land under cultivation, save that occupied by shepherds belonging to some sheep-farmers. With regard to this very district Mr Donald Macleod in his book, which I sent you, says, "And I recollect when 2,000 able-bodied young men could be raised within the same circuit in 48 hours!".'

She defended her friend the Duchess with vigour and passion. Since the publication of the *Affectionate and Christian Address* some Americans had been asking why they should be lectured by an Englishwoman who 'turned her tenants out into the snow, and ordered the cottages to be set on fire over their heads.'

As to those ridiculous stories about the Duchess of Sutherland, one only has to be here, moving in society, to see how excessively absurd they are. I was associating, from day to day, with people of every religious denomination and every rank of life. I have been with dissenters and with churchmen; with the national Presbyterian church and the free Presbyterian; with Quakers and Baptists. In all these circles I have heard the great and noble of the land freely spoken of and canvassed, and if there had been the least shadow of a foundation for any such accusations, I certainly should have heard it.

Mr Eric Findlater was one Free Church minister whom she had obviously failed to consult. On National Fast Day at Lochearnhead, shortly after Loch's death, he had preached a windy but impassioned sermon against the proprietors, against sheep-farmers, against factors such as Evander MacIver of Scourie who was now serving the second Duke of Sutherland as ably as Patrick Sellar had served the first, against eviction, and against the Godless substitution of men by sheep. Mr Findlater was naturally overconfident of the Judgment awaiting the landlords

('Already may they discern the forth-putting of the hand that wrote on the royal palace walls of Babylon the ominous words *Mene, Mene Tekel Upharsin !*') but the theme of his sermon was so popular that he was encouraged to publish it, in green covers, price sixpence.

A ravenous spirit of avarice seems to have spread like an epidemic and seized on all those who were the owners of property in the Highlands. They hastened to be rich, and in the determination to succeed they cast away all claims of gratitude and justice. They became so blinded with this lust after riches that the strong bond which had for ages knit chieftain and clan became as withes which were broken in a moment – ancestral associations were cast to the winds – those whose fathers had bled and fought and died for their fathers were henceforth to be cast out – and a sheep was now to rank higher than a man.

But to Mrs Stowe what had taken place in the Highlands was 'an almost sublime instance of the benevolent employment of superior wealth and power in shortening the struggles of advancing civilization'. Had not Mr Loch written that Sutherland farmers now desired hot baths and water-closets in the houses which the Estate built for them? Were there not eight bakers in the county, and forty-six grocers nearly all of whom sold shoe-blacking, 'an unmistakable evidence of advancing civilization'? If there had been abuses in the early days of Improvement, the Duchess Harriet could scarcely be held responsible for them now. 'Everywhere I have heard her kindness of heart, her affability of manner, and her attention to the feelings of others spoken of as marked characteristics.' No one apparently, none of those churchmen and dissenters, those national and free Presbyterians, Quakers and Baptists (where had she found *nonconformists* in Sutherland?), none of them had told Mrs Stowe what her dear, dear friend's son and daughter-in-law had been doing on their Ross-shire estates in 1852.

In March that year forty people, eighteen sub-tenants and their families living in Coigach at the mouth of Loch Broom and at the western end of Destitution Road, heard that they were to be served with writs of removal in the names of the Marquess and Marchioness of Stafford. Young Lord Stafford, who was twenty-three, had ambitions to be as great an Improver as his grandfather and Coigach was his first attempt at clearance. The sub-tenants were paying rents to William Mackenzie & Company of Ullapool, two merchant brothers who held a lease on Coigach from Stafford and who now wished to be relieved of it. He proposed to remove all the people because his factor said they were 'altogether unable to occupy beneficially the large extent of hill-pasture attached to their little allotments of land.' There was, of course, another sheep-farmer waiting in the wings to take possession as soon as lease and land were vacant.

At the beginning of March the Mackenzies told Sheriff-Substitute Cameron in Dingwall that the people were threatening to resist the writs and to deforce any officer bringing them. Cameron asked the Lord Advocate for soldiers, but was told to test the strength of the resistance first, and then rely on the County Police. If this failed, then might he have bayonets. He went to Ullapool with the Procurator-Fiscal, with Stafford's law-agent, and with a body of Sheriff-Officers. William Mackenzie advised him against going by road to Coigach, 'so hostile are the inhabitants of Ullapool and the surrounding country'. He offered the use of his boat, and even here there was a difficulty, the wives of the crewmen pleading with their husbands not to take the oars. 'The wife of one,' said the *Inverness Courier*, 'finding her appeals ineffectual, placed an infant, which she held in her arms, on the beach and walked away, leaving the little mortal crying bitterly in the hearing of both parents!'

On the shore at Coigach the boat was met by the people, standing in the now customary battle-order, the women and boys in the van, the men to the rear. They were civil and threw no stones, but refused to let the Sheriff pass to the township. Another boat now came from Ullapool, with Andrew Scott the factor, and with the writs of removal. When Scott joined Cameron, shouting threats against the wind, a group of women and boys ran to his boat, took the writs from the thwarts, burnt them and dragged the boat two hundred yards up the beach. One of the Mackenzies, Alexander, liking none of this, and feeling that

the responsibility for violence might be his company's told Scott
that he and his brother wished to withdraw their renunciation
of the lease. Though he was in a fury, the factor had to accept it.
'The Messrs Mackenzie being then the tenants for another year,'
said the *Courier*, 'the service of the summonses became unnecessary. Mr Scott and his crew were carried back in Mr Mackenzie's boat with the Sheriff's party to Ullapool, where they
arrived about midnight.' The people had won, and Andrew Scott
gave the young Marquess what comfort he could. 'It was a distinguished triumph of brute force over law and order,' he said,
'and while it continues in the ascendant the rights of proprietors
must remain in abeyance.'

Sunny Memories provoked a long and bitter reply from Donald
Macleod, then in exile in Canada. He made selections from his
earlier writings, polished them and improved them, and published
them as *Gloomy Memories*. He said that he could prove his facts
with 'a cloud of living witnesses', Sutherland emigrants living
near him in British North America. And he would allow her no
pardon for her friend.

I agree with you that the Duchess of Sutherland is a beautiful, accomplished lady who would shudder at the idea of taking a faggot or a
burning torch in her hand to set fire to the cottages of her tenants,
and so would her predecessor, the first Duchess of Sutherland, likewise would the late and present Dukes of Sutherland. Yet it was done
in their name, under their authority, to their knowledge, and with
their sanction. The dukes and duchesses of Sutherland, and those of
their depopulating order, had not, nor have they any call to defile
their pure hands; no, no, they had, and have plenty of willing tools
at their beck to perform their dirty work.

He accused Harriet Stowe of being paid by the Duchess to
write 'your panegyric'. This was unjust and untrue. She was a
simple, impressionable woman, an amateur reporter who did not
know how or where to find the truth. She could believe no evil
of a woman who so admired *Uncle Tom* and so passionately supported the abolition of slavery. Shoe-blacking, savings-bank,
post offices, fifty thousand barrels of herrings and forty thousand
fleeces were civilization, and the Gaelic tongue was an obstacle

to them, if Mr Loch said so. In his efforts to persuade her (or, rather, his readers) Macleod foolishly exaggerated the happiness of the Sutherlanders before the Improvements began. 'Now, Madam, I can tell you, and hundreds will back me, that before 1812 there were thousands of bakers in Sutherland. There were 26 shops in the county, and 31 blacksmiths. The Sutherland people never knew what want was until they became subject to Loch's iron sway.' This was nonsense, of course. More accurately, he reminded her of the crimes against humanity that had been committed in the county during the responsible lifetime of her Duchess. He told her of houses dragged down, townships destroyed, families separated. He told her that armed men had guarded the Duke's salmon and trout rivers during the Famine, when the people had lived on sea-weed. More armed men, with Newfoundland dogs, 'watched the mussel scalps to preserve them from the people, and to keep them to supply the fishermen on the opposite side of the Moray Firth'. Men could not work, marry, or worship except by the delegated authority of the husband of a woman 'who is so religiously denouncing the American statute which denies the slave the sanctity of marriage, which separates, at the will of the master, the wife from the husband, the children from the parents.'

The results of James Loch's Improvements were not to be read in his book, or seen from the windows of Dunrobin. 'If you took the information and evidence upon which you founded your *Uncle Tom's Cabin* from such unreliable sources, who can believe one-tenth of your novel? I cannot.'

'Send your deer, your roes, your rams to fight!'

AT the beginning of the Crimean War, General Officers in Whitehall turned instinctively to the Highlands for the blood and the bone to expend upon it. They remembered the Napoleonic wars (much too well and much too often, some of them) when the mountains had been a prodigal source of superb foot-soldiers.

In his feathered bonnet, tight red coat and black Government tartan, the Highland soldier had been present in company, regimental or brigade strength at every battle from Walcheren to Waterloo, and in every country where this first world war was fought. Highlanders were the earliest native regiments raised by imperial Britain, and like all such levies they had first been used for the subjection of their own people and then for the defeat of others. Their history and their pride committed them to war as the proper realization of man, and they went into battle shouting slogans that had been heard at Harlaw, and to pibrochs that had been played at Culloden. In 1815 it was stated in Scottish newspapers, and generally believed, that 14,000 men of the Black Watch alone had been killed or disabled since 1803, and that casualties in other Highland regiments had been equally bitter. 'So firm and prevalent is this belief,' complained David Stewart of Garth, 'that when young men enter those regiments it is considered much the same as if a sentence of death had been passed upon them.'*

But the dead of one war are used to inspire recruits for the next, and in April 1854, the lairds of Sutherland, Argyll, Seaforth and Gordon were asked to muster their young tenantry in new battalions of the regiments that carried their names. On the evidence that lay in War Office files, there was reason to believe that the response would be as bountiful as it had always been. During the American Revolution more than eleven thousand men had been raised for the Fraser, Argyll, Macdonald, Atholl and Seaforth Highlanders. Two thousand of them had been Frasers from Lord Lovat's country. In thirty years the Seaforth family filled five battalions with the sons of its tenants. Between 1793 and 1815, 72,385 Highlanders served in forty line, fencible or reserve battalions, seven regiments of regular militia, and a number of companies of local militia. 'Moral, well-principled and brave,' said David Stewart, 'they have never failed in any kind of duty entrusted to them.'

---

*In fact, said David Stewart, of 20,500 men who served in five Highland regiments, 668 only were killed in action, 235 of them in the Black Watch.

It was not only the great lords who were responsible for supplying the British Army with the equivalent of seven or eight
infantry divisions during the French Wars. Sir James Grant of
Grant raised a fencible regiment of five hundred men from his
estates in Strathspey and Glen Urquhart, and in the following
year he found another thousand for a regular battalion. Alan
Cameron of Erracht mustered eight hundred men in Lochaber
for the 79th, and the small gentlemen of Ross and Lewis provided the same number for a second battalion of the 78th. Tacksmen did the recruiting for the chiefs and the proprietors, gathering men by persuasion and by threat, and for every company of
a hundred men they brought to the colours the laird was granted
the right to dispose of commissions for a captain, two lieutenants
and an ensign. Not only were Highland regiments of value to the
Government as élite troops, they were also much cheaper to raise.
'To the south of those hills,' said David Stewart, 'no recruits
could be raised without money. In the north money had its influence, but, in raising soldiers, it was less regarded than the
character and family of the person recruiting, and with whose
fortunes the young soldiers connected themselves.' An influence
just as strong, of course, was the power which tacksman and
laird had to evict or punish their tenants-at-will.

Probably no one district made a greater contribution of men
than the Isle of Skye. Four thousand were enlisted there between
1793 and 1805. According to a letter which Donald Ross wrote
to the *North British Mail* in 1854, the island's roll of service by
1837 had amounted to:

Lieutenant- and Major-Generals	21
Lieutenant-Colonels	48
Majors, Captains, Subalterns	600
Pipers	120
N.C.O.s and Men	10,000

Ross said that Skye had also provided the country with four
Colonial Governors, one Governor-General, a Chief Baron of
England, and Judge of the Supreme Court of Scotland.

Though Highland regiments had their spectacular mutinies

these were invariably over points of honour, or the result of broken promises. The stubborn discipline of British line regiments was created by the whip and the gallows, and English soldiers accepted this with a brute stoicism and a perverse pride. Outside their red ranks a man could be hanged for stealing five shillings, and armies have always reflected the worse features of the systems they defend. In Highland regiments, however, crime was uncommon and punishment rare. 'To the young Highlanders,' said Stewart, 'the dread of corporal punishment not only checks their military propensity, and prevents their entering the army, but it conveys to their minds a greater deal of horror and shame than death itself. When a Highlander is brought to the halberts* he considers himself as having lost caste. He becomes, in his own estimation, a disgraced man, and is no longer fit for the society of his friends. To them, therefore, or to his native countrymen, he can never return.' A soldier who is docile in barracks and a fury in battle is an ideal, and the Highlandman of the French wars was unique. But if army commanders begin a new war with the tactics and weapons of the last, they frequently assume, also, that they will be employing the same type of man. In 1854 they were as mistaken in this as ever.

Of thirty-three infantry battalions that were sent to the Crimea, three only were Highland – the 42nd, the 79th and the 93rd. By autumn, when Colin Campbell's Highland 'Brigade' at Balaclava consisted of the 93rd Sutherlanders only, a bewildered question was being asked in the Press, in Parliament, in pulpits, and, somewhat fretfully here, in Windsor Castle: *Where are the Highlanders?*

There was no immediately apparent explanation for the failure of the recruiting campaign. In England it was difficult enough to get men for the Army, but this had always been the case. Figures published by *The Times* that summer showed that the population of the northern shires of Scotland had increased, and if the growth was not as great as in other parts of Britain quite

---

*A combined axe and pike carried by sergeants. A man ordered for flogging was spread-eagled on a frame made from four of these weapons.

clearly there were more men in Argyll, Sutherland and Inverness than there had been in 1793. An unconsidered fact was that districts where thousands of young soldiers had once been found were now empty except for shepherds and sheep. The parishes of Farr and Kildonan, for example, which had once supplied most of the men for the 93rd when the regiment was formed, could scarcely muster a company of young men now, even were they willing. The glens of Ross, where the 78th and the 42nd had found their battalions, were deserted, and there were few Camerons in Lochaber for the 79th. It was not realized, and could not be understood in London, that in the past the lairds had raised their regiments as much by threat of eviction as by appeals to clan loyalties, and that although their rents had been low their tenantry had been great. Now rents were high and the people no longer lived on the land. For fifty years eviction for profit had dispersed them, to the coasts or the colonies, and had destroyed the old influence of the chiefs. 'My people have been set wandering,' said the bard Calum Campbell Macphail, 'many are the places to which they have been scattered . . .'

> When the strife begins
> the poor man will be needed.
> The gentry will be calling for him
> over the face of the hills.
> Echo will answer
> 'Do not be afraid in this day of stress
> when you have an abundance of hornless sheep.'

Betrayed and bitter, the people who remained turned their backs on the recruiters. To the Isle of Skye, so fruitful in the past, went a Captain Otter. 'After beating about all winter in the lochs and bays,' said Donald Ross, 'with all sorts of music, flags, ribbons, and tempting offers printed in Gaelic and English he only succeeded in getting one Skyeman to enlist, and after getting him he found the poor wretch was not worth the keeping and dismissed him.' In Breadalbane, where a Campbell lord had once put sixteen hundred of his tenants' sons into a fencible regiment, his own son (the evicting capercailzie enthusiast) was now 'sarcastically recommended to try how the present residents in the Black Mount, sheep, would look with red coats on.' The young men of Ross, unattracted by a bounty of £2 which proprietors were offering to every recruit, took to the hills when British warships anchored in the Cromarty Firth, and the newspapers, unwilling to admit the truth, said that the credulous fellows believed that the Russian fleet had arrived. Lord Macdonald went to the Isles and asked men to remember how their fathers and their grandfathers had served with the 78th. 'You remember Sollas!' he was advised, 'when you would have sent soldiers against us. What security have we that in a very short time we would not be called upon to clear out our kin and our friends to make room for sheep?' Throughout the Highlands men came to recruiting meetings in angry protest. They bleated and they barked. Spokesmen among them stood up and told the landlords 'Send your deer, your roes, your rams, dogs, shepherds and game-keepers to fight the Russians. They have never done us any harm.'

The Duke of Sutherland was among the first to receive the Government's appeal for recruits, and because the 93rd was already under orders for Scutari it was thought that he would have no difficulty in raising a second battalion to join it. No doubt he thought so too. His mother had raised the regiment, a thousand men, and a thousand more for a fencible regiment to serve against the Irish. With an extraordinary lack of perception, he asked James Loch to go to Sutherland and arrange the matter. The Commissioner was 74 and within a few months of his death, but he went to work like a loyal and conscientious servant who requires no reward but continued employment. He toured the county for six weeks with no success. 'More fruits of the Loch Policy', said the *Northern Ensign*, after the fishermen of Golspie had booed him from the town. The writer was Donald Ross again:

In Sutherland not one single soldier can be raised. Captain Craigie, R.N., the Duke's Factor, a Free Church Minister and a Moderate Minister, have been piping for days for volunteers and recruits; and yet, after many threats on the part of the Factor, and sweet music on the part of the parsons, the military spirit of the poor Sutherland serfs could not be raised to fighting power. The men told the parsons 'We have no country to fight for. You robbed us of our country and gave it to the sheep. Therefore, since you have preferred sheep to men, let sheep defend you!

At last the deaf old Duke travelled north from London, and called a meeting of all the male inhabitants in the parishes of Clyne, Rogart and Golspie. Not all came, but four hundred were there to cheer him politely as he stepped from his carriage in Golspie. He was accompanied by four clerks who sat at a table before the Inn, and who laid upon it piles of notes and coin. 'The Duke addressed the people very seriously,' one of the crowd wrote to Donald Macleod in Canada, 'and entered upon the necessity of going to war with Russia, and of the danger of allowing the Czar to have more power than he holds already, of his cruel and despotic reign in Russia, etc., likewise praising the Queen and her government, rulers and nobles of Great Britain, who stood so much in need of men to put down and keep down the tyrant of Russia.' Every man who enlisted in the 93rd would be given, there and then, a bounty of £6, or £3 if he chose some other corps. This money would come from the Duke's private purse.

He then sat down, and platform and people stared at each other in silence. He rose again, 'his anxious looks assuming a somewhat indignant appearance', and he asked for an explanation. He got it from an old man. 'I am sorry for the response your Grace's proposals are meeting here, but there is a cause for it. ... It is the opinion of this county that should the Czar of Russia take possession of Dunrobin Castle and of Stafford House next term that we couldn't expect worse treatment at his hands than we have experienced in the hands of your family for the last fifty years. ... How could you expect to find men where they are not, and the few of them which are to be found among the rubbish or ruins of the country have more sense than to be decoyed by chaff to the field of slaughter. But one comfort you have. Though you cannot find men to fight, you can supply those who will fight with plenty of mutton, beef and venison.'

Macleod said that one man only was enlisted at this meeting, and he was a silly man who believed that thereby 'his bread was baked for life, but no sooner was he away to Fort George to join his regiment than his place of abode was pulled down, his wife and family turned out, and only permitted to live in a hut from which an old female pauper was carried a few days before to the churchyard.' Macleod said that the Duke, who was away south to London again, knew nothing of this, but it had been done in his name by the Factor.

When the recruiters left the Highlands, without the men they had hoped for, Donald Ross jeered at the astonished landlords. 'Let them bring out their cooks and their housemaids with pokers and broomsticks, and their flunkeys and coachmen with switches and pitchforks!' But the young men of Sutherland, remembering their ancestors and those few of their kin who were dying of cholera and cold before Sebastopol, did not wish it to be thought that they were cowards. They called a public meeting and drew up an address to the newspapers.

We have no country to fight for, as our glens and straths are laid desolate, and we have no wives nor children to defend as we are forbidden to have them. We are not allowed to marry without the consent of the factor, the ground officer being always ready to report every case of marriage, and the result would be banishment from the county. Our lands have been taken from us and given to sheep farmers, and we are denied any portion of them, and when we apply for such, or even a site for a house, we are told that we should leave the country. For these wrongs and oppressions, as well as for others which we have long and patiently endured, we are resolved that there shall be no volunteers or recruits from Sutherlandshire. Yet we assert that we are as willing as our forefathers were to peril life and limb in defence of our Queen and country were our wrongs and long-endured oppression redressed, wrongs which will be remembered in Sutherlandshire by every true Highlander as long as grass grows and water runs.

But to reverse history and overturn a profitable economy in return for six hundred willing recruits to the 93rd was a ridiculous proposal, and it was given less thought by the landlords than it received space in the Press. As the war continued, so did

the little evictions. Some disbanded men of the 93rd came home
to the parish of Lairg to find that a factor known to them as
Domhnal Sgrios, Donald Destruction, had cleared their families
and pulled down their houses. They caught him at his work,
stripped him naked and beat him with switches of gorse, and
though this may have raised their spirits higher than hearing
Colin Campbell call upon them to stand firm at Balaclava, it did
not give them back the land. Over all the Highlands the earth
now belonged to the Lowlander and to the Great Cheviot.
'Heavy, sorrowful my heart, going through the glen,' said John
Maclachlan of Rahoy.

> On an April morning I no longer hear
> bird-songs, or the lowing of cattle on the moor.
> I hear the unpleasant noise of sheep
> and the English language, dogs barking
> and frightening the deer.

The slow attrition of the people went on, small removals as
the sheep-walks changed hands, grew in size, or were broken
into lots. Thirty years after Knoydart, and sixty since Strathnaver, the cause of the people was taken into politics by the
Land Restoration League and by a League for the Nationalization
of Land. On Skye and Lewis crofters fought with police, Marines
and Royal Scots. Before Lord Napier and his Commissioners of
Inquiry, old men and old women remembered their childhood in
the Year of the Burnings. The Land Leagues had their poet in
Mary Macdonald of the Songs, and with her they believed that
'Deer and sheep will be wheeled away and the glens will be
tilled. The cold, ruined houses will be raised up by our kinsmen.'
But Lord Adam Gordon had seen the future more clearly a century before. The people did not return to the Highlands. When
Australian mutton and Australian wool, bred and sheared by the
children of emigrants, destroyed the wealth of the True Mountain Sheep, the land was given to the deer and the sporting rifle.
In time, spruce and fir were regimentally planted over the ruins
of the townships and the enduring green of the potato gardens.
Men accepted the removals as inevitable, a casualty of progress,

though Sinclair of Ulbster had hoped for something better from the animal he brought to the north. And in 1845, Delane's unknown Commissioner had written from the Inn at Ardgay :

What, then is the remedy? Employment. Give employment to the people. Create employment. Pursue a course directly the opposite in its tendencies to that now pursued. Do not make employment more scarce by turning the hills and glens into sheep-wilds. Make many yeomen out of one sheep-farmer. A people, the mass of whom it is evident can now only just live, cannot create employment. That is a duty his Grace of Sutherland *ought* to perform ... Promote factories; surely with water-power costing nothing, and wool at your doors, you can make cloth as cheaply as it can be made in Yorkshire. This will employ your population instead of driving them to Canada ... Abandon the tenant-at-will system; give leases, or make such agreement as shall secure the tenant as well as the landlord; and independence of spirit, and improvement, and enterprise, will rapidly follow.

At Culloden, and during the military occupation of the glens, the British government first defeated a tribal uprising and then destroyed the society that had made it possible. The exploitation of the country during the next hundred years was within the same pattern of colonial development – new economies introduced for the greater wealth of the few, and the unproductive obstacle of a native population removed or reduced. In the beginning the men who imposed the change were of the same blood, tongue and family as the people. They used the advantages given them by the old society to profit from the new, but in the end they were gone with their clans.

The Lowlander has inherited the hills, and the tartan is a shroud.

APPENDIX

Principal Characters

AIRD, The Rev. Gustavus. Minister to the people of Glencalvie.

BAILLIE, James. Banker, merchant and landowner, who put Glenelg under sheep.

CHISHOLM, William. Tinker and 'gypsy' of Strathnaver, whose mother-in-law Patrick Sellar was accused of murdering.

CHISHOLM, William. 24th Chief of Clan Chisholm who began the clearance of Strathglass.

ELLICE, Edward. M.P. for St Andrews Burghs. Bought Glenquoich on the Glengarry estates, a critic of the administration of the Poor Law in the Highlands.

GEDDES, Thomas. Lowland sheep-farmer whom Lockhart-Ross of Balnagowan brought to the North.

GILLANDERS, James. Factor to Robertson of Kindeace and other lairds. Evictor of Strathcarron and Strathconon.

GILLESPIE, Thomas. Lowland grazier who brought sheep to Glengarry and Strathglass.

GORDON, Colonel John, of Cluny. Bought South Uist and Barra and was responsible for wide and brutal clearances there.

LOCKHART-ROSS, Sir John of Balnagowan. Retired admiral. Began sheep-farming in the Highlands.

LOCH, James. Commissioner for the Marquess of Stafford's Estates in Scotland and England. Creator of the Policy of Improvement.

MACDONALD, Lord. Godfrey William Wentworth, Fourth Baron of the Isles, descendant of the Macdonald chiefs of Sleat. Authorized the clearing of his people on North Uist and Skye.

MACDONELL, Alistair Ranaldson. 15th Chief of Glengarry. The 'True Highlander' and model for 'Fergus MacIvor' in *Waverley*. The great clearances of Glengarry began under his chieftainship.

MACDONELL, Josephine. Wife of the 16th Chief of Glengarry who cleared Knoydart in 1853.

MACDONELL, Marjorie. 'Light-headed Marjorie', wife of the 14th

Chief of Glengarry, who brought Thomas Gillespie to the Highlands.

MACKENZIE, the Rev. David. Minister at Achness in Strathnaver, and later of the Parish of Farr.

MACKENZIE, Sir George Steuart, of Coul. Mineralogist, agriculturalist. Author of A *General View of Ross and Cromarty*. An advocate of clearance and sheep-farming.

MACKID, Robert. Sheriff-Substitute of Sutherland, who brought Patrick Sellar to trial.

MACLAUCHLAN, Thomas. Presbyterian divine and Gaelic scholar, writer against the evictions.

MACLEOD, Donald of Geanies. Sheriff-Depute of the County of Ross. Suppressed the Sheep Riots of 1792 and 1820.

MACLEOD, Donald. Stonemason of Strathnaver. Author of *Gloomy Memories*. Prolific writer against the clearances and the Loch Policy.

MACNEILL, Sir John. Chairman of the Board of Supervision of the Scottish Poor Law Act.

MATHESON, James. Made a fortune trading in China. Bought the Lewis Estate for £190,000, also Achany in Sutherlandshire. A liberal and generous proprietor. Later knighted. M.P. for Ross.

MULOCK, Thomas. Journalist and Baptist Minister. Father of Mrs Humphrey Craik. Attacked the Duke of Sutherland and other proprietors in the *Inverness Advertiser*.

ROBERTSON, William. 6th laird of Kindeace, in whose name writs of removal were first issued against the Glencalvie people.

ROBERTSON, Charles. 7th laird of Kindeace, a Major in the 78th Highlanders. Son of the above.

ROSS, Donald. Lawyer of Glasgow. Wrote of the evictions in Strathcarron and the destitution in Knoydart.

SAGE, the Rev. Donald. Minister at Achness during the last clearance of Strathnaver. Son of the Minister of Kildonan.

SELKIRK, 5th Earl of. Founder of the Red River Settlement in Canada to which the Kildonan people emigrated.

SELLAR, Patrick of Morayshire. Advocate, later a prosperous sheep-farmer. Factor to the Marquess of Stafford, charged with homicide after the first Strathnaver evictions.

SHOEMAKERS' David Ross Senior, David Ross Junior, and Alexander Ross, tenants at Glencalvie who were known as *Greusaich* – Shoemaker. Evicted in 1845.
Also William Ross in Greenyards.

SINCLAIR, Sir John, of Ulbster in Caithness. President of the Board of Agriculture (which he created). Brought improved methods of agriculture and stock-breeding to northern Scotland, and also the Great Cheviot Sheep.

STEWART, David of Garth. An officer of the 42nd in 1792 and later a major-general and governor of St Lucia. In his *Sketches of the Highlanders* he defended the people against the Improvers.

STOWE, Harriet Beecher. Author of *Uncle Tom's Cabin*, friend of the second Duchess of Sutherland. Wrote *Sunny Memories* in support of the Sutherland family and the Loch Policy.

SUTHERLAND, Duchess-Countess of. Elizabeth Gordon, daughter of the last Earl of Sutherland, *Ban mhorair Chataibh*, the Great Lady of Sutherland. Married the 2nd Marquess of Stafford who acquired through her the great estates of Sutherland.

SUTHERLAND, 1st Duke of. George Granville Leveson-Gower, 2nd Marquess of Stafford. The largest landowner and probably the richest man in Britain of his time. Authorized the Loch Policy of Improvement in Sutherland.

SUTHERLAND, 2nd Duke of. George Granville Leveson-Gower succeeded his father, the above, in 1833. Continued the work of Improvement and clearance.

SUTHERLAND, 2nd Duchess of. Harriet Howard, daughter of the Earl of Carlisle, Mistress of the Robes to Queen Victoria. Invited Mrs Stowe to Sutherland. Attacked by Thomas Mulock and Donald Macleod.

TREVELYAN, Sir Charles. Assistant-Secretary to the Treasury. Administered Irish relief works in 1845, also relief during the Highland Potato Famine of 1846. Chairman of the Highland and Island Emigration Society.

YOUNG, William. One-time corn-chandler of Morayshire. Became the first Commissioner and later the Chief Factor under Loch for the Stafford estates. Responsible for early evictions in the west. Became a rich sheep-farmer.

Chronology

Two periods of major clearances: 1782–1820; 1840–1854

1762 Sir John Lockhart-Ross inherits Balnagowan and introduces sheep-farming to the north.

1782 Thomas Geddes, a Lowland sheep-farmer, takes a lease on Balnagowan land.

1783   Thomas Gillespie rents a sheep-walk on Glenquoich from Macdonell of Glengarry.

1784   The Forfeited Estates, administered by the Crown since the Jacobite Rebellion, are restored to their owners.

1785   First large clearances on Glengarry's estates.
        Marriage of Elizabeth, Countess of Sutherland, to the Marquess of Stafford.

1786   Large emigrations to Canada from Knoydart, on Glengarry's property.

1790   The Great Cheviot brought to Ross and Caithness.

1792   THE YEAR OF THE SHEEP.

1800   First clearances in Sutherland, small numbers to the north of the River Oykel.

1801   STRATHGLASS. Beginning of the evictions.

1802   Disbanded men of the Glengarry Fencibles leave for Upper Canada.

1807   SUTHERLAND. Ninety families removed from the parishes of Farr and Lairg.
        The Northern Association of Gentlemen Farmers and Breeders of Sheep resolve to obtain a Royal Charter to extend their activities in Inverness, Ross, Sutherland and Caithness.

1809   SUTHERLAND. William Young and Patrick Sellar take employment with Lord Stafford. Removals from the parishes of Dornoch, Rogart, Loth, Clyne and Golspie.
        STRATHGLASS. More large clearances.

1812   SUTHERLAND. Patrick Sellar clears wide districts in Assynt.

1813   SUTHERLAND. Removals in lower Kildonan. The 'rebellion' of the Gunns.
        James Loch becomes Lord Stafford's Commissioner.

1814   THE YEAR OF THE BURNINGS. First clearance of Strathnaver.

1815   The Society of True Highlanders formed by Alistair Ranaldson Macdonell of Glengarry.
        James Loch publishes a brief account of the Improvements completed and proposed for Lord Stafford's estates in Sutherland.

1816   THE TRIAL OF PATRICK SELLAR.

1817   An annual sheep and wool market established in Inverness.

1819   SUTHERLAND. Final clearance of Strathnaver and Upper Kildonan.

1820   ROSS. The Culrain Riots and evictions in Strathoykel.

1821   SUTHERLAND. Riots and evictions at Gruids.

1825   The kelp industry, in decline since the end of the French Wars, is now destroyed by the abolition of the excise duty on salt. The lairds of the Isles, particularly Clanranald, begin the sale of their estates.

1829   Lord Stafford buys Lord Reay's Country.

1830   Emigration increases with destitution. According to the northern Press this year 'a fever of emigration is raging in the county of Sutherland'.

1831   The Marchioness of Stafford, Countess of Sutherland, tours Lord Reay's Country.

1832   CHOLERA.

1833   Death of Lord Stafford who, six months before, was created Duke of Sutherland.

1836   FAMINE.

1839   Death of the Duchess-Countess of Sutherland.

1841   SUTHERLAND. Rioting and deforcement in Durness.

1842   ROSS. First attempt to deliver writs of removal to the people of Glencalvie.

1845   ROSS. Glencalvie cleared. Delane of The Times sends a Special Commissioner to report.
Failure of the potato crop in Ireland and famine.

1846   FAMINE following the potato blight.
Establishment of Destitution Relief Boards in Glasgow and Edinburgh.

1847   Food riots.

1849   GLENELG evictions.
SOLLAS evictions from Lord Macdonald's land on North Uist.

1850   STRATHCONON evictions by James Gillanders and others.

1851   SOUTH UIST AND BARRA. Evictions by Colonel Gordon of Cluny.

1851   The Skye Emigration Society formed under the chairmanship of Thomas Fraser, Sheriff-Substitute of the island.
STRATHAIRD evictions on Skye.

1852   The Highland and Island Emigration Society formed under the patronage of Prince Albert. It absorbs the Skye Society. The Land and Emigration Commissioners offer ships and assistance.

1853   SKYE. Lord Macdonald clears the last of the people from Boreraig and Suishnish.

KNOYDART. Mrs Macdonell of Glengarry, with the trustees of her son's estate, serves writs of removal on the last of her sub-tenants there.

Harriet Beecher Stowe's first visit to Britain, and her meeting with the second Duchess of Sutherland.

1854   ROSS. Last evictions from the property of Robertson of Kindeace in Strathcarron. 'The Slaughter at Greenyards' and 'The Massacre of the Rosses'.

KNOYDART. The Lord Advocate orders an inquiry into the the state of paupers there following the evictions.

Failure of the recruiting campaign in the Highlands.

1856   Harriet Beecher Stowe's second visit to Britain. She stays at Inverary and Dunrobin to gather 'notes on the clearances', and publishes them in *Sunny Memories*.

A Writ of Removal

The old Tolbooth Gaol in Tain now forms part of the Sheriff Court House. It is the 'sharp-pointed house' feared by the young men of Glencalvie, and there Peter Ross and Ann Ross waited for their trial in 1854. In a small upper room, the only part in use, are stored copies of writs of removal issued in Easter Ross over a century ago. Sixty years of tragedy are bound in strong tape and buried in dust. The room is rarely entered, and I was the first for many years. I found only one writ relating to Glencalvie or Strathcarron, and that follows here. I can think of no explanation for its date, 1846. By all contem-porary accounts, the Shoemakers were gone from Glencalvie in 1845.

SUMMONS OF REMOVAL
Major Charles Robertson of Kindeace
VS
Donald Macleod, Esquire & Others

1846
Allan MacIntyre
Sheriff Clerk

Call per John Mackenzie
Summons of Removing
Major Charles Robertson of Kindeace
against
Donald Macleod, Esq., residing at Kingsburgh, Isle of Skye.

David Ross, Snr., alias Greishich, residing at urlar of Glencalvie
David Ross, alias Greishich, residing at urlar of Glencalvie
Alexander Ross, alias Greishich, residing at urlar of Glencalvie.

JOHN JARDINE, Esquire, Advocate, Sheriff of the shires of Ross and Cromarty, to sundry officers in that part conjunctly and severally, specially constituted greeting. Whereas it is humbly meant and shewn to me by Major Charles Robertson of Kindeace, presently residing in Edinburgh, Heritable Proprietor of the Land and other parts after mentioned, that by the Act of Sederunt of the Lords of Council and Session, dated the fourteenth day of December, one thousand seven hundred and fifty-six, entitled 'An Act Anent Removings', it is provided 'That where a Tenant hath not obliged himself to remove without warning, in such case it shall be lawful to the Heritor or Setter of the Tack, either to use the order prescribed by the Act of Parliament made in the year fifteen hundred and fifty-five entitled 'An Act Anent the Warning of Tenants', and thereupon pursue a warning of Ejection, or to bring his Action of removing against the Tenant before the Judge Ordinary; and such action being called before the Judge Ordinary at least forty days before the term of Whitsunday, shall be held as equal to a Warning executed in terms of the foresaid Act; and the Judge shall thereupon proceed to determine in the Removings in terms of the Act, in the same manner as if a Warning had been executed in terms of the foresaid Act of Parliament.'

I. That Donald Macleod, Esquire, residing at Kingsburgh in the Isle of Skye, is tenant, subtenant, or Possessor under the Pursuer of the Lands and Grazings of the urlar of Glencalvie or part thereof, lying within the Parish of Kincardine, and Sheriffdom of Ross on a Title of Possession which will expire as to the Houses, Gardens and Grass on the said Possessions, at and against the term of Whitsunday next, and as to the Arable land under Crop at the Separating of the Crop from the ground, in the year one thousand eight hundred and forty-six.

II. That David Ross, alias Greisich Senior, residing at urlar of Glencalvie, is Tenant, Subtenant or Possessor under the Pursuer of a Dwelling house and other premises and pertinents thereto attached at urlar of Glencalvie, lying within the Parish of Kincardine and Sheriffdom of Ross, on a Title of Possession which will expire at and against the term of Whitsunday next, in the year one thousand eight hundred and forty-six.

III. That David Ross, alias Greisich Junior, residing at urlar of Glencalvie, is Tenant, Subtenant or Possessor under the Pursuer of a Dwelling house and other premises and pertinents thereto attached at urlar of Glencalvie, lying within the Parish of Kincardine and Sheriffdom of Ross, on a Title of Possession which will expire at and against the term of Whitsunday next, in the year one thousand eight hundred and forty-six.

IV. That Alexander Ross, alias Greisich, residing at urlar of Glencalvie, is Tenant, Subtenant or Possessor under the Pursuer of a Dwelling house and other premises and pertinents thereto attached at urlar of Glencalvie, lying within the Parish of Kincardine and Sheriffdom of Ross, on a Title of Possession which will expire at and against the term of Whitsunday next, in the year one thousand eight hundred and forty-six.

V. That the Pursuer is desirous that the said Donald Macleod, Esquire, David Ross alias Greisich Senior, David Ross alias Greisich Junior, and Alexander Ross alias Greisich, shall remove from the said Possessions respectively occupied by them at the terms above mentioned, and to obtain Decree of Removal against them accordingly in order that the Pursuer or others in his name may enter thereto and possess the same.

Therefore the said Defenders ought and should be declared and ordained by Decree and Sentence of me or my Substitute.

1. To flit and Remove themselves, Bairns, Family, servants, subtenants, cottars and dependants, Cattle, Goods and gear, forth and from possession of the said Subjects above described with the pertinents respectively occupied by them, as aforesaid, and to leave the same void, redd and patent, at the respective terms of Removal above specified, that the Pursuer or others in his name may then enter thereto and peaceably possess, occupy and enjoy the same in time coming. And

2. In the event of their opposing this action to make payment to the pursuer of the sum of Ten pounds Sterling, or such other Sum as shall be modified at the Expenses of Process, besides the Expense of Extracting and Recording the Decree to follow thereon.

All in terms of the Act of Sederunt and the laws and daily practice of Scotland, used and observed in the like cases in all points as if alleged. MY WILL IS HEREFORE, I commend you that on sight hereof, ye pass and lawfully Summon, warn and charge the Said Defenders personally, or at their dwelling places, to appear before me or my Substitute within the ordinary Court place at Tain upon the seventh day next after Court day, or if not on the next Court day thereafter, in the hour of course, with continuation of days to answer at the instance of the said Pursuer in the matter libelled. That is to say to hear and see the premises verified and proved and Sentence and Decreet given and pronounced therein *ut supra*, or else to allege a reasonable Cause to the Contrary. With Certification According to Justice given under the hand of the Clerk of Court at Tain, the Fifth day of March, Eighteen hundred and Forty-six years.

Allan McIntyre,
Sheriff Clerk Depute.

ACKNOWLEDGEMENTS

MY gratitude to those who have helped me with this book cannot be adequately expressed. They gave not only information and advice, but time and encouragement, and some the hospitality of their homes. I particularly wish to record my debt to the following:

Robert Bannerman, of Crieff, for sending me his own writings on Kildonan where his ancestors once lived. Dr Evan Barron of the *Inverness Courier*, who made the files of his newspaper available to me, and who gave me a copy of his father's three-volume index of it. Dr H. Fairhurst, of the Department of Archaeology, Glasgow University, for advice and warning of what might be the truth of the Strathnaver burnings. Ian Grimble, author of a book on the Trial of Patrick Sellar, who showed a writer's understanding of the problems of another and kindly allowed me to use his translations from Sismondi's works. Miss Anne Henderson, of Winnipeg, for information about the Kildonan settlers from whom she is descended. Rory Mackay of Inverness, whose sustained interest in the progress of this book has been a great encouragement, and whose knowledgeable advice has been invaluable. A. H. M. Munro, Sheriff Clerk Depute at Tain, who opened the sharp-pointed house for me. Robert Munro, of the *Highland News*, who gave a newspaperman's time and attention to my inquiries about Strathcarron. Samuel Maclean of Plockton, schoolmaster and Gaelic bard, and an authority on the poetry of the Clearances, who had time and patience for a non-Gaelic speaker. Donald Ross of Letchworth, for his many letters and his knowledge of Strathcarron. Mrs Annie Macleod Stenhouse, great-niece of Donald Macleod of Strathnaver, for her patience. And finally Iain Cameron Taylor who opened many doors, not the least of which was that to his own home.

OFFICIAL PAPERS, PRINTED & MSS

Home Office Correspondence (Scotland), 102–5 on the Ross-shire Sheep Riots. 1792.
The Sheriff Clerk's Records, Tain, Ross-shire. 1800–1850.
Hansard.
Reports from the Select Committee appointed to inquire into the

Islands and Highlands of Scotland, and into the practicability of affording the proper relief by means of Emigration. 1841.

Periodic Reports of the Central Board for the Relief of Destitution in the Highlands and Islands of Scotland. 1848–52.

Reports of the Free Church Committee on Destitution. 1847.

Report to the Board of Supervision by Sir John MacNeill on the Western Highlands and Islands. 1851.

Periodic Reports of the Highland and Island Emigration Society. 1852–3.

House of Commons Papers, (Poor Law, Scotland), Vol. XLVI. 1854.

House of Commons Papers, N. 163. 1855.

Report of the Commissioners of Inquiry into the Conditions of the Crofters and Cottars in the Highlands and Islands of Scotland (The Napier Commission). 1884.

NEWSPAPERS AND MAGAZINES

Celtic Magazine   John o' Groats Journal
Edinburgh Chronicle   Military Register
Edinburgh Courant   Notes and Queries
Gentleman's Magazine   North British Mail
Glasgow Herald   North Star
Glasgow National   Northern Ensign
Inverness Advertiser   Scots Magazine
Inverness Courier   Scotsman
Inverness Journal   The Times

ANONYMOUS PAMPHLETS AND PAPERS

A Word on Highland Destitution and its Remedies. Edinburgh, 1851.

Emigration from the Highlands and Islands of Scotland to Australia. London, 1852.

The Emigrants Guide – practical and authentic information. Westport; 1832.

Emigration – Who should go, what to take, etc. London, 1843.

Hints to Emigrants respecting British North America – by an Emigrant. Quebec, 1831.

Lectures on the Mountains, or Highlands, and the Highlanders as they were and as they are. 1860.

Sutherland as it was and is, or How a Country May be Ruined. Edinburgh, 1843.

BIBLIOGRAPHY

ADAM, Margaret I. 'The Highland Emigration of 1770'. *Scottish Historical Review*, vol. XVI, 1919.

'The Causes of the Highland Emigrations of 1783–1803'. *Scottish Historical Review*, vol. XVII, 1920.

'Eighteenth-century Highland Landlords and the Poverty Problem'. *Scottish Historical Review*, vol. XIX, 1921.

AIRD, Gustavus. *The Families of Douglas of Mulderg and Robertson of Kindeace*. 1895.

BAIN, Robert. *History of the Ancient Province of Ross (The County Palatine of Scotland)*. 1899.

BAKEWELL, Thomas. *Remarks on a Publication by James Loch entitled 'An Account of the Improvements', etc.* 1820.

BARRON, James, *The Northern Highlands in the Ninteenth Century. Newspaper Index and Annals.* 1903.

BLACKIE, John Stuart. *The Scottish Highlands and the Land Laws.* 1885.

BLUNDELL, Odo. *The Catholic Highlands of Scotland.* vol. II, 1917.

BROWNE, James. *A Critical Examination of Dr MacCulloch's Work.* 1825.

BRUCE, James. *Destitution in the Highlands,* letters reprinted from the *Scotsman.* 1847.

CARMICHAEL, Alexander. Carmina Gadelica. 1900.

DAY, John Percival. *Public Administration in the Highlands and Islands of Scotland.* 1918.

FRASER-MACKINTOSH, C. *Letters of Two Centuries.* 1890.

GIBBON, J. M. *The Scots in Canada.* 1911.

GOWER, Lord Ronald. *My Reminiscences.* 1885.

Stafford House Letters. 1891.

GRANT, Elizabeth. *Memoirs of a Highland Lady,* edited by Lady Strachey. 1898.

GRAY, Malcolm. *The Highland Economy, 1750–1850.* 1957.

GUNN, the Rev. Adam, with MACKAY, John. *Sutherland and the Reay Country.* 1897.

GRIMBLE, Ian. *The Trial of Patrick Sellar*. 1962.

HALDANE, A. R. B. *New Ways through the Glens*. 1962.
The Drove Roads of Scotland. 1952.

KENNEDY, John. *The Days of the Fathers in Ross-shire*. 1897.

KER, Andrew. *A Report of the State of Sheep Farming along the Eastern Coast of Scotland and the Interior parts of the Highlands.* 1791.

KNOX, John. *A Tour through the Highlands of Scotland and the Hebride Isles in 1786*. 1787.

LEES, J. C. *History of the County of Inverness*. 1897.

LOCH, Gordon. *The Family of Loch*. 1934.

LOCH, James. *An Account of the Improvements on the Estates of the Marquess of Stafford*. 1820.
A Memoir of George Granville, late Duke of Sutherland. 1834.

MACCULLOCH, John. *The Highlands and Western Isles of Scotland.* 1824.

MACDONALD, D. F. *Scotland's Shifting Population, 1770–1850*. 1937.

MACKENZIE, Agnes. *Scotland in Modern Times, 1720–1939*. 1947.

MACKENZIE, Alexander. *A History of the Highland Clearances*. 1883.
The Isle of Skye in 1882–3, also a full report of the Trial of Patrick Sellar. 1883.

MACKENZIE, Sir George Steuart. *General View of the Agriculture of the Counties of Ross and Cromarty*. 1813.

MACKENZIE, W. C. *History of the Outer Hebrides*. 1903.

MACLAUCHLAN, Thomas. *The Depopulation System in the Highlands.* 1849.

MACLEAN, Samuel. 'The Poetry of the Clearances'. *Transactions of the Gaelic Society of Inverness*, vol. XXXVIII.

MACLEOD, Donald. *Gloomy Memories in the Highlands of Scotland.* 1857.
History of the Destitution in Sutherlandshire. 1841.

MACLEOD, Norman (the Elder). *Destitution in the Highlands, a Speech*. 1837.

MARTIN, Chester. *Lord Selkirk's Work in Canada*. 1916.

MEIKLE, Henry W. *Scotland and the French Revolution*. 1912.

MILLER, Hugh (the Elder). *Sutherland and the Sutherlanders*. 1844.

MITCHINSON, Rosalind. *Agricultural Sir John, the Life of Sir John Sinclair of Ulbster*. 1962.

MULOCK, Thomas. *The Western Highlands and Islands of Scotland socially considered, with reference to the proprietors*. 1850.

NAISMYTH, John. *Observations on the different Breeds of sheep, and the State of Sheep-farming in the Southern Districts of Scotland.* 1795.

PENNANT, Thomas. *Tour in Scotland and Voyage to the Hebrides.* 1774.

ROBERTSON, Alexander. *Barriers to National Prosperity* (written under the pseudonym of R. Alister). 1853.

Extermination of the Scottish Peasantry (written under the pseudonym of R. Alister). 1853.

Where are the Highlanders? of the Highland Regiments and Highland Clearances. 1856.

ROBERTSON, James. *General View of the Agriculture in the County of Inverness.* 1808.

ROBERTSON, John. *The Rosses of Glencalvie.* 1844.

ROBERTSON, P. *The Trial of Patrick Sellar, as originally prepared by Mr Sellar's junior counsel (P. Robertson), newly edited by Alexander Mackenzie.*

ROSS, Donald. *The Scottish Highlanders.* 1852.

The Glengarry Evictions, or Scenes at Knoydart. 1853.

The Massacre of the Rosses. 1854.

The Clearing of the Glens. 1854.

Real Scottish Grievances. 1854.

Letters on the Depopulation of the Highlands. 1856.

SAGE, Donald. *Memorabilia Domestica*, edited by his son. 1889.

SELKIRK, Earl of. *Observations on the Present State of the Highlands.* 1805.

SELLAR, Thomas. *The Sutherland Evictions of 1814.* 1883.

SINCLAIR, Sir John. *General View of the Agriculture of the Northern Counties, and Islands of Scotland.* 1795.

STEWART, David, of Garth. *Sketches of the Character, Manners and Present State of the Highlanders of Scotland.* 1822.

STOWE, Harriet Beecher. *Sunny Memories of Foreign Lands.* 1857.

SUTHERLAND, 5th Duke of. *Looking Back.* 1957.

WALPOLE, L. A. 'The Humanitarian Movement in the Early nineteenth Century to remedy Abuses on Emigration Vessels'. *Transactions of the Royal Historical Society*, vol. XIV, 1931.

INDEX

Note: (P) indicates proprietor; (T) tacks man or tenant; (S) sheep-farmer; (A) factor, commissioner or other agent of the proprietor; (C) the 'commonality', as they were generally termed, of sub-tenant, out-servant, cotter, etc.; (E) for those who were evicted; and (B) for bard. Place names are listed under SCOTS TOPOGRAPHY, and an asterisk marks those that also appear under CLEARANCES.